RELIGION AND VIOLENCE
IN EARLY AMERICAN
METHODISM

RELIGION IN NORTH AMERICA

Catherine L. Albanese and Stephen J. Stein, editors

Religion and Violence in Early American Methodism

Taking the Kingdom by Force

Jeffrey Williams

INDIANA UNIVERSITY PRESS
Bloomington and Indianapolis

This book is a publication of

Indiana University Press

601 North Morton Street
Bloomington, Indiana 47404-3797 USA

www.iupress.indiana.edu

Telephone orders	800-842-6796
Fax orders	812-855-7931
Orders by e-mail	iuporder@indiana.edu

Library of Congress Cataloging-in-Publication Data

Williams, Jeffrey, [date–]
  Religion and violence in early American Methodism : taking the
kingdom by force / Jeffrey Williams.
     p. cm. — (Religion in North America)
  Includes bibliographical references and index.
  ISBN 978-0-253-35444-0 (cloth : alk. paper) 1. Methodist
Church—History—18th century. 2. Methodist Church—History—
19th century. 3. United States—Church history—18th century.
4. United States—Church history—19th century. 5. Violence—
Religious aspects—Christianity. 6. Language and languages—
Religious aspects—Christianity. I. Title.
  BX8231.W49 2010
  287.0973'09033—dc22
                                        2009034078

1 2 3 4 5 15 14 13 12 11 10

To Michele

Contents

Foreword

In this study of early Methodist literature on both sides of the Atlantic, Jeffrey Williams explores the language used by Methodists as they spoke and wrote of their religious experiences and as they dealt with social conflicts of one kind or another. Williams's chronological framework extends from the time of John and Charles Wesley until the mid-nineteenth century. The documents he scrutinizes include sermons, worship materials, letters, tracts, and other publications. Williams examines the rich tapestry of the language the Methodists employed in these documents as they spoke of their religious experiences and as they engaged in social struggles of various kinds. That language included a variety of conflict-oriented and violent rhetoric. He shows how the Methodists' use of diverse metaphors, including the language of violence, was employed in their discourse regarding spirituality and daily life.

This volume is a strongly revisionist work on early American Methodism. Williams counters the familiar narrative about the "sweetness" and "melting times" of the early Methodist movement and denomination with an alternative picture of angry warriors struggling against the devil, waging war with themselves and even with God, in the fight for virtue and heavenly reward. He does not deny the earlier picture of Methodism; there is no simplism here. But Williams shines a steady light on another way of talking and living among early Methodists that, perforce, must modify what we think of all those melting times.

Methodism is understudied in American religious history and therefore deserves all the new attention it can receive. In this important new look at Methodist history, Williams inserts his revisionism within a theoretical religious studies framework and discourse regarding the role of violence in religion. He takes his cue from René Girard, whose seminal work *Violence and the Sacred* has been largely responsible for the recent scholarly emphasis on the role of violence in religion. To his credit, Williams does not force his work into Girardian categories. Rather, he uses Girard as a springboard for his own narrative, and he certainly does not give us theory masking as history.

This volume breaks new ground by its focus upon the violent dimensions of Methodist spirituality involving themes of warfare, aggression, conflict, and pain, in contrast to the standard accounts of the Methodist tradition dealing with comfort, home, and peace. Williams shows how Methodist preachers and their hymnody called for the soldiers of Christ to arise, to wage war against Satan's dominions that included frivolity, adornment, injustice, and slavery, and to take the kingdom by force. But he also carries the story forward to the Civil War era and shows how over time Methodist preachers turned the spirituality of warfare with God into moralities of refinement and domesticity.

In sum, this volume forces us to reconsider some commonplace assumptions concerning early Methodism that have long been standard judgments. It is therefore a volume that demands attention from those who are especially comfortable with established axioms regarding the early Methodist tradition. It also invites attention from students engaged in courses on early American religions or in classes focused on violence, warfare, peacemaking, and/or conflict resolution. We stand in Jeffrey Williams's debt for this important, provocative, and instructive study.

Catherine L. Albanese and
Stephen J. Stein, series editors

Acknowledgments

I owe an enormous debt of gratitude to the many people who helped bring this book to fruition. The staff at the Honnold/Mudd Library at Claremont Graduate University, the Library of Claremont School of Theology, the archives at Duke University, the United Methodist Archives Center at Drew University, and the Mary Couts Burnett Library at Texas Christian University all provided helpful assistance in locating materials and providing research space.

Ann Taves read and commented upon countless drafts while I was a graduate student. Jack Fitzmier, Ellen Marshall, and Mark Juergensmeyer provided important insight into how I might turn my ideas into a book. Two of my colleagues at Brite Divinity School and Texas Christian University, Mark Toulouse and Steve Sherwood, read and commented on important parts of the book. Russell Richey provided an enormously helpful reader's response. Lisa Barnett performed a herculean task as my student assistant entrusted with helping me sift through a century of Methodist periodical literature. *Methodist History* kindly published parts of the first two chapters of this book.

The wonderful people at Indiana University Press, Dee Mortensen and Laura MacLeod, along with the series editors Catherine Albanese and Stephen Stein, had an unwavering faith in this project since I first proposed it.

I missed too many days in the lives of Joshua, Aiden, and Samuel while writing this book. I hope that someday they might pick up a dusty copy and finally know why Daddy was gone so often.

My wife Michele not only read drafts of this work, she provided much-needed encouragement and support. Her patience in the midst of my impatience, faith in the face of my doubt, and peace in place of my contention are a marvel. I can honestly say that the book would have never seen the light of day without her. I dedicate this book to you, Michele, with all my love.

RELIGION AND VIOLENCE
IN EARLY AMERICAN
METHODISM

⛨

INTRODUCTION

Soldiers of Christ Arise, and put your armor on,
Strong in the strength which God supplies thru his eternal Son;
Strong in the Lord of Hosts, and in his mighty power,
Who in the strength of Jesus trusts is more than conqueror.

—*Charles Wesley, "Soldiers of Christ Arise"*

Early Methodist leader Charles Wesley originally, and quite appropriately, set the tune of this hymn to Handel's *March*. We know the hymn today as "Soldiers of Christ Arise." Its origins stretch back to a much longer poem, sixteen verses in all, that Charles composed no later than 1742. The selection has appeared in Methodist hymnals for two and a half centuries, sung by everyone from poor farmers in tiny clapboard churches to the world's elite. Unlike many hymns that have failed to stand the test of time, "Soldiers of Christ Arise" has become a classic that continues to enjoy a place in the official United Methodist hymnal.

But if hymns of similar content indicate important themes and values within a religious community, "Soldiers of Christ Arise" now stands out awkwardly. Though Methodists, like many other Christians, can still open their hymnals and loudly sing "stand up, stand up for Jesus, ye soldiers of the cross," ask in the words of Isaac Watts "am I a soldier of the Cross?" or bellow "onward, Christian soldiers, marching as to war, with the cross of Jesus going on before," there are few other hymns in the United Methodist hymnal that overtly refer to Christians as soldiers or to some aspect of the Christian life as a battle. Two of these hymns, including "Soldiers of Christ Arise," are more than two centuries old, and their presence is fading.[1]

The relative absence of hymns of military glory and epic battle in today's mainline churches in America masks a much more vibrant past. In fact, "Soldiers of Christ Arise" is the last remaining song in the United Methodist hymnal that also appeared in a curious section of the famous *A Collection of Hymns for the Use of the People Called Methodists,* compiled by Charles Wesley's older and more renowned brother John in 1780. The elder Wesley intended his *Collection of Hymns* to be inexpensive, widely disseminated, exhaustive, and highly adaptable. He organized the hymnal around various experiences of the Christian life, with the section of twenty-eight hymns that included "Soldiers of Christ Arise" tucked neatly between seventy-four hymns Wesley labeled "For Believers Rejoicing" and eleven hymns labeled "For Believers Praying." Wesley provocatively named the section in between "For Believers Fighting."[2]

The preacher also utilized "Soldiers of Christ Arise" in another significant early Methodist publication. In 1742, John Wesley appended all sixteen verses of Charles's poem, then known as "The Whole Armour of God," to the end of his seminal document *Character of a Methodist.* Wesley used the document to define and defend the growing British Methodist movement against confusion and criticism. Wesley firmly established the character or mark of a Methodist in experiential terms: "one who has 'the love of God shed abroad in his heart by the Holy Ghost given unto him'" and affectionate terms as one who loves both God and neighbor. The Methodist, insisted Wesley, not only puts these experiences and affections into practice by obeying God's commandments, praying without ceasing, and performing good deeds, but she also attains a form of sinless perfection that Wesley defined as sanctification.[3]

Through a dramatic rhetorical shift, Wesley cast aside the language of intimacy evoked through his repeated use of terms such as "love" and "joy" and closed the *Character of a Methodist* with his brother's now famous call for "soldiers of Christ" to arise, stand "against your foes," and "wrestle, fight, and pray." Wesley might have used the body of his essay to define Methodists as ones who experienced the love of God and expressed that love to humanity, but his conclusion left no doubt that his followers were also warriors prepared for battle, strong, powerful, and confident in victory.

Wesley's followers responded to his call to battle in profound ways. Wesley's chief lieutenant, John Fletcher, warned Christians about failing to see the necessity of fighting. To view the Christian life in any way other than a battle was "THE GRAND device of Satan" to deny humans their salvation (emphasis in original). By contrast, Fletcher contended that the kingdom of heaven "permits certain kinds of 'violence'" as the appropriate means to wage the "good fight" against what he identified as two primary opponents. First, the Christian battled "those lords who reign over us—the world, the flesh and the devil. These rebels must be turned out." The believer's other opponent was none other than God, against whom converts, like the patriarch Jacob in the Hebrew Bible, "wrestle" for divine blessings. Salvation, for Fletcher, could never be achieved in any way other than struggle against both of these forces. "None prevail but those 'who take the kingdom by violence. . . . Weariness, care, friends, fear and unbelief must all be thrown aside when we seek to see God face to face and to be brought into the light of his life."[4]

Across the Atlantic, where Methodism enjoyed its most profound success in the eighteenth and nineteenth centuries, "New World" Methodists also communicated the importance of the believer's warfare in the experiential literature—diaries, autobiographies, biographies, and hymnals—they popularized. In these works, American Methodists waged the battles to which leaders like John Wesley and John Fletcher called them, and they hoped that by recording their victories and defeats their readers would enlist alongside them in the fight to conquer evil. The most influential leader within the early Methodist community, Francis Asbury, verified as much. The superintendent-turned-bishop filled his published journals with entries of Satan's constant "assaults," against which Asbury committed to "either fight or die." By steadfastly resisting these attacks with "sword in hand," Asbury explained that he gained power over Satan and joined with other Christians to "be more than conquerors."[5]

Many American Methodists literally embodied Asbury's fight not only in their encounters with Satan, but also in their encounters with God. Describing his experience of sanctification, itinerant preacher Benjamin Abbott recalled that the "spirit of God" came upon him and he "fellfalt [sic] to the floor, and lay as one strangling in blood." Fearing that Abbott might die, his wife and children wept at the sight of his lifeless body. "But I had not power to lift hand or foot, nor to speak one word" while he "felt the power of God, running through every part of my soul and body like fire consuming the inward corruptions of fallen depraved nature."[6] In countless similar narratives, Methodists spoke of falling to the ground under the power of God "as if shot," writhing on the ground, sometimes in extreme physical pain, and shouting for mercy, portraying their conversions as battles in which God ultimately struck them down as soldiers at war in order to resurrect them to new life.

Assuming as we must that Methodists were anything but careless in referring to important aspects of the religious life in terms of war, violence, and aggression, we ought to ask certain fundamental questions. What did Methodists mean when they described their religious lives as battles? What exactly was the nature of this warfare and who were the enemies? How did language of violence, fighting, and warfare relate to other core Methodist values that promised joy, peace, and hope? Perhaps even more importantly, did this martial rhetoric have any relation to Methodist perceptions of or participation in acts of physical violence and aggression?

This book explores these questions through a careful examination of the religious world of early American Methodists and the social implications of that religious world. The militant rhetoric of "Soldiers of Christ Arise" was an essential component of American Methodist theology, experience, and practice. While early Methodists often spoke of the love and intimacy they enjoyed with both God and their fellow Christians, they believed that such bonds emerged through intense struggle and conflict. The religious life was nothing less than a battle against a wide array of forces, malevolent and benevolent. By bodily and spiritually "fighting the good fight" and "taking the kingdom by violence," even as they were "wounded" or "killed" by God in the process of justification and sanctification, American Methodists sought salvation, holiness, and religious community.

These battles not only exercised a critical role in how early Methodists described the practice of the Christian life, they also had important implications for Methodist perceptions of and participation in social violence. Precisely speaking, the former battle could never be equated with other types of violence such as involvement in the state's warfare or even run-of-the-mill brawling between angry enemies. The "good fight" took the form of a spiritual battle against spiritual forces for individual salvation and social transformation. If humans hoped to realize the salvation of their souls and the reform of their nation, they needed to fight spiritual forces and their own sinful natures. Very few Methodists, if any, would have applied the same necessity to the temporal conflicts around them or would have argued that one's salvation depended upon fighting another human being.

In fact, at certain points in their history American Methodists constructed an inverse relationship between their militant struggle for the Christian faith and human warfare, arguing that their enlistment in God's army for the most cherished prize of eternal redemption overshadowed the trivial contests of politicians. Even more strongly, some defined war as inherently sinful so that Christians could not participate in it without compromising their spiritual condition. In such instances, the battle for salvation became a potent force for discouraging participation in social violence.

However, in other important cases Methodists identified certain political or social conflicts that seemed to necessitate violent social action. Methodists commonly observed Satan's corrupting influence in society—in slavery, poverty, and war, for instance—in ways that brought social issues into the Christian's warfare as part of the overall struggle against sin. Some of these issues seemed to warrant action that moved beyond spiritual war on the part of the believer. These issues called the Christian to take up arms and physically wound or kill their opponents. In such instances, the lines between the believer's struggle for salvation and the earthly battle became blurred and the latter became closely intertwined with the former. The community's enemies became minions of Satan and acts of physical violence became a sacred duty in the battle for salvation. As a result, the believer's holy violence intended to lead to salvation provided a powerful justification for social violence.

Despite the prevalence of a highly conflicted, one might even say violent, religious world communicated within the pages of Methodist sermons, hymns, autobiographies, and journals, and its varying connection to systems of social violence, the conflicted aspects of Methodists' religious world have received little serious attention within the resurgence of scholarship on early American Methodism. There are, I believe, a few reasons for this lacuna. First, some of the finest work on American Methodist spirituality has focused on later expressions of spirituality that were not amenable to the militant rhetoric and action of an earlier era. A. Gregory Schneider's work on Methodism and domesticity is the most significant recent critical analysis of early American Methodist spirituality.[7] Schneider sees Methodist spirituality playing an important role in the evolving cultural embrace of domestic ideology over the course of the first half of the nineteenth century among white middle-class Americans. He seizes upon

Methodism's emphasis on intimate bonds of affection, a religiosity rooted in the domestic realm, and an otherworldliness focused on a heavenly abode of perfection as direct contributors to the growth of domesticity.[8]

Unfortunately, the closest Schneider comes to observing the type of militant spirituality considered here is in what he calls Methodist spirituality's "active passivity." Schneider uses this term to refer to Methodist notions of spiritual transformation that included the roles of God and the human being. Methodists commonly spoke of salvation as an act of God alone, a theological commitment that rendered adherents relatively passive in the process of gaining salvation. However, Methodists simultaneously emphasized that seekers needed to search out and vigorously take hold of the very grace that made them passive.[9] Methodists sought a sinless perfection that required intense effort, even as believers recognized that ultimately holiness came as an act of God.

Although Schneider's idea of active passivity begins to capture a sense of the militant effort Methodists believed they ought to apply to their spiritual lives, the fact that Schneider overlooks the martial language Methodists relied on to narrate their spiritual lives requires a reconsideration of Methodist spirituality. Much of Methodist spirituality had a rougher edge than the refined domestic ideology of home and affection. It spoke of bloody battles against the minions of evil and slayings at the hands of a warrior God. Particularly among the earliest generations of Methodists, the militant became one of the central modes for defining the Christian life, not only in terms of the nature of the discourse used to describe the quest for holiness, but also in the theological descriptions of conversion, the bodily practices that reflected this theology, and participation in physical encounters with Satan, all of which departed significantly from the rhetoric of domesticity.

The difference between the type of spirituality described by Schneider and that presented here likely has less to do with sources or interpretation and more to do with time. Although the periods under consideration in this book and in Schneider's work overlap, the emphasis in the former is on the late eighteenth and early nineteenth centuries, whereas Schneider deals mainly with the early to mid-nineteenth century. American Methodism underwent a process of transformation that by the mid-nineteenth century led the community to abandon fighting as a central aspect of its spirituality. Schneider's work captures this movement, while the arguments made here better represent Methodist spirituality in the decades immediately prior to and following the turn of the century.

A second reason that previous histories of early Methodism have overlooked the highly contested practices and discourse that I argue were so prevalent is that historians of early Methodism have tended to emphasize the positive and refined aspects of Methodism's "experimental" or "heart" religion (e.g., love, joy, and peace) or the socially salubrious implications of what historians imagine to be the fruits of conversion and sanctification.[10] Early Methodist literature certainly took pains to stress that Methodists truly experienced love, joy, and peace and that these affections were evidence of the "new birth." It is equally difficult to deny that early Methodist religious experience could facilitate a countercultural environment that created, if even briefly, space for marginalized peoples to express freely their inner experiences and in some cases exert significant religious influence. Unfortunately, the process of privileging the resolution of conversion and sanctification has resulted in a lack of appreciation for the pervasive struggle and terror that preceded conversion, not to mention that which endured long after the experience ended. Even converted and sanctified believers continued to "fight" in ways that had profound consequences for their spiritual, emotional, and in some cases even physical health.

A final reason that historians have not given serious attention to the battles and warfare of Methodist religious life is that accounts of physical spasms, shouting, falling, Satanic assaults, and suicidal thoughts do not conform to the idyllic image of early Methodism that many historians have sought to portray. Scholars have called the early Methodist community "Edenic," egalitarian, and innocent.[11] This idealism reflects what Nathan Hatch has argued is a tendency of "modern church historians . . . to focus on those dimensions of their own heritage that point to cultural enrichment, institutional cohesion, and intellectual respectability."[12] A long-time itinerant preacher driven mad by what he perceived as Satan's attacks or the devout "mother of Israel" who considered killing herself simply do not fit into the historiographical caricature. If we are to achieve a deeper understanding of early Methodism, we must consider more seriously language of "wounding," "killing," "wrestling," and "crucifying" alongside references to "melting," "love," "peace," and "fraternity." Methodists not only credited the former terms with making the latter possible, but also made warfare and struggle a permanent component of the Christian life. Notions of struggle and warfare became enmeshed within the theology, practices, and experiences of early Methodists in ways that made them critical to living the Christian life.

By giving attention to the meaning and significance of Methodism's cosmic battles, this book is situated within a lively area of American religious history influenced by both popular studies and ethnography. Historians such as David Hall, Leigh Schmidt, Robert Orsi, and Colleen McDaniel have made space for religious practices and experiences to take center stage over the more traditional historical focus on institutional formation and formal theological expression.[13] The values, perspectives, and meaning religious adherents found in religious practices and experiences are understood, in this approach, to be essential for gaining insight into the lives of those in the past, those who shared very different assumptions about the world that otherwise would remain lost to the twenty-first-century interpreter.

The method employed in this book also recognizes that historical inter-pretation does not stop at the point of reconstructing the meaning religious adherents found in their practices and experiences, but can also be informed by the use of theory, in this case a broader body of literature on religion and vio-lence. A significant literature of varying quality exists that seeks to demonstrate religion's influence in violent acts, whether particular acts of violence, say the First Crusade, or violence more generally. However, only recently have scholars given serious attention to the ways violence often helps give structure and mean-ing to religion. The work of René Girard is perhaps the most notable attempt to explain how violence shapes religious thought and practice. Girard contends that religion emerges out of social acts of violence. In every culture, mimetic rivalry among members of the community sets off violence that the community can only assuage through the scapegoating, in most cases the murder, of an innocent victim. Of course, the community must not recognize that the victim is inno-cent. Through misrecognition, the community considers the victim the cause of the disorder and concludes that the death of the victim will not only deliver the community from the violence besetting it, but will also become the source for the founding of a united society. After the event, myths and rituals, the very basis of religion for Girard, arise to retell and re-enact the "founding" murder, passing on to future generations rules for the maintenance of society and passing on the assumption that God decrees violence as the necessary mechanism for the creation and protection of social order.[14]

Girard's theory offers a complicated and compelling picture of the relation-ship between religion and violence by suggesting that violence and religion have integral connections, if not by necessity, then at least in practice.[15] Although

Religion and Violence in Early American Methodism departs from Girard in important ways, the book follows Girard by exploring the role of violence in the formation and performance of religion, in this case within a particular religious tradition in America. By drawing from the work of Girard and others, this book offers a fully textured portrait of the meaning and significance of American Methodists' cosmic battles.

The present discussion of Girard's work and my own sensitivity to how Methodists understood their experiences and practices make it important to take a moment to discuss my use of the word "violence." I have already loosely applied the term to certain aspects of Methodist religious life, but I do so with special care in order to avoid misrepresenting Methodist thought and practice. Precisely speaking, characterizing aspects of Methodist religion as violent does not present a problem. We saw earlier that John Fletcher referred to the Christian's struggle for redemption as requiring the use of violence. John Wesley frequently used the term to describe the power of religious experience. For instance, Wesley referred to a man who "was suddenly seized with violent trembling all over." In another case, Wesley wrote in a letter to John Manners that a Mr. Timmins's struggle for redemption was "violent" after which he fell to the ground "as dead," his body even growing cold.[16] Methodists' description of their spirituality as violent suggests that it is consistent with their own use of language to appropriate the term in this book.

However, what Methodists meant by using violence for spiritual ends, or undergoing a violent experience in the process of salvation, varies significantly from most modern conceptions of the term. The *Oxford English Dictionary* defines violence as "the exercise of physical force so as to inflict injury on, or cause damage to, persons or property."[17] As with any term, the definition is both helpful and problematic when read back on a historical community. The idea that violence is the exercise of "physical" force is consistent with Methodist assertions that their battle was a very real struggle that included a physical element. Methodists repeatedly noted their suffering in both mind and body at the hands of God and Satan. Nevertheless, Methodists considered the primary significance of their battles to strike at a spiritual level, namely the eternal state of their soul and Satan's control over the world. As a result, the application of "physical force" does not fully capture what Methodists meant when they described the religious life as violent. Methodists' battles for salvation had as much, if not more, to do with spiritual opponents and spiritual implications than physical ones. We must be wary, then, of at least initially limiting the term "violence" to only physical force. Methodists believed that the use of spiritual force that resulted in harm to spiritual enemies might equally be identified as violent.

We compromise our ability to reconstruct the early Methodist use of the term "violence" if we add a popular sense of the word to the formal sense of the application of physical force to cause damage or injury. In many cases, when someone calls an act violent there is an assumption about the morality or legality of that act. We not only mean that an action is the exercise of physical force intended to cause damage to persons or property, but we also assume that the exercise of that force is illegal or immoral. There is a negative connotation to calling something an act of violence. In everyday usage we would call a mugging violent, but we tend not to call the defensive counterstrike of the victim violent, though it certainly entails the exercise of physical force intended to cause damage. We call it self-defense. We do so because we want to distinguish between appropriate and inappropriate uses of force.

Methodists might have thought that certain experiences that constituted their "violent" religious world were immoral, as when they suffered Satan's attacks, but it is highly unlikely that Methodists would have seen other, perhaps most, aspects of their combative spirituality as immoral or illegal. The acts of violence they thought they needed to apply against the spiritual forces of evil and that God applied to believers were all, to them anyway, necessary for human redemption and holiness.

If we are to avoid compromising our representation of early American Methodism by imposing an anachronistic definition of violence on Methodist religious life, we must establish a clearer understanding of the term for the purposes of this work. I will use a less value-laden definition of violence as: *the use of force in order to cause injury or harm to someone or something.* This definition does not limit the actors, objects, or the means of force to "physical" or "spiritual." I reserve the morality or immorality of the actions for explicit discussion, particularly in the final chapter.[18]

To unearth the religious and social significance of Methodism's redemptive violence, the book moves chronologically from Methodism's emergence in the mid-eighteenth century to the decline of the religious significance of "holy violence" in the mid-nineteenth century. Chapter 1 traces the roots and nature of what came to be known as the "good fight" in the Methodist tradition through a close examination of the life and thought of Methodism's founder, John Wesley.

Wesley called his followers to participate in a bodily and spiritual battle both as warriors who triumphed over sin, the world, and Satan, and as victims who were "wounded" or "killed" by God in order to be saved. Christians could only assure themselves of eternal salvation by succumbing to a divine wounding even as they aggressively subdued their spiritual enemies.

Chapter 2 introduces American Methodism by examining disputes over the American Revolution within the transatlantic Methodist connection. John Wesley defended Britain's right to suppress the American rebellion, but in doing so he differed from his American followers who offered religious reasons for neutrality. A careful examination of Wesley's arguments on the one hand and his American followers on the other reveals that an essential factor in Methodist perspectives on the Revolution was whether Methodists came to see their spiritual battles as bearing on the political conflict. If, as Wesley determined, the outcome of the Revolution influenced the greater battle between good and evil, then Wesley could begin to cast aside his otherwise strong denunciation of physical violence and urge Christian participation in violence that he elevated to a sacred duty. On the other hand, if Methodists could not establish a clear connection between the political and spiritual battles, or if they saw the former as detrimental to waging the latter, then the importance of the spiritual battle discouraged participation in the political.

The third chapter traces the evolution of the battle for salvation in the early American republic. As Methodists grew exponentially in the years following the American Revolution, the community embraced new converts who responded to the call to participate as soldiers for religious redemption. However, while for some the body remained a very real part of the battle, as evident in the emergence of what came to be known as the "jerks," an experience that violently convulsed people's bodies, others began a subtle effort to alter the nature of the cosmic battle by restricting the physical body from the fight. Whether they struggled with God or Satan, many began to contend that physical harm would not befall the Christian in the contestation of the inner dimensions of the good fight for salvation.

While chapter 3 uncovers the changes in American Methodist spirituality, chapter 4 explores the changes in their perspectives on social violence. The first generation of American Methodists who opposed the Revolution gave way to a new generation, many of whom had fewer scruples about participation in violent activity. I contend that American Methodists increasingly intertwined their spiritual battles with social and political struggles surrounding them, particularly the War of 1812 and Methodism's westward expansion across the continental United States. In so doing, Methodists found a motive for sacralizing both individual and communal acts of violence.

Chapter 5 chronicles the decline of the cosmic battle in American Methodism during the middle decades of the nineteenth century. Although the image of the Christian life as a battle never disappeared, it faced profound challenges from within and outside of Methodism that ensured that fighting the good fight became far less important for one's salvation and the creation of spiritual communities than expressing and experiencing nurturing acts of love. Even so, conceptions of a cosmic battle between good and evil assumed particularly prominent and important roles during the Civil War. Methodists, both North and South, described the war as a divine battle and motivated followers to enlist with the argument that good Christians not only loved their country, they were the only thing that stood between the nation's victory and its destruction.

The concluding chapter brings the importance of Methodism's spiritual battles into conversation with recent theoretical literature on the intersection between religion and violence and, in the process, considers what the battles Methodists fought in the eighteenth and nineteenth centuries might mean for the twenty-first century's struggle with religiously inspired violence. The scholarship of René Girard, Maurice Bloch, and others serves as an interpretive lens to help determine how religious struggles and contestation give rise to religious change and how social violence converges with the religious struggles that adherents identify as redemptive. While early American Methodists demonstrate that the "violence" that helps constitute a religious world can prove to be a disincentive to social violence, they also confirm the all-too-soluble boundaries between redemptive and social battles. In all these ways, Methodists have something to offer those interested in the intersection between religion and violence. In a world now beset by terrifying and horrific acts of religiously inspired violence, it is more than mere curiosity to consider whether the history of a mainstream American Protestant community in the eighteenth and nineteenth centuries has something to offer to conversations on religion and violence.

ONE

FIGHTING THE GOOD FIGHT

I found more and more undeniable proofs that
the Christian state is a continual warfare
[emphasis in original].

—*Works 19:149*

The very thing that Mr. Stinstra calls "fanaticism" is no
other than heart religion, in other words, righteousness,
and peace, and joy in the Holy Ghost.

—*Works 22:287*

These concise entries from the journals of John Wesley reveal a great deal about what Wesley considered constitutive of the Christian life. "True" religion brought righteousness, peace, and joy.[1] The experience of salvation included literally feeling "the love of God shed abroad in our heart . . . producing love to all mankind, and more especially to the children of God." Through justification and sanctification, believers not only set out on a path to eternal bliss in the world after, but they also experienced temporal benefits in the form of an intimate relationship with the divine, a holiness of living that freed Christians from the wicked constraints of the present world, and reordered relations with their fellow human beings.[2]

Yet "continual warfare" also plagued Christ's disciples. Wesley insisted that Christians faced a trio of fierce enemies in sin, the "world," and Satan. The powerful attacks of the latter, according to Wesley, caused immeasurable, and in some cases even life-threatening, mental and physical anguish. Likewise, the realities of a fallen world and the hardened cravings of the sinful self required Christians to mount an aggressive attack on of the forces of evil. The bitter conflicts between Christians and their enemies left Wesley to conclude that battle was an inescapable feature of Christian living.

Wesley countered the tribulations inherent in the Christian's warfare by often casting the struggle in triumphalist ways, calling it a "good fight," a reference to 1 Timothy 6:12: "Fight the good fight of faith, lay hold on eternal life, whereunto thou are also called, and hast professed a good profession before many witnesses." For Wesley, though the fight was bitter, true Christians were not embattled victims; they were conquering heroes. As such, the Christian was as much an aggressor as an object of attack in a lifelong battle against both internal and external forces for their own redemption and the renewal of society.[3]

Wesley's image of the Christian as a victor over evil converged with his description of a very different conflict between humans and the divine, one in which God spiritually, and in many cases even bodily, "wounded" Christians in order to deliver them to salvation. To become conquerors, believers needed first to be conquered by God in ways that Wesley believed caused many to scream, fall to the ground, choke, and tremble. In these instances the body became engulfed in the bitter and destructive contest for salvation.

The hope for righteousness, peace, and joy in the midst of continual warfare seems quite paradoxical. How could Christians experience peace and joy while participating in battle? To Wesley this mix of peace and joy with fighting and warfare was no paradox; fighting constituted a critical mechanism for the realization of peace. Christians needed to be "wounded" to become "soldiers of Christ" who "fought the good fight" against the forces of evil, not only because believers encountered terrible attacks from Satan and those under Satan's dominion, but also because Wesley credited the struggle and suffering of fighting with a Christian's ability to conquer sin, realize his or her redemption, and reorder his or her communities according to God's perfect law. Wesley believed that Christians literally participated in a battle for their souls *and* bodies that made righteousness, peace, and joy possible. The process of understanding the importance of warfare and violence in Wesley's imagining of the Christian life begins with the origins of such notions in his early life.

The Emergence of the "Good Fight" Against Sin and "the World"

The basis for Wesley's characterization of the Christian life as a fight or battle evolved in significant ways over the course of the first half of his life. Wesley learned from a young age that at its most foundational level the Christian's warfare was a vigilant struggle against sin. Though High Church Anglicans, Wesley's parents, Samuel and Susanna, appealed to reforming elements within the Anglican tradition and the continental Pietists to steer themselves and their children from what John would later call "the dry and dead carcass" of Latitudinarian and Deistic elements within the Church of England.[4] Central to Wesley's religious upbringing was a highly disciplined commitment to root out sin and conform his will to God's pleasure. In Susanna's famous letter to John on child rearing, Susanna commented that parents could do nothing better for their children than to take pains to subvert the power of self-will, which she saw as the source of all sin:

> As self-will is the root of all sin and misery, so whatever cherishes this in children ensures their after-wretchedness and irreligion.... Religion is nothing else than the doing the will of God, and not our own; that the one grand impediment to our temporal and eternal happiness being this *self-will*, no indulgence of it can be trivial, no denial unprofitable. Heaven or hell depends on this alone. So that the parent who studies to subdue it in his child, works together with God in the renewing and saving a soul; the parent who indulges it does the devil's work, makes religion impracticable, salvation unattainable, and does all that in him lies to damn his child, soul and body, for ever.[5]

Susanna's aim for John, as for all her children, was a life lived in obedience to God's command to holiness, a call that the Wesleys recognized required significant effort and discipline to combat inbred sinfulness.

Wesley's assumptions about the foundational conflict between human sinfulness and the requirements of holiness strengthened during his years as a student, and later as a Fellow, at Oxford. Wesley's reading of Thomas à Kempis,

Jeremy Taylor, and others continued to inspire him to pattern all his thoughts and actions on Christ. These authors also struck a particularly personal chord that caused Wesley to develop serious doubts about his spiritual state. If Wesley aimed for a life lived in imitation of Christ, he found himself wanting. The young Wesley countered such doubts by turning to ever more careful and even extreme methods of disciplining his behavior and desires in the hope that pious action would reflect a changed inner spiritual condition. Wesley's "exacter" diary, which he began as an Oxford Fellow in 1734, reveals Wesley at perhaps his most extreme period of self-analysis. Here Wesley constructed a rating system whereby he could hourly measure on a scale of one to nine the degree of his "temper and devotion" toward God. On November 26, 1735, for instance, Wesley recorded that he experienced "Lively zeal" three times and a "7 rating five times" over the course of the day. He added that he enjoyed "Fervent ejaculatory prayers twelve times."[6] On February 21 of the following year, Wesley showed a bit more variation, reaching a 7 rating once between 5:00 and 6:00 AM, a 5 rating between noon and 1:00 PM as well as between 6:00 and 7:00 PM, and a 4 rating twice between 4:00 and 6:00 PM.[7] While such attention to detail might border on the obsessive, it clearly demonstrated the strict discipline and care the young Wesley felt necessary to apply to his spiritual life. Only through an intricate examination of the self and one's spiritual successes and failures in the midst of the day's many distractions could one hope to stem the tide of sin and grow in grace. Struggle, striving, and conflict against sin, always apparent in Wesley's spirituality, became increasingly critical to Wesley's religious imagination.

More than simply a focus on internal sin, Wesley also directed his efforts against the effects of sin on his surroundings, particularly after 1730. Wesley and his "Holy Club" peers spent much of their time ministering to the poor, sick, and imprisoned. The aims of this work were more charitable and evangelistic than direct attempts to overturn the structures that gave rise to suffering. Nevertheless, Wesley's interests clearly strayed beyond his own internal state to the health of society in general, a characteristic that remained part of Wesley's interests for the remainder of his life. In like manner, his relatively conservative approach to addressing the social effects of sin also remained intact throughout his life.

Throughout the 1730s, Wesley's lingering doubts that his strivings against sin proved efficacious played an essential role in the continued evolution of his understanding of the Christian's warfare. In the months preceding Wesley's so-called conversion in 1738, Wesley clearly criticized his spiritual life as nothing more than a "works righteousness" that deprived him of true pardon from God (justification).[8] The influence of the Moravians, particularly Peter Böhler, led Wesley to see justification as an instantaneous act of God arising through faith alone. Wesley's Moravian mentors also influenced him to insist that an inner witness in the form of the Holy Spirit's testimony confirmed that the person was a "child of God."[9]

Wesley found great solace in an understanding of justification that freed him from a sense of works righteousness. Yet he also sought to avoid the quietism of his Moravian advisers who advocated seeking justification in "silence and retirement." Wesley, influenced by his longstanding commitment to root out evil, countered that while faith alone rather than "works" could justify, humans had the responsibility to actively observe the means of grace, prayer, Bible study, and the sacraments, in the process of seeking justification.[10]

Wesley's struggle for justification by faith without falling into the errors of quietism led him to particularly martial language to describe the experience of justification and, later, sanctification. Wesley's Aldersgate conversion in 1738 laid claim to providing Wesley with a direct witness from the Holy Spirit to the forgiveness of his sins. In his post-Aldersgate reflections, Wesley adopted an image of his past efforts as a series of deliberate, though always fruitless, battles. Wesley's lament of his pre-Aldersgate state is telling: "In this vile, abject state of bondage to sin I was indeed fighting continually, but not conquering."[11] Wesley claimed that his recurring struggle and defeat ceased with his Aldersgate experience and instilled a new identity in him as a "conqueror" of sin.[12] Thereafter, Wesley's writings made prominent the notion of the Christian life as a fight in which the converted believer transformed into a conqueror. In fact, in his 1746 sermon "The Spirit of Bondage and of Adoption," Wesley associated fighting and conquering not only with setting the believer on the path to conversion, but also with constituting the essence of Christian identity:

> Art thou daily fighting against all sin; and daily more than conqueror? I acknowledge thee for a child of God. O stand fast in thy glorious liberty. Art thou fighting, but not conquering, striving for the mastery, but not able to attain? Then thou are not yet a believer in Christ. But follow on; and thou shalt know the Lord. Art thou not fighting at all, but leading an easy, indolent, fashionable life? O how hast thou dared to name the name of Christ! Only

to make it a reproach among the heathen? Awake thou sleeper! Call upon thy God, before the deep swallow thee up.[13]

The practice of fighting urged in this sermon played an important role in many of the hymns that occupied such a prominent place in the early Methodist community.[14] Wesley intentionally organized his most important hymnal, *A Collection of Hymns for the Use of the People Called Methodists,* "under proper heads, according to the experience of real Christians." Critical to this organization is a section of hymns provocatively titled "For Believers Fighting."[15] These particularly militant hymns vividly portrayed believers as beleaguered or, in the words of one selection, "surrounded by a host of foes" and "stormed by a host of foes within."[16] The hymns respond to such dire straits by calling forth an aggressive response on the part of Christ as the believers' defender. Hymns such as the following depict Jesus' victory on behalf of believers:

> Yet God is above, Men, devils, and sin
> My Jesus's love the battle shall win
> So terribly glorious His coming shall be
> His love all-victorious shall conquer for me.[17]

Although several hymns attest to Jesus' role in achieving the victory, a belief that Wesley's larger theological system supported, more often the hymns portrayed an active response from believers who strove to slay their enemies through prayer, the exercise of faith, and virtuous living. Take, for instance, this dramatic call to Christian action:

> Urge on your rapid course,
> Ye blood-besprinkled bands:
> The heavenly kingdom suffers force,
> 'Tis seized by violent hands;
> See there the starry crown
> That glitters through the skies;
> Satan, the world, and sin tread down,
> And take the glorious prize![18]

This hymn's identification of "bands" underscores the fact that believers fought as a collective army of saints as well as individuals. Many of the hymns certainly take an individualistic tone, as in the plea, "equip *me* for the war / And teach *my* hands to fight" [emphasis added].[19] But the struggle, like the context in which Methodists sung these hymns, was social, a reality that required the efforts of an army amassed "in close and firm array."[20] Similarly, another hymn commanded:

> Fight the good fight of faith with me,
> My fellow-soldiers, fight.
> In mighty phalanx joined,
> To battle all proceed.[21]

The popularity of these hymns helped disseminate the fight among Methodists of all classes. But if hymns helped convey and spread the importance of the individual and collective fight against sin, they took a backseat to Wesley's theology and cosmology when it came to providing the central foundation for the Christian's warfare. For Wesley, the cosmos existed in a state of conflict, torn asunder by various competing spiritual and temporal forces. Sin acted as the major force in creating this state of affairs. The fall of Adam and Eve introduced sin into the world and corrupted all human beings, distorting the *imago Dei* or human likeness to the divine being, rendering humans prideful, ignorant, self-loving, and disobedient.[22] From their spiritual height as the image of God, humans descended to became "the image of Satan" and fell victim to physical death and, more importantly, spiritual death.[23] Wesley insisted on the centrality of this doctrine:

> Is man by nature filled with all manner of evil? Is he void of all good? Is he wholly fallen? Is his soul totally corrupted? Or, to come back to the text, is 'every imagination of the thoughts of his heart evil continually'? Allow this, and you are so far a Christian. Deny it, and you are but an heathen still.[24]

The fall of humankind rendered the earth a kind of battlefield in which humans existed in constant animosity with one another, the spiritual world, and even nature itself. The world labored under the power of darkness, groping for life and hope but more commonly existing in a state of suffering, despair, and death. God's grace, which preserved some measure of light, was all that prevented the world from falling into utter ruin.

Wesley's embrace of the doctrine of total depravity denied humans any natural capacity to perform good or warrant salvation. However, Wesley's emphasis on prevenient grace, expressed most clearly in his sermon "On Working Out Our Own Salvation," provided the foundation for transcending depravity.

Humans were "dead in sin by nature" and therefore unable to attain salvation on their own merit, but God did not leave them to their own feeble powers. God granted every person enough grace to desire the good, differentiate the bad, and exercise their conscience.

> Everyone has sooner or later good desires. . . . Everyone has some measure of that light, some faint glimmering ray, which sooner or later, more or less, enlightens every man that cometh into the world. And everyone, unless he be one of the small number whose conscience is seared as with a hot iron, feels more or less uneasy when he acts contrary to the light of his own conscience. So that *no man sins because he has not grace, but because he does not use the grace which he hath* [emphasis added].[25]

Wesley's understanding of the grace given to each human being supported his conviction that humans could "work" toward their salvation by responding to the grace God had given them and by pursuing the good, which would result in further outpourings of grace that could lead to salvation. Wesley also insisted that because of the strength of sin in each person's life, the ability to work toward salvation became an extremely difficult enterprise. Humans had to "agonize" to "enter the straight gate" by fasting, reading the Scriptures, and attending to the sacraments with the utmost seriousness, care, and caution. Even more, humans assumed this active role even though their effort could never be sufficient in its own right to merit salvation. Salvation could come only through an act of divine grace.[26] Nevertheless, Wesley created a system by which human effort played an essential role *as a response to grace*. The responsibility of the Christian to "strive" and "agonize" created a conflictual paradigm in which Christians became active participants who needed to struggle against opposing powers of evil.[27]

The effect of the combined doctrines of total depravity and prevenient grace created a powerful dynamic in Wesley's theology that allowed Wesley to assert the depths of sin but also establish the power of humans to overcome their enslavement to it. This dynamic provided the foundation for Wesley's aggressive attack against sin. Humans could not overcome the power and pervasiveness of sin on their own. But through the infusion of divine grace that permitted a militantly aggressive effort, humans could to a large degree become free from sin's malicious hold.

Wesley's doctrine of sanctification extended the prospect for triumphing over sin beyond that of many of his evangelical peers. Wesley allowed that Christians could actually live free of sin, though he clarified that this state did not overcome humanity's Fall to the degree that humans could recapture an "Adamic perfection" in which the understanding and affections were so perfected that, like Adam, people had the ability "always to speak and act right" as well as avoid all error.[28] Even sanctified Christians continued to commit errors in judgment that could lead to mistakes in practice. Rather, Wesley meant that the sanctified could obtain freedom from evil thoughts and tempers while being empowered to fulfill the two great commandments to love God and neighbor.

> This is the sum of Christian perfection: it is all comprised in that one word, love. The first branch of it is the love of God: and as he that loves God loves his brother also, it is inseparably connected with the second, 'Thou shalt love thy neighbor as thyself.' Thou shalt love every man as thy own soul, as Christ loved us. 'On these two commandments hang all the law and the prophets:' these contain the whole of Christian perfection.[29]

As he did in his theory of justification, Wesley asserted that sanctification came only through grace by faith rather than works. However, Wesley ensured that he did not leave human effort out of sanctification by continuing to parallel the work of justification and sanctification. Just as they did in justification, Christians needed to pursue acts of repentance, piety, and mercy in their pursuit of sanctification. Wesley insisted that though these actions were neither of the same sense nor degree as the role of faith in bringing about sanctification, they remained significant and thus further ensconced believers in a spiritual world of conflict in which humans needed to pursue holiness with the same vigor with which they sought their justification. Grace awaited those who actively strove for the blessing.[30]

This dualistic battle between holiness and sin extended to what Wesley ambiguously called "the world." The "world" served as Wesleyan shorthand for all earthly things that kept people from God, such as the love of money, the pleasant company of sinners, or participation in evil structures such as slavery. Wesley called "friendship" with this world "spiritual adultery" in which the hearts of believers became corrupt and their sinful desires inflamed. As a result, Wesley directed Christians to break off all relations with the world, including all unnecessary contacts with nonbelievers, even as he simultaneously called converts to demonstrate love toward nonbelievers by ministering to them through the proclamation of the Gospel and providing for their temporal needs.[31] Unfortunately, the break with the world did not come easily because human desire remained firmly oriented toward the material rather than the divine.

The intimate connections between human desire and the world's impediments to holiness inevitably led Wesley to call the warrior back to the self, which Wesley identified as a corrupt entity requiring "sacrifice" through a "crucifixion" modeled by Jesus. Wesley admonished believers to "crucify" themselves to the world in order to liberate themselves from the bondage of sin and enjoy the pleasures of communion with God.[32] When converts embraced Christianity, Wesley contended, they entered into a life of sacrifice that Wesley saw embodied in Jesus' command: "And he said to them all, 'If anyone will come after me, let them deny themselves, and take up their cross daily, and follow me.'"[33] Wesley's understanding of "taking up the cross" required the believer to deny the self and the self's desires and embrace the will of God, an activity that though displeasing to the person breaks his or her desire for sin and conforms them to the will of God.[34]

Wesley's followers clearly perceived the difficulty of reforming the human will when the process of self-denial, by necessity, resulted in suffering and pain.

> In order to the healing of that corruption, that evil disease which every man brings with him into the world, it is often needful to pluck out as it were a right eye, to cut off a right hand. . . . The tearing away of . . . desire and affection when it is deeply rooted in the soul is often like the piercing of a sword.

Here Wesley mixed his metaphors of redemption, comparing sin to a disease and the cure to a wound received in battle. Both ways of understanding the process relied upon the necessity of pain. "It is essentially painful; it must be so by the very nature of the thing. The soul cannot be thus torn asunder, it cannot pass through the fire, without pain."[35]

Wesley's words denote how the struggle extended beyond a mental effort to control the desire for material comfort. The Christian's warfare demanded a willingness to sacrifice, suffer, and die. Some eighteenth-century British Methodists experienced this command in literal form through physical harm, and for a few even death. In the 1740s, for instance, Wesley and his followers faced mob attacks and persecution, the most of serious of which occurred in Wednesbury, where in 1743 a mob physically assaulted Methodist followers and besieged their homes and shops. Assailants dragged Wesley himself through the streets and later beat him, though he claimed that he miraculously did not feel pain.[36] In fact, attacks like this ultimately functioned positively for Wesley in helping him situate his movement within the early Christian tradition of persecution and martyrdom.[37]

The external dangers Wesley's followers faced from angry mobs were compounded by the battle's internal emotional and psychological toll, a fact that created a great deal of controversy for Wesley and the early Methodist community. Methodism's opponents questioned whether the intense struggles, acetic behavior, and "false" sense of inspiration from God they called enthusiasm would prove destructive to mind and body. Such arguments haunted Wesley from his Oxford days because of the death of his fellow Oxford Methodist, William Morgan. In the search for an explanation for the passing of a promising young man, some within the Oxford community, including Morgan's father, cast an accusing gaze Wesley's way by suggesting that Wesley's "rigorous" fasting regimen and socially questionable ministry to the poor, sick, and imprisoned drove the young man mad.[38]

Wesley took a measured response to his critics immediately following the Morgan affair. In his letter to Morgan's father, Wesley denied claims of excessiveness.[39] In particular, Wesley asserted that William gave up fasting more than a year before his death. Wesley also defended the propriety of the group's outreach to the poor, infirm, and imprisoned, largely on the grounds that they sought advice and approval from various authorities, including Wesley's father. Nevertheless, Wesley later admitted that many in the throes of conversion and even those who had already undergone the new birth experienced significant psychological struggles. The most serious of these were often pejoratively identified as "religious melancholia," a condition in which sufferers experienced "humiliation, terror of conscience, despair, suicidal inclinations, self-accusations of blasphemy and the unpardonable sin, and fear of having sinned away the day of grace."[40] Opponents seized on victims of melancholia as evidence that Methodism represented a false religion that corrupted the psyche of its followers.[41]

Although Wesley blamed some of the most serious cases of mental suffering on illness and denied that others resulted from the proper practice of the Christian life, he offered his most direct explication of mental turmoil in the religious life in two noteworthy sermons, "The Wilderness State" and "Heaviness Through Manifold Temptations." In these sermons, Wesley reduced many of the conditions that his opponents perceived as melancholia to the strictness and struggles inherent in his idea of Christian living as a form of warfare. In fact, Wesley linked the two sermons for publication with "The Wilderness State" preceding "Heaviness Through Manifold Temptations." These sermons carefully balanced Wesley's recognition that many of his followers suffered mental turmoil, some of which he thought was beneficial, with a desire to attribute much of the blame for the most serious manifestations to sin. He achieved this balance by separating the various conditions into two qualitatively different categories: "heaviness" and "the wilderness state." Heaviness was a significant psychological and even physical burden that "sinks deep into the soul" and lingers "as a settled temper." It was an intense feeling of grief or sorrow that Wesley commonly observed among believers. Unlike the wilderness state, which originated most frequently in a person's sin, heaviness arose from the "manifold temptations" of sickness, disease, poverty, and death that Satan used to "inject unbelieving, or blasphemous, or repining thoughts" into the minds of believers. These negative effects of heaviness, however, functioned positively for Wesley as a test of faith that one could see as a form of divine grace.[42] By emphasizing the origins of heaviness in temptation rather than one's own sinfulness and the potential for growth that might come through heaviness, Wesley created a space for recognizing the religious benefits of what many of his opponents saw as a psychological danger.

Wesley countered that in stark contrast to heaviness, the wilderness state was neither as common nor as beneficial as the condition of heaviness. The wilderness state was a retreat into "darkness" that resulted in a total loss of faith, love, joy, and assurance in ways that mirrored the diagnosis of religious melancholia. Wesley believed that the state arose from sin, sloth, or ignorance and presaged the departure of God's spirit from the person.[43] The experience did not originate with God nor was it a tool through which God nurtured believers in the faith. Wesley even admitted that for many, the attending mental and physical anguish could be utterly devastating. Such was the terrible case of a woman Wesley encountered in Salisbury, who, though a convert, fell into what Wesley called a "black despair" that ultimately led to madness.[44]

Interestingly, one of the very causes Wesley attributed to inducing the wilderness state was a failure to "'agonize' continually 'to enter at the strait gate'" and "'strive for the mastery'" that was so characteristic of the good fight. Not surprisingly, then, Wesley's cure for the wilderness state took the form of a renewed battle against sin. By "putting away" all sin, repenting, and "shak[ing] yourself from the dust" by "wrestl[ing] with God for the mighty blessing," one might hope to emerge from the darkness of the wilderness into the light of God's love.[45]

Wesley's recognition of the potentially negative psychological states that the battle created never dissuaded him from stressing that the Christian's warfare was the necessary means for Christians to achieve the righteousness, peace, and joy for which they longed. Wesley reminded his followers that their redemption transformed them from death to life. Justification brought with it "the peace of God" and "joy unspeakable" that was "full of glory."[46] Christians could rejoice in their experience of the love of God that sanctified them from all sin and permitted them to "love all mankind, and more especially to [love] the children of God" even as this love "expelled the love of the world, the love of pleasure, of ease, of honour, or money; together with pride, anger, self-will, and every other evil temper—in a word, changing the 'earthly, sensual, devilish' mind into 'the mind which was in Christ Jesus.'"[47]

Wesley reinforced this hope of triumph and redemption through battle in his frequent narratives of the life and death of his followers that he inserted in his published journals. By encountering the testimonial evidence of believers who successfully defended themselves against the attacks of sin and Satan, readers could be heartened to learn that even in death the redeemed believer could gain the victory.[48] Katherine Murray's narrative included in Wesley's published journals is typical of both the struggles and confidence Wesley anticipated for his followers. The narrative opens with Murray's initial struggle against sin and the "workings" of God that convicted her of sin at the age of thirteen. Her conviction steadily grew over the next several years until she received a frightening vision of the Lord that caused her to cry out and faint. This event set off a process of intense anguish in which "sleep departed from her; her food was tasteless, and she mingled her drink with weeping." At the same time, Katherine committed herself "never to rest till she found rest in him whom alone her soul desired."[49]

The resolution of Katherine's suffering in her conversion provided reassurance to readers that God would deliver the earnest seeker. For Katherine, conversion included the reception of yet another vision, this time of Christ in majesty, who assured her that her sins had been forgiven. In common fashion, however, victory in one phase of the war merely opened up a new battlefront. Katherine now had to fight Satan, who terrorized her into thinking she was eternally damned. Her successful resistance throughout the course of her life led to a final and most crucial fight with Satan immediately prior to her death. Wesley informs us that while on her deathbed the "devil made his last effort" to shake Katherine from her faith. "She was in a violent struggle about half an hour. Then she stretched out her hands and said, 'Glory to Jesus! O love Jesus! Love Jesus! He is a glorious Jesus! He has made me fit for himself.'" She continued, "I have long been drinking wine and water here; now I shall drink wine in my Father's kingdom." After uttering this proclamation, Katherine died and "breathed her soul into the hands of her Redeemer."[50]

The victories of Katherine Murray and her coreligionists demonstrated to others the ability to persevere under the conflicts of the Christian life and offered encouragement that death could be met with confidence and joy rather than doubt and fear. Believers could even long for death and the final release from sin that accompanied it.[51] The living celebrated a "good death" as Wesley did in a hymn sung before "the most beautiful corpse" he had ever seen:

> Ah, lovely appearance of death! What sight upon earth so fair!
> Not all the gay pageants that breathe, Can with a dead body compare![52]

Wesley stressed that whether in life or death the converted and sanctified believer was a conqueror. Though often beset by the world and their own sinful cravings, Christians were empowered by divine grace to become soldiers of Christ dedicated to victory over the forces of evil. Wesley implored Christians to act vigorously in pursuit of salvation. If they failed to consider seriously the real war surrounding them, they could fall prey to complacency and enter the trap of Satan that destroyed body and soul. If watchful, however, Christians could gain victory in the "good fight," free themselves from sin, and bask in the pleasures of divine love.

The Battle Intensified: The Christian's Fight Against Satan

Katherine Murray's death narrative presents the Christian's fight as not only against sin and desire for the comforts of a fallen world, but also against Satan. The power that Wesley and his fellow Methodists granted Satan ran counter to the Enlightenment's skepticism about the supernatural and the direct intervention of the divine in earthly events. Wesley insisted on the pervasive influence of spiritual powers, both benevolent and malevolent, in the daily affairs of human beings. Wesley testified to horrifying demonic possessions, cases of witchcraft, and miraculous wonders, begging skeptics to account for these through scientific or natural means.[53] In this way, Wesley reflected what H. C. Erik Midelfort has called "the awkward and ungainly transition to secular modernity" in the eighteenth century.[54] The effects of the Enlightenment, the rise of modern science, and disillusionment with the controversial witchcraft trials of the seventeenth century undermined eighteenth-century belief in supernaturalism, demons, and miracles, though the process was far slower to take root and more uneven than many have presumed. Belief in wonders, in contrast to enlightened skepticism, endured and even flourished in many areas of eighteenth-century western Europe, both Catholic and Protestant.[55]

Wesley's England exhibited the tensions and contradictions prevalent in Europe as a whole. Claims of demon possession and witchcraft continued throughout the early modern period. John Milton's epic poem *Paradise Lost* gave new life to literary images of Satan in the seventeenth century and joined Dante Alighieri's fourteenth-century poem *The Divine Comedy* as Western literature's most detailed and influential depiction of Satan, demons, and hell. The figure of the devil and the demonic ability to harm remained a fixture in the consciousness of most early modern English, but three factors bequeathed to the eighteenth century a more moderate demonology. First, the widespread Protestant belief that the age of miracles ceased with the writing of the New Testament directly influenced the means with which English Protestants addressed demon possession. In the face of preternatural assaults, English Protestants rejected dramatic exorcisms as superstitious and more often turned to what they identified as natural means to overcome possession, including prayer, fasting, and Bible reading.[56] Here natural means for expelling evil intermixed with preternatural causes to retain the explanatory power that belief in devils and possession entailed for intractable cases of sickness, suffering, and natural disasters, while reducing dependence on supernatural intervention to cure them.

A second factor in the moderation of English demonology is that though cultural expressions of Satan's physical appearance and belief in his role in witchcraft persisted in early modern England, Protestants increasingly emphasized mental temptations as Satan's most powerful tool. The main site of conflict with Satan shifted away from the body to the conscience. In response, prayer, faith, and an understanding of the meaning of temptation became the most important weapons to counter Satan's attacks. The impact was not a decline in demonism, but a change in its power and implications away from the body and toward the mind.[57]

Finally, by the turn of the eighteenth century, the philosophical, religious, and scientific transformations generated by the likes of Descartes, Locke, and Newton began to profoundly influence English thought and culture. The intellectual elite envisioned the universe functioning independent of the actions of spiritual beings, instead operating in an orderly fashion according to natural laws. Rationalism insisted that religion ought to be subjected to rational analysis, and empiricism emphasized the priority of sense observation as the foundation of knowledge. These shifts left little room for the influence of demonic powers in the workings of the world, a result that Jeffrey Burton Russell argues helped pave the way for the emergence of notions of the devil as simply a function of the human personality, a symbol of human evil rather than a literal, embodied creature.[58]

English Protestants' increased scrutiny of the devil did not translate into a wholesale purging of the Evil One. In fact, the eighteenth century witnessed vigorous debates about the devil. In England, this controversy appears in the continued popularity of early modern defenses of demons and witchcraft, including a text influential on John Wesley, *Saducismus Triumphatus; or, Full and Plain Evidence Concerning Witches and Apparitions,* but also in the ways that eighteenth-century English writers engaged in fierce contestations over the interpretation of New Testament passages describing demonic possession.[59] In 1737, Anglican clergyman Arthur Ashley Sykes (c. 1684–1756), motivated by his assumptions about the incredulity of demonic possession, sought to recast the interpretation of biblical passages normally associated with Satanic affliction. In *An Inquiry Into the Meaning of the Demoniacks in the New Testament,* Sykes sought to challenge the traditional interpretation of possession narratives on two fronts. First, Sykes asserted that ancient writers used the Greek word "daimon" as a literary device to describe wicked human beings rather than Satan's fallen angels. By referring to one's opponents as seducing spirits that tempt humans to do evil, biblical writers, Sykes argued, harnessed a powerful rhetorical argument in order to discredit their enemies and discourage believers from associating with them.[60]

When he turned to the miracles of Jesus, which seemed to suggest that Jesus literally exorcised demons from the bodies of stricken followers, Sykes resorted to a different understanding of "daimon," one influenced by Greek cosmology that equated demons with the souls of the dead rather than devils. These creatures were not generally thought to possess human bodies, but only to cause natural illnesses that science could now explain. Thus, the malevolent work of a dead soul made the "demoniack" infirm. In Sykes's view, Jesus had no intention of suggesting human beings were physically possessed by demons. Rather, the Son of God merely used common language to convey the essential message of his power over sickness.[61]

The strength of opposition to Sykes's works from the likes of Anglicans Thomas Church and Leonard Twells and from the Newtonian antitrinitarian William Whiston illustrates the devil's vitality, even within educated circles.[62] Sykes's critics attacked his departure from what they considered the "literal" and most obvious reading of both the Old and New Testament's claims to demonic possession. Marshalling their own biblical passages, defenders of Jesus' exorcism of evil spirits hoped to show that the New Testament authors and the church's own traditions understood "daimon" to be an apostate spirit who had the power to harm and possess human beings. These writers further countered that their reading of extra-biblical sources showed that ancient readers did not universally understand demons to be only the souls of the dead.[63]

These interpretive controversies reached their highest pitch in the very year John Wesley underwent his Aldersgate experience. Though Wesley did not interject himself into these particular arguments, he revealed his predilections in his later ministry and writings. David Hempton has recently summarized the positive influence of several aspects of the Enlightenment on Wesley and the early Methodist movement, including Wesley's "indebtedness to Lockean empiricism and sensationalist psychology, his endorsement, within limits, of the scientific method, his boyish enthusiasm for all kinds of experimentation, his fundamentally optimistic emphasis on human progress," and some of Wesley's most deeply held commitments to "religious toleration, advocacy of slavery abolition, concern for bodily and mental health, and dislike of all persecution and violence."[64] While the influence of Enlightenment was significant, it did not seem to substantially influence Wesley's demonology or his belief in the miraculous in general. Wesley's thought in these matters remained largely traditional. Wesley's diaries record fantastic tales of supernatural visions of heaven and hell and miraculous wonders. In Wesley's telling, bodies literally burned before his face, the dead haunted the living, and Satan, whom Wesley described as the "prince of this world," the "enemy" of Christian souls, and "the god of this world," assumed the most destructive role within the cosmos.[65] Though Wesley discussed Satan and demons more frequently in his journals than in his sermons, he set forth his most clearly articulated ideas about the origin and work of Satan and demons in his sermon "Of Evil Angels," published in 1783.[66] Like so many before him, Wesley acknowledged that Christians inevitably struggled against evil spiritual beings. These creatures were once holy angels, but their apostasy forced God to cast them from heaven. Full of rage and malice, "Satan and all his angels are continually warring against us" by looking for any moment of weakness or vulnerability to exploit to destroy humankind.[67]

With his Protestant forebears, Wesley strongly emphasized Satan's capacity to tempt believers to sin and doubt. Satan's "fiery darts" often took the form of mental assaults that provoked questions in believers' minds about their own salvation, undermined their desire to perform good works, and aroused evil "passions or tempers."[68] Wesley even explained that no evil was committed in the world, even that by humans, apart from the leading of Satan and his demons.[69]

But "Of Evil Angels" also exposes Wesley's more traditional view that Satan's work extended beyond merely mental temptation. Departing from many of his contemporaries, Wesley clearly emphasized Satan's threat to the body. Wesley explained to his followers that "[i]f he [Satan] cannot entice men to sin he will (so far as he is permitted) put them to pain" by causing diseases, "accidents," and nervous disorders that either incapacitated or killed people.[70]

If Wesley presented his most intentional reflections about Satan and demons in "Of Evil Angels," he offered his clearest picture of the devil ravaging mind, body, and soul in his journals. Wesley repeatedly bemoaned cases of Satan's assaults, particularly during his relation of his followers' conversion narratives. In these narratives, Wesley chronicled the devil's temptations to sin and doubt as more than nuisances that delayed conversion. He portrayed such attacks as provoking horrifying mental anguish, as in his publication of a Quaker woman's conversion narrative in which Satan inspired visions of hell along with a belief that devils continually surrounded her. The woman explained that her trauma became so great that she feared she would go insane.[71] For others, Satan's temptation went so far as to cause them to contemplate suicide.[72]

Wesley made clear his belief that Satan's attacks continued after conversion in his repeated warning drawn from 2 Corinthians 2:11 not to let Satan "gain an advantage" and in his dramatic accounts of his followers' deaths.[73] Again and again these narratives related Satan's final attempt at derailing a person's salvation in the days and even moments prior to death.[74] Those like Lucy God-shall, who found herself facing death in "darkness and heaviness," had to fight against Satan's attempt to "sift them like wheat" during their moments of greatest weakness.[75]

Wesley's journals also confirm the belief he articulated in "Of Evil Angels" that Satan's work extended beyond mental temptation to bodily affliction. Wesley attributed uncontrollable bodily movements, including running, jumping, and laughter, as well as many physical illnesses to the work of Satan.[76] Wesley's as-sociation of some bodily afflictions with witchcraft exposed a particular tension with many eighteenth-century religious leaders. For instance, Wesley diagnosed Sally Simpson, who in 1760 experienced horrible bodily afflictions, including suddenly falling to the ground, choking as if someone was strangling her, beat-ing herself, speaking incoherently, and attempting to throw herself on the house fire, as bewitched.[77]

Wesley described even worse physical cases than Simpson's in his accounts of Satan's direct invasion of the body through possession. Take, for instance, the terrifying case of Sally Jones. Wesley found her:

> . . . on the bed, two or three holding her. It was a terrible sight. Anguish, horror, and despair, above all description, appeared in her pale face. The thousand distortions of her whole body showed how the dogs of hell were gnawing her heart. The shrieks intermixed were scarce to be endured.

In the midst of her trials, Sally received a vision of Satan and cried out, "Come, good devil come. Take me away. You said you would dash my brains out. Come, do it quickly. I am yours. I *will* be yours. Come just now. Take me away." When Wesley returned to the woman four days later, he found that "her pangs in-creased more and more; so that one would have imagined, by the violence of the throes, her body must have been shattered to pieces."[78]

On another occasion, Wesley referred to a letter he received describ-ing a woman against whom "Satan raged vehemently." The letter explained that the woman had to be tied to the bed to protect her from killing herself. Nevertheless:

> He [Satan] caused her to roar in an incommon manner, then to shriek, so that it went through our heads, then to bark like a dog. Then her face was

distorted to an amazing degree, her mouth being drawn from ear to ear, and her eyes turned opposite ways and starting as if they would start out of her head. Presently, her throat was so convulsed that she appeared to be quite strangled. Then the convulsions were in her bowels, and her body swelled as if ready to burst. At other times she was stiff from head to foot as an iron bar, being at the same time wholly deprived of her senses and motion, not even breathing at all. Soon after, her body so writhed, one would have thought all her bones must be dislocated.[79]

In classically Protestant form, Wesley did not resort to exorcism to heal the demon-possessed. Rather, Wesley's approach to ridding evil spirits followed the typical method of prayer, fasting, and Bible reading, though Wesley also occasionally included hymn singing as well.[80] Some found relief relatively quickly while others labored on for some time with only occasional respite.

Wesley recommended a similar response to those suffering from Satan's assaults that fell short of bodily possession. First, Wesley called his followers to "put on the whole armour of God" defined simply in "Of Evil Angels" as "universal holiness."[81] Holiness gave strength to the believer to stand firm against "all the force and stratagems of the enemy." Second, Wesley reminded believers to make use of the "the shield of faith" and the "helmet of salvation" to resist Satan's temptations.[82] These defensive weapons used against Satan's most powerful "malice and rage" allowed the believer to turn the tide of the battle and assume the offensive, to "attack in the name of the Lord, and in the power of his might; and 'he [Satan] will' soon 'flee from you.'" A vigilant watch against sin and fervent prayer for power became the critical weapons of the offensive warrior. Even so, Wesley clarified that the believer finally earned victory through God's deliverance of the loyal soldier. "If you continue" to fight, Wesley said, "the God whom you love and serve will deliver you." The converse is apparent. Those who did not fight would fall prey to Satan's destructive power.[83]

The nature and importance of Satan's aggressive attack of both mind and body, when coupled with the power of sin and the temptation of the world, confirmed Wesley's claim that the Christian life was nothing less than continual warfare. In response, Christians fought in the hope that by "treading down" the evil threats plaguing them they might gain victory over their foes. Constant vigilance helped ward off any moment of weakness that could spell ruin for the soldier of God and, more importantly, ensured the glorious prize of eternal life.

Fighting and the Religious
Experience of the Divine

Those seeking respite from the terror and exhaustion of battle against sin, the world, and Satan found little solace in many of Wesley's depictions of the believer's interactions with God. In addition to the war against their trio of dark enemies, Wesley also insisted that believers became victims within a divine battle to deliver humanity to salvation. This form of conflict moved beyond the Christian's battle against evil to dominate critical aspects of human interaction with a God defined as inherently good.

Wesley identified the foundation of this divine struggle in the enmity that characterized the preconverted relationship between humanity and the divine. Human sin awakened divine judgment, most commonly when people willingly interfered with the divine plan. For instance, Wesley witnessed an example of "awful providence" after a man cursed, blasphemed, and "hindered the work of God." Wesley recalled that "God laid his hand upon him" and two days later he died.[84] For Wesley, divine justice demanded the punishment of all evildoers, whether in this life or the next.

Even the intimate relationship with God, which Methodists claimed was one of the fruits of the new birth, depended upon believers retaining obedience to God's commands. If they failed in this responsibility, they too could experience divine wrath. Francis Coxen, a former follower who Wesley explained opted to pursue a less rigorous faith, is a good example. While walking home one evening, Coxen mysteriously fell to the ground with a broken leg. Wesley said that Coxen knew immediately what happened to him. God had "overtaken" him because of his disobedience. Unfortunately, even Coxen's repentance could not save his mortal life, though Wesley indicated that it at least saved him from eternal damnation.[85]

Wesley made human rebellion and divine punishment common features of the divine-human interaction. He saw the conversion process as the most conflict-ridden aspect of the relation between God and humanity. Wesley often characterized the process of conversion as humans "wrestling" God for deliverance from sin.[86] Wrestling God seems to derive from the biblical narrative of the patriarch Jacob wrestling the angel of the Lord in Genesis 32:22–32. In this passage, the angel accosted Jacob at the ford of Jabbok but could not overpower him. The angel proceeded to dislocate Jacob's hip but still Jacob refused to relent until the angel gave him a blessing. John's brother Charles memorialized the event in his hymn "Wrestling Jacob," which Isaac Watts said "was worth all the verses he himself had written."[87] In John Wesley's *Explanatory Notes Upon the Old Testament,* Wesley wrote that Jacob's encounter with the angel for a blessing consisted of both a corporeal and spiritual wrestling. Wesley concluded believers should follow Jacob's examples and struggle with God for divine favor. "Those that would have the blessing of Christ must be in good earnest, and be importunate for it." Christians must aggressively contend with God for what they seek and maintain their faith in God's rewards despite discouragement.[88]

The command to wrestle with God might suggest a disinclination on God's part to bestow divine favor upon human beings, but Wesley argued otherwise. The only reason Jacob did not succumb to the angel, Wesley insisted, was that "it was not on his own strength that he wrestled, nor by his own strength that he prevails; but by strength derived from heaven." God empowered Jacob to wrestle the angel in the first place. Wrestling with God was therefore not an attempt to obtain what God refused to bestow, but to demonstrate the commitment and desire of the person undertaking the conflict. Jacob's willingness "that all his bones be put out of joint than he will go away without" the blessing made him exemplary for believers. Wesley concluded that Jacob's faith in divine blessing despite discouragement pointed the believer to a life committed to vigilantly contending with God through divine power for spiritual and temporal blessings.[89]

In the published form of his sermon "The Wilderness State," Wesley underscored just how important the believer's pursuit of divine blessings through fighting might be. In the course of the sermon Wesley referred to Matthew 11:12 to reinforce the struggle that Christians must endure to "strive for the mastery." Wesley commanded Christians to "take the kingdom of heaven by violence," by which he meant that Christians must rush into the kingdom like "those who are taking a City by Storm."[90] Christians, like soldiers, must use every effort to realize their redemption.

Wesley nuanced his understanding of this aggressive expression of piety as critical to the struggle against God by arguing that Christians could never claim the status of conqueror like they could against sin, the world, and Satan. The battle with God placed the divine in the role as conqueror over the defeated human. God must "wound" or "kill" the believer as part of the conversion process.[91] Such experiences found their antecedents in biblical narratives such as

James 4:12: "There is only one Lawgiver and Judge, the one who is able to save and destroy." By referencing such passages, Wesley constructed an image of God as a warrior who vanquished converts in order to deliver them to salvation.

Wesley's link between the conversion experience and a divine wounding harks back to English and American Puritans who spoke similarly in the seventeenth century. Thomas Hooker's massive seventeenth-century analysis of the movement of the soul toward salvation identified a "Holy kind of violence" that saved sinners from the entrenched hold of sin over them.[92] The power of sin required an equally powerful counterforce to tear humans away from their ignorance and blindness. That such "violence" could take bodily shape in experiences like falling out or feeling physical pain did not appear in any widespread way among Protestants, however, until the eighteenth century, when the experience became a particularly prominent and contentious part of the religious revivals then occurring on both sides of the Atlantic. Revivalist supporters from a host of denominations, from Presbyterian and Congregationalist to Baptist and Methodist, attributed bodily exercises to the work of God.[93] In most cases, the person trembled, groaned, screamed, and/or fell motionless to the ground "as dead" under divine power.[94] Wesley told of both men and women who were "seized with violent pain" that included feeling "just as if a sword was running through them; others, that they thought a great weight lay upon them, as if it would squeeze them to the earth." Further accounts included people who felt they were "quite choked so that they could not breathe" and some "that it was as if their heart, as if all their inside, as if their whole body, was tearing all to pieces."[95] Still others found the very signs of life departing from them, as did one woman whom Wesley recalled showed almost no signs of breath or a pulse.[96]

For converts who underwent such bodily experiences, the theological language of death and new life in Christ assumed tangible forms, and the trauma to the convert was often considerable. Some found only temporary relief from their conditions after the passing of days and even weeks.[97] Wesley recorded in his journals that one woman suffered such horrible bodily forms of conviction that she had to be tied to her bed, while another suffered so greatly that Wesley recalled, "you would have imagined she could not live a moment."[98] In the face of such suffering, Wesley admitted it was sometimes even difficult for him to watch.[99]

The gravity of such experiences that served as a precursor to the feelings of joy and love that marked, albeit in some cases temporarily, the resolution of conversion, raise important questions about Wesley's understanding of the function of bodily religious experiences. What connection did such experiences have to the theological claim that the person moved from spiritual death to new life? Ann Taves argues that Wesley attributed bodily experiences of falling, trembling, and the like to the natural effects of what Wesley called the "witness" or "testimony" of the Holy Spirit to the person of their sinfulness and rightful damnation. The individual's awakening to her or his own sinfulness shocked the person to such a degree that the only response could be to scream, cry, tremble, and even faint at the depths of his or her own degradation. God did not directly cause the bodily movements, and they were not supernatural. Rather, Wesley saw the movements as natural responses of humans to the supernatural testimony of the spirit.[100]

Taves's interpretation likely reflects Wesley's most careful analysis of bodily exercises, though at various points Wesley offered far more ambiguous accounts. Even in moments when he seemed to attribute bodily movements to one source, Wesley opened up the possibility for their origins in another. In one revealing passage of his journals, Wesley attributed bodily exercises to the witness of the spirit, but then also explained "I have no doubt but it was Satan 'tearing' them, as they were 'coming' to Christ." Similarly, Wesley wrote of a woman who attended one of his meetings and experienced "violent fits" in which she "strongly convulsed from head to foot and shrieked in a dreadful manner." Wesley concluded that an "unclean spirit did tear her indeed." Thus, bodily effects could originate from Satan's attempt to disrupt the conversion process as well as from divine conviction.[101]

On the other hand, Wesley suggested that people could also experience bodily exercises as a natural response to God's love. Like those exercises that resulted from conviction, these experiences also flowed from a divine influence and were a human response to a divine witness rather than a direct act of God. However, the witness was not one of wrath or condemnation as in the cases mentioned above, but love. Wesley recalled a woman named Margaret who could not speak or move because "the love of God so overflowed her soul."[102] Similarly, Wesley received a letter describing a revival near Everton in which a man "was so filled with the love of God during morning prayer that he dropped down and lay as one dead for two hours."[103]

Finally, Wesley described ambiguous occasions of bodily exercises that suggest God might have been more directly involved in the movements than simply testifying through the Holy Spirit. Wesley's language suggests God was the first cause of the experience. In narrating bodily movements, Wesley referred to "the hand of God pressing them [those falling] to the earth."[104] Wesley also wrote of what he called a "peculiar" case in which a woman cried aloud like others under conviction. What made the woman's case unusual was that she felt "the sufferings of Christ," including "sharp bodily pain, as if she had literally suffered with him."[105] Other people, Wesley said, felt "the terrible wrath of God" course through their bodies.[106] These examples show that whether because of imprecision in his language or genuine ambiguity in his thinking, Wesley could imply a direct role for God in causing bodily exercises.

It is important to note that the prospect of a more direct role for God in bodily experience is not alien to other ways that Wesley imagined divine action. Wesley's broader theological system allowed God to cause bodily pain and discomfort to bring about some greater good, including salvation. God had to subdue human hearts, break their wills, and eradicate their sinful attachments to the world. These changes could only come through an act of divine power likened to a wound or even a death. In Wesley's third discourse on the Sermon on the Mount, he explained how God caused suffering, particularly in the form of persecution, in order to chastise the wayward and foster spiritual growth. Physical suffering became the "medicine" by which God "healed" humans of their sins and their attachments to the world and created a deeper communion with the divine.[107]

More generally, E. Brooks Holifield found that Methodists imputed religious significance to physical suffering by identifying it with the suffering of Christ. Suffering allowed Christians to imitate Christ and in the process come to more fully understand the sacrifice that Christ made for human beings. At the same time, suffering could permit Christians to better identify with other sufferers and thus more effectively engage them in acts of love.[108]

All these examples suggest that Wesley's writings sustain at least three possible ways of interpreting the causes of what he considered legitimate bodily exercises: a natural human response to the witness of the spirit concerning either a person's sin or God's love, direct divine force, and Satan's resistance to the person's conversion.[109] Good reason exists to think that a combination of these could also account for bodily exercises. Wesley's analysis of bodily movements in the second volume of his journals explained that those who could give a coherent relation of their experiences said that "the Word of God" in the form of the testimony of the spirit "pierced their souls" and convinced them of "inward, as well as outward, sin. They *saw and felt* the wrath of God abiding on them and were afraid of his judgments" [emphasis added]. In addition to the wrath displayed by God, Satan attempted to convince them that they could not be saved and struck their bodies with pain that resulted in their "loud and bitter cries" as well as their falling to the ground, feelings of being torn, and so on.[110] In this passage God and Satan both caused bodily effects.

Stephen Gunter suggests that by the end of Wesley's life the preacher's views on bodily movements changed such that Wesley doubted that God played even an indirect role in their manifestation.[111] For Gunter, bodily exercises resulted from the level of anxiety seekers felt when confronted by claims about their impending damnation. The mental stress derived from fears about their damnation caused people to fall out and scream. Gunter contends that largely under the influence of Charles Wesley, John began to emphasize a more optimistic message to people, saying that if they were earnest seekers of God they would eventually receive saving grace. This message lessened people's fears and the concomitant mental anxiety, thus taking away the cause of bodily exercises.[112] Ann Taves has argued, however, that while Wesley acknowledged that bodily experiences declined after a few years, he never claimed that they disappeared altogether nor was he ever willing to grant that God did not play a role in at least some of the experiences.[113]

Wesley's association of bodily religious exercises with "the *natural* consequences" of divine conviction and his willingness to allow that Satan also occasionally imitated these exercises for demonic purposes seems to have been Wesley's most refined theological reflection on bodily experiences.[114] Yet the ambiguity with which he addresses the issue in his writings can only leave his interpreters to puzzle over whether Wesley might have entertained other possible relationships between the divine and bodily religious experiences. In all cases, Wesley steeped the experience of conversion in aggression. Christians had to wrestle God with the effort of an attacking army even though victory could come only in defeat as God "wounded" believers both metaphorically and literally in order to heal them. Only after God's successful battle with the penitent could the believer claim redemption.

The reward for success in this conflict, according to Wesley, included spiritual redemption as well as temporal power and authority. "They that by faith have power in heaven, have thereby as much power on earth as they have occasion for. . . . Those that resolve though God slay them yet to trust in him, will at length be more than conquerors."[115] Though their battle might be difficult, believers could take solace that God would provide for both their spiritual and temporal needs. An integral part of this provision entailed the formation of a religious community bound by the shared experience of the new birth. Wesley explained in "The Marks of the New Birth" that conversion gives rise to a love of God *and neighbor* that extended to the willingness to sacrifice all things, even one's life, for another.[116] While this ethic applied to all humans, whether redeemed or not, it imposed itself most strongly on those who shared the intimate bonds of the new birth and could truly call their fellow believers "brothers" and "sisters" in Christ. This new community, formed in the present world through a reconstituted relation with God, prefaced the final heavenly state in which "an intimate" and "uninterrupted union with God" will lead to "the continual enjoyment of all the creatures in him!"[117]

John Wesley's spirituality depended heavily upon the notion of conflict between saint and sinner, good and evil, the redeemed and the demonic. Although Wesley sought the salvation of human beings from all sin, a restored relationship with the divine, and an intimate community of faith bound together by the new birth, he argued that Christians could only realize these aims through intense struggle defined in terms of warfare. That Christians participated in a fight extended from metaphorical ways of understanding believers' struggle to overcome sin in their life to very tangible encounters with Satan, human beings, and even the divine that could leave humans physically and psychologically wounded. Simply stated, Christians needed to fight, and Wesley celebrated when a believer reached the end of his or her life having "conquered" sin, Satan, and the world. Through fighting the good fight, even as God conquered penitents in conversion, believers moved from enmity with the divine to an intimate relationship in which they worked for the transformation of their communities and the fruits of redemption for eternity in heaven.

The battles Wesley found so important for the Christian life also came to shape Wesley's view of temporal struggles, whether in the form of England's wars or personal conflicts between individual human beings. Wesley often discouraged Christians from using force against other human beings. The Christian's battle was not against "flesh and blood." Yet at various points throughout his life, Wesley allowed for the possibility that aspects of the Christian's fight might intersect with that of the state. In this intersection the boundaries of the good fight became more permeable and contested as Wesley's followers struggled to apply the fight to their own lives and communities. Most preserved the idea that fighting provided one of the central means of facilitating spiritual growth and creating communal relations. Yet within different economic, political, and theological contexts, Wesley's followers either could not or would not adhere to Wesley's exact formulations of the good fight and who the object of that fight might be. While some focused on a purely spiritual fight, others justified social violence by rooting it within the context of the good fight against sin, the world, and Satan. For nearly all Methodists, the terms of warfare dramatically shifted from Wesley's design.

TWO

CONTESTING THE GOOD FIGHT

Warfare and the American Revolution

John Wesley firmly entrenched the Christian life in a physical and spiritual battle with God and the forces of evil that required Christians to enlist as soldiers to "fight the good fight" and take "the kingdom by violence." The militant ways that Wesley described the Christian life raise the question of whether a relationship existed between Christians' battle against sin and the temporal struggles of war. Did the violent nature of early Methodists' spiritual battles—Satan's ravaging the body, God "killing" penitents, Christian "warriors" committing themselves to unceasing acts of vigilance against the evil in their souls and societies—lead adherents to commit acts of physical violence against other human beings? Or did the nature of the battle against sin render armed conflict against human beings meaningless?

This chapter explores these questions through an examination of Methodist contestations over the American Revolution. The warfare Wesley portrayed as essential to the practice of the Christian life occupied a complicated and at times contradictory relationship to bodily violence between humans. Wesley simultaneously championed an aggressively militant expression of Christian spirituality while often advocating peaceful and nonviolent interactions between human beings. The true believer battled sin, the world, and Satan while ideally displaying love toward saints and sinners alike. But by no means did Wesley imagine himself a pacifist.[1] He believed that certain occasions could necessitate violent physical responses that transformed the Christian into a soldier for God *and* country. By examining Wesley's rationale for the Christian's participation in war we can begin to identify the boundaries and intersections Methodists constructed between the wars fought among nations and those fought for salvation. Wesley did not always make the two forms of fighting mutually exclusive. Rather, his justification of the state's warfare depended heavily upon his ability to both conceptualize the war in terms of the battle against evil and embrace the use of the weapons of the state to fight the Christian's war.

Across the Atlantic, many Methodists in America refused to participate in or condone the Revolution, casting their resistance in religious terms. These Methodists rejected Wesley's conflation of the Christian's religious battle with armed political conflict. This rejection did not come by way of a less vibrant or expansive notion of the Christian's warfare. Quite to the contrary, American Methodists shared Wesley's insistence on the importance of the "good fight" and the terrifying dangers that plagued all those who entered into it. Rather, American Methodists refused to read the political conflict through the lens of their battles against evil. American Methodists constructed an inverse relationship between the two forms of warfare. They emphasized that their participation in the battle leading to spiritual liberty left them with little interest in the military struggle for liberty's political correlate. These Methodists insisted that war distracted them from their greater battle for salvation. Some even rendered war entirely inconsistent with a Christian life that they defined as inherently aggressive and dangerously contested.

I argue in this chapter that though the holy violence of the good fight for salvation played a divergent role for Methodists in the Revolution, the battle is an essential piece in the puzzle of Methodist motivations for war and peace. The very same commitments that discouraged Wesley's American followers, and at times even Wesley himself, from resorting to violence could, when applied to the public realm, provide an equally powerful justification for horrendous violence.

John Wesley and War

The warfare that inhered in Wesley's theology and practice of the Christian life did not demand that Christians commit physical violence against other human beings. Christians might be ardent soldiers of God who waged a battle against the powers of evil and even suffered in order to realize their salvation at the hands of a warrior God, but they did not target other humans as meaningful opponents in their "good fight." Wesley often insisted that the believer did not fight against "flesh and blood, but with principalities and powers, and spiritual wickedness in high places."[2] Wesley made this battle against spiritual forces his primary concern. Those who wandered from it exposed themselves not only to physical death, but also eternal punishment.

Wesley's focus on battling spiritual rather than earthly forces intersected with his deeply conservative political philosophy. Wesley regularly warned his followers to steer clear of "preaching politics." Instead, he called for quiet obedience to ruling authorities, a position that Wesley found biblical precedent for in Romans 6:1–6: "Everyone must submit himself to the governing authorities . . . he who rebels against the authority is rebelling against what God has instituted and those who do so will bring judgment on themselves." Wesley translated this ethic into a mandate for passive obedience and nonresistance to the government that he believed characterized a good Tory.[3]

This incredulity about the Christian's role in politics informed Wesley's brief treatise "How Far is it the Duty of a Christian Minister to Preach Politics?" written during the hostilities of the American Revolution. In this document, Wesley reiterated his ethic of silence concerning politics even as he sought to make space for what he thought could be rare occasions for Christians to enter the political fray to defend their rulers from "palpably false" rumors. Wesley preferred that his followers focus their attention on preaching "repentance towards God, and faith in our Lord Jesus Christ." The risk that political involvement might factionalize his followers and divert them from focus on their eternal condition was simply too great to countenance active political involvement. More practically, since Wesley's opponents often attacked Methodists as Jacobites, avoiding political involvement seemed most wise. Enforcing political disinterest, however, discouraged Methodists from developing a theological justification for challenging social and political injustices and denied them the opportunity to develop a constructive political philosophy that complemented their theology.[4]

Wesley's public rule against political involvement did not prevent him from occasionally and unsystematically speaking to political and social issues he thought important, particularly slavery, education, the use of money, and war. On most of these occasions, Wesley's social ethic, informed by his understanding of the Christian's responsibility to love God and neighbor, played a significant role in motivating a sometimes biting critique of his fellow citizens and England's ruling authorities. Wesley tried to root this ethic of love to humans in his soteriology. Wesley insisted that God's love extended to all human beings and that redemption itself originated in this love. Thus, while he interpreted justification in a legal sense of the "pardon" of sinful humans from their just punishment, he described the process of pardon as God's love for humanity leading God to offer the "Beloved" Son to suffer in humanity's place. Further, the love of God and Christ that effected this pardon resulted in a new relationship between God and believers in which God "loves and blesses and watches over us for good, even as if we had never sinned."[5]

Wesley attempted to push beyond an intellectual assertion of the reality of this love to insist that Christians actually experienced God's love in a direct and affective way. Through "the new birth," believers literally felt the love of God "'shed abroad in [their] heart[s]'" that produced joy and peace with God. In response, believers expressed love back to God both emotively, as God became "the joy of their heart," and by seeking "all things needful whether for their souls or bodies" from God.[6]

Wesley also credited this experience of divine love to fundamentally transforming the nature of the Christian's interactions with other human beings. God's expression of love experienced in justification and sanctification allowed humans, and in fact obligated them, to display love to others such that love for God and neighbor became the very sign of the perfected life. Conversely, the failure to love and the concomitant lack of faith that attended this failure ensured eternal punishment.[7]

Wesley used the paradigm of the experience of God's love shaping the believer's responsibility to others as the basis for social action, or as Wesley stated, "the never-failing remedy for all the evils of a disordered world."[8] In "Thoughts Upon Slavery," for instance, Wesley adopted a largely rationalist argument based on natural rights to condemn the Atlantic slave trade. However, Wesley interlaced this argument with a theological commitment to the image of a God of love and justice who both calls sinful humans to spiritual transformation leading to compassion for their fellow human beings, and also punishes slaveholders according to how they treated their slaves.[9]

Wesley's theological framing of slavery as a form of sin underscores his recognition that sin existed within social structures as well as the individual heart, in the external world, and within the self. Like the sin within the individual, social sins arose through the influence of Satan as well as human corruption. The Christians' struggle against sin and Satan, then, included a struggle against sinful social behavior. Wesley made this dual struggle clear in his urging of Christians to "take the kingdom by force." Wesley envisioned the kingdom's manifestation in the renewed hearts of individuals, but also in the renewal of society that culminated in the eschatological vision of a heavenly kingdom of perfection in which Christ reigned in glory.[10]

Wesley imagined the means of realizing the social dimensions of the kingdom, at least ideally, through the spiritual weapons of Gospel preaching, holy living, and the expression of love to enemies. Wesley particularly emphasized the motive of love as a force for social action in his hope that his followers would become peacemakers. In his exposition of the Sermon on the Mount in which Jesus calls the peacemaker blessed, Wesley explained that the peacemaker's task of showing love to the world extended to all human beings regardless of whether they were friends or foes.

> But in the full extent of the word a "peacemaker" is one that as he hath opportunity "doth good unto all men"; one that being filled with the love of God and of all mankind cannot confine the expressions of it to his own family, or friends, or acquaintance, or party; or to those of his own opinions; no, nor to those who are partakers of like precious faith; but steps over all these narrow bounds that he may do good to every man; that he may some way or other manifest his love to neighbors and strangers, friends and enemies.[11]

This responsibility to love others prevented the Christian from harming her fellow humans. In his famous sermon "The Use of Money," Wesley forbade Christians from any occupations that harmed either themselves or their neighbors in substance, body, or soul.[12] Even more, Wesley's condemnation of self-defense in response to the mob attacks that dogged the preacher and his followers throughout the 1740s and into the early 1750s extended such prohibitions to particular acts of violence. Though the persecution of Methodists often only rose to the level of nuisance, it could become dangerous, as it did when mobs harassed Methodist preaching and class meetings by shouting, throwing stones, beating people, and destroying property.[13] Bodily harm sometimes resulted, even for Wesley, who at various times received blows significant enough to bloody him.[14] Nevertheless, Wesley repeatedly cautioned his followers not to respond in kind.[15] On at least one occasion Wesley even protected a man whose disturbance of his preaching drew the ire of Wesley's followers.[16]

Though Wesley forbade his followers from physically defending themselves against mob attacks, he did not leave his follows without protection of any kind. Wesley acknowledged that Methodists had recourse to the court system, but he also mysteriously promised that God would do the fighting for believers to protect them from harm and deliver them from having to use force. Take for example an occasion when an angry mob beat Wesley. One of his followers, Joan Parks, reportedly fought in Wesley's defense. Wesley confronted Parks and asked her if she had indeed fought for him, to which Park adamantly responded, "No; I knew God would fight for his children."[17] Similarly, after escaping the persecution plaguing the town of Wednesbury, Wesley concluded that "the Lord fought for us" so that Wesley and his followers could "hold their peace."[18] In such cases, God's "fighting" seems to have meant miraculous intervention that moderated the belligerent spirit of the mob or protected those under attack from actual harm.

Wesley offset his opposition to inflicting violence against other humans by ascribing benefit to suffering mob attacks. Wesley certainly cautioned his followers against intentionally seeking out persecution, but mob attacks also helped Wesley confirm the validity of his ministry.[19] Wesley believed that members of his movement, like the martyrs of the early church, fulfilled the biblical promise that those who served God would suffer persecution.[20] Wesley also came to see violent persecution as a blessing that produced spiritual maturity.[21] He proclaimed as much after a particularly brutal assault left his face bloodied: "what a blessing it is when it is given to us, even in the lowest degree, to suffer for his name's sake."[22]

Wesley's emphasis on the believer's responsibility to engage humans in love, and the meaning that he found in suffering violence rather than inflicting it, provided a significant ethical base for early Methodists. Wesley sought to focus

his followers' attention on their spiritual state and the war against sin and evil being fought around them, but he did not use this focus to dismiss the Christians'
obligation to contribute to the human communities around them. The experience of God's love that every Christian enjoyed required believers to demonstrate
love to those they encountered. In fact, love became a tool for conquering Satan's
dominion and achieving God's kingdom within the hearts and communities of
Christians. This commitment to challenging enemies on a spiritual battlefield
through love rather than force made participation in social violence deeply problematic for the obedient practice of the Christian life. Because even social evils
ultimately emerged out of sin, the most successful counterattack occurred at the
spiritual level.

Nevertheless, when British Methodists, including Wesley, gathered in London in 1744 for their first joint conference amidst heightened conflicts between
France and England, they strayed from Wesley's refusal to commit bodily harm
in their answer to the question of whether the moral law allowed a Christian to
bear arms as a soldier for the state. The official minutes record their affirmative
response. "There is no command against it [bearing arms] in the New Testament," and secondly, "because Cornelius a Soldier is Commended there [the New
Testament], and not mentioned to have laid them [his arms] down."[23]

This statement appears to make the issue of military service relatively clear
for British Methodists. In reality, bearing arms for the state and warfare in
general represented a far more complex problem. First, how could Methodists
balance participation in war with Wesley's prioritization of spiritual weapons,
particularly effective Gospel preaching and acts of piety and love? More specifically, how could Christians love their enemies if they served in a profession that
required participants to kill those enemies on the battlefield? Similarly, how
could Wesley reconcile his claims about the spiritual value that came from suffering violence with the action of the soldier who inflicted violence?

Wesley's concern that his followers not become engulfed in political struggles to the exclusion of the greater battle for salvation posed a second problem for
Methodists' defense of war. On at least one occasion this concern led Wesley to
distinguish Christianity from the "savage cruelty" of warfare. Wesley considered
the nation's wars far more banal than the cosmic battle for salvation, and thus
to be avoided when possible. In turn, Wesley recognized that even soldiers in a
temporal king's army needed to enlist to "fight a better fight" in which the word
of God became "mightier than arms."[24] Christians could never earn salvation by

committing acts of physical violence against humans, but violence could easily derail the path to eternity in heaven.

Finally, Wesley's theological association between sin and war also proved problematic for condoning participation in war. In his sermon "The Doctrine of Original Sin," Wesley answered his own question about the origins of war. "From whence comes that complication of all the miseries incident to human nature—war? Is it not from the tempers 'which war in the soul?'"[25] By connecting the internal struggle against sin with the external conflicts of nations, Wesley inextricably bound the act of war with sin. How could Christians, whom God called to holiness, participate in an act arising from sin?

One might think that given the connections between sin and war, the distraction that war posed to pursuing the greater battle of salvation, and Wesley's belief that Christians fought their battles with spiritual rather than temporal weapons, Wesley would have denounced war and the Christian's responsibility in it as an impassible barrier to holiness. But Wesley did not renounce war. Wesley never fully explained his rationale for the Christian's participation in war, but his writings reveal the tensions inherent in his call for radical discipleship in the midst of a life lived within traditional social boundaries. Wesley's views on the role of government and the responsibilities of Christians to participate in the civic realm meant that he would have to overlook both the boundaries he set against the use of physical violence and also the concomitant role those boundaries played in promoting holiness.

The right to wage war rested in Wesley's views on the origins of power. Wesley denied that individuals ever had the right to take a life or grant that power to another. Rather, God alone held the power of life and death and granted that power to the king as God's appointed ruler. This power defined the king's right to legitimately wage war and punish the wicked.[26] Thus, governments held the power to kill through war and through capital punishment of criminals.[27] Of course, the sovereign needed to avoid using this power indiscriminately. In accordance with the just war tradition, the sovereign could only summon the nation to war for defensive purposes to counter a foreign aggressor or suppress internal rebellion.[28] When such instances arose, loyal citizens, whether Christian or not, had the responsibility to support the ruler by participating in warfare. The obligation of citizens to support their ruler trumped Wesley's concern for Christians' avoiding political rancor. Rather, as loyal subjects, Christians were commanded by God to submit to the ruling authorities that maintained order and liberty according to their own divine calling. Wesley's approval of the 1744 conference action legitimating military service formalized this rule and led to his offer to raise a company of troops from among the Methodist societies in Great Britain to defend England during the Seven Years' War and to support Thomas Webb's attempt to recruit British Methodists for a similar task during the American Revolution.[29] Wesley's permissive stance toward war stretched the boundaries of legitimate fighting to include the participation of believers in forms of physical violence and rendered those pursuits theologically justifiable.

The palpable tensions in Wesley's views on war, a symbol of sin and a distraction from the pursuit of salvation and perfect love on the one hand, and the responsibility of obedient citizens submitting to the just actions of a divinely instituted sovereign on the other, appeared most clearly during England's war with the American colonies. Wesley moved from initial support of the colonists and a theological castigation of the impending war as the product of sin on both sides, to depicting the struggle as a just war in which the righteous nation of England became the instrument of divine punishment for the sins of the colonies. Wesley bound these shifting positions together by tying them to his views on the intersection between the battle against sin and evil that posed essential implications for the redemption of God's people.

In 1766, Wesley wrote that he could not "defend the measures which have been taken with regard to America." Though he did not identify which measures he opposed, Wesley likely was referring to the taxation measures pursued by George Granville in the 1760s, including the Revenue Act of 1764 and Stamp Act of 1765.[30] Wesley's letters to Lords Dartmouth and North nearly a decade later made clear that Wesley imagined the complaints of the colonists, "an oppressed people" as he called them, "nothing more than [a demand for] their legal rights, and that in the most modest and inoffensive manner which the nature of the thing will allow."[31]

This rather demure portrait of the Americans' "modest and inoffensive" quest for their rights as citizens would face a serious challenge as the winds of war blew stronger throughout the 1770s. For the moment, however, Wesley continued to view the Americans' claims as legitimate political concerns, and he hoped for a peaceful resolution. Merely a month before the Battle of Lexington, Wesley wrote the preachers in America to admonish them toward neutrality: "It is your part to be peace-makers, to be loving and tender to all, but to addict yourselves to no party. In spite of all solicitations . . . say not one word against one side or the other."[32]

By November 1775, the battles of Lexington, Concord, and Bunker Hill dimmed Wesley's hope for a peaceful resolution and caused his mood to grow dark at the prospect of widespread war. Wesley countered with a passionate plea against war in a sermon we now know as "National Sins and Miseries."[33] The sermon painted an apocalyptic vision of the impending war with the colonies by predicting God's judgment upon the sins of the English, particularly their lying, luxury, sloth, and profaneness. Comparing England to the people of Israel in 2 Samuel 24, whom the angel of the Lord punished because of King David's sin, Wesley postulated that this same angel would destroy England. Wesley went on to depict a terrifying picture of the citizens of both England and the American colonies as having lost all reason and morality and devolving into sheer madness, rage, and murder. In such a state, said Wesley, those "foaming with rage . . . ready to tear out one another's throat, and to plunge their swords into each other's bowels" cast aside all liberty and proper obedience to the sovereign. Wesley further lamented that people's iniquities had brought the "fell monster" of war upon Britain's colonies, ushering nothing but terror and death as the people's "blood is poured on the earth like water," an image Wesley may have borrowed from the Psalmist's mourning: "Their blood have they shed like water round about Jerusalem; and there was none to bury them."[34]

Wesley had never spoken so vehemently and pessimistically about the prospect of war with the colonies. Yet his sermon also held out hope that should the people repent of their sins and put away their evil deeds they might stay the hand of God. Because he saw the true cause of the war as resting with the sins of the people, Wesley explained that the purification of the people's hearts and lives could heal the nation and avoid a war he believed would surely lead to its destruction.[35]

Wesley offered a similar argument that the colonies and mother country shared responsibility for a conflict that had its ultimate roots in sin in 1775, though by the end of that year he began laying the groundwork for a profound transformation in his estimation of responsibility for the war and his opposition to the war itself. After reading Samuel Johnson's *Taxation No Tyranny* months earlier, Wesley became convinced that American complaints about the violation of their liberties lacked the proper moral and legal foundations. In turn, Wesley revised and reprinted Johnson's essay as "A Calm Address to Our American

Colonies." Wesley insisted that the colonists, like the inhabitants of England, enjoyed civil and religious liberty and that independence could only result in either anarchy or tyranny. Further, Wesley powerfully underscored what he considered the hypocrisy of the Americans by emphasizing that though they spoke of forming a government of the people and chafed when they believed they were denied representation in government, they upheld the very same violations of liberty by denying women and children the right to vote.[36]

While Wesley now recognized some of the problems inherent in the colonial campaign, he, unlike Samuel Johnson, was not ready to lay full blame on the Americans. Rather, Wesley linked American unrest to "designing men" in England who intended to overthrow the monarchy.[37] Wesley's reference to English rebels associated the American conflict with controversies John Wilkes stirred in the 1760s and early 1770s. Wilkes gained famed for championing the rights of the people to directly elect their representatives and, more seriously, for his public criticisms of the king and his ministers. In 1768, Wilkes's election to Parliament was overturned and his seat awarded to the runner-up, Henry Luttrel. This action roused intense debate about the privileges of Parliament and the validity of popular elections, to which Wesley responded in several essays, including "Free Thoughts on the Present State of Public Affairs" (1768, 1770), "Thoughts Upon Liberty" (1772), and "Thoughts Concerning the Origins of Power" (1772).[38] In these tracts, Wesley not only defended the king against what he considered false charges, but he also castigated Wilkes's claims to resting political power in the hands of the people. Wesley countered Wilkes by rooting the origins of power theologically in God, who transferred power to the ruling authorities serving as God's representative.[39]

Wesley's inclination to either spread the blame for hostilities between the Americans and British or more squarely focus on discontent among radical segments in England prevailed for only a limited time. A new perspective on the colonial crisis profoundly influenced his willingness to discourage armed violence. With the publication in 1776 of "Some Observations on Liberty," Wesley moved to condone war. His arguments depended heavily on his ability to see England and America in dualistic categories of good and evil. Wesley began to portray the American cause as a form of sin whose corruption brought divine punishment. In important respects, "Some Observations on Liberty" drew from several of Wesley's earlier essays on English politics. As he did when confronting the upheaval posed earlier in the decade by John Wilkes, Wesley argued that true liberty consisted of both religious and civil liberty. "Religious liberty is, a liberty to choose our own religion." Civil liberty "is a liberty to dispose of our lives, persons, and fortunes, according to our own choice, and the laws of our country." In both cases, Wesley believed the Americans enjoyed these liberties to the same degree as their cousins in Great Britain. Just as he did in "A Calm Address to the American Colonies," Wesley emphasized that Americans spoke in contradictions when they demanded representation in a government formed by the people when they denied so many people the right to vote.[40]

But Wesley departed from his previous statements concerning the colonial controversy by employing a theological argument he first used in 1772 against John Wilkes to challenge the fundamental principle that government emerged from the people. Government, insisted Wesley, could never emerge from the people because only God could grant power. Rulers were "delegates" or "ministers" of God to govern the people.[41] Because God invested England's government with the power to rule, Wesley associated obedience to the government with obedience to God. Conversely, loyalty to the king flowed naturally from loyalty to God. As Wesley so often expressed: "Those who fear God, honour the King."

By associating loyalty to God with loyalty to the crown, Wesley associated sinners with enemies of the state, since corruption necessarily spread beyond the individual to the community as a whole.[42] These interconnections between government and religion reflected Wesley's sense that government played an important role in promoting and maintaining morality among its citizens even as religion played a vital role in the preservation of the government. Although Wesley never provided a systematic treatment of his views on religion and politics, he imagined the government playing an integral role in religion through its support for and participation in religious functions, its "advancement of moral behavior, the suppression of openly ill conduct, and the establishment of peace and mutual goodwill."[43] This important role for the government certainly did not mean that Wesley refused to ever question the government or call it to account when it wavered from its divinely prescribed role. More often than not, however, Wesley championed passive obedience and nonresistance to the government he saw as ordained by God. In these terms, proper Christian behavior became nearly synonymous with obedience to the king.

Given the theological defense of Britain's government as divinely sanctioned, Wesley, almost by default, had to consider active rebellion against that order as posing religious significance unless he could find some reason to believe that the government had abandoned or abused its divinely prescribed role. "Some Observations on Liberty" allowed Wesley to draw out the religious implications of American treason. Wesley portrayed American attempts to gain independence as posing grave implications for the exercise of religion and the preservation of social order that existed to promote religion. Because Wesley already established that the Americans possessed liberty, he postulated that a far more sinister motive captured them. The Americans really sought independence from the monarchy rather than liberty. As a result, their aims stirred a deeply ingrained fear within Wesley that republican forms of government "unhinge all government, and . . . plunge every nation into total anarchy," thereby destroying civil and religious liberty.[44]

The Americans' decision to arm themselves against the sovereign in an unlawful manner and "illegally and violently" deny religious and civil liberties to the king's people transformed England's role in the war to a defensive act against colonial aggressors. Wesley infused this argument with religious language when he identified the Americans as "unrighteous" and therefore liable for the blood shed during war. With this argument, Wesley completely cut ties with his pleadings in "National Sins and Miseries," discussed earlier, in which he promoted shared responsibility for the hostilities because of the sins of both the English and the Americans. Wesley now portrayed the English as a righteous community "daily wrestling with God in prayer for a blessing upon their king and country." The righteous mother country now possessed the moral and ethical grounds to fight a just war to suppress rebellion.[45]

Wesley further developed the duality between American sin and English righteousness in his 1778 sermon "The Late Work of God in North America." Using Ezekiel 1:16 as the sermon's basis, Wesley attempted to discern the "wheel within the wheel" of divine providence in the midst of the colonial conflict. Throughout the sermon, Wesley cast the colonists as sinners whose wealth led to "pride, luxury, sloth, and wantonness" as well as the "evil disease" of "independence." God's providence used the corrective punishment of war to strike at the root sins of the people. Readers could not help but see the implications for the British military forces. If the colonists' sins had provoked God's punishment of war, then the British military served as God's instrument for that punishment. Wesley did not stop there. The preacher defined Britain's war efforts as part of the larger war for redemption by casting the war as "the destruction of Satan's kingdom, and the promotion of the kingdom of his dear Son; that they should all minister to the general spread of righteousness and peace, and joy in the Holy Ghost." This interpretation of the war as the extension of God's battle against sin and evil allowed Wesley to conflate spiritual and political ends. The defeat of the Americans would result in both "liberty from sin" and the civil liberty of property and personhood, all manifestations of one larger form of liberty: "the glorious liberty of the children of God."[46]

It only took Wesley a year to relinquish his interpretations of the controversy as a political matter of Americans asserting their natural and lawful rights or the result of the shared sins of England and America. While Wesley interpreted the conflict in either of these ways he could not condone war. Wesley's theology even offered a harsh denunciation of war when he could see it as resulting from the sins of both parties. The role of sin in causing war and the Christian's responsibility to overcome sin by exhibiting love to all people motivated Wesley to speak out against war. This understanding helps explain Wesley's temporary reversal of course in 1776 with his publication of "A Seasonable Address to the More Serious Parts of the Inhabitants of Great Britain," which again identified both the sins of England and the colonies as the cause of the war. In this essay, Wesley repeatedly cast the war as an "evil" battle between brothers that ultimately resulted from the wiles of Satan. Wesley took particular aim at British involvement in the Atlantic slave trade and also contended that the British maliciously fomented war among Native peoples in order to plunder their resources. Wesley went further by castigating the people for their neglect of the worship of God that he believed provoked God's extraordinary wrath. This argument rendered the struggle between the colonies a "divine contention," but not one in which God sided with one combatant over another. Rather, God's wrath fell upon both parties "to punish the inhabitants of the earth for their iniquity."[47]

Wesley followed this declaration of the shared sins of the people with a call to repentance rather than war. He also created a critical role for Christians in reconciliation. Wesley postulated that Christians might be the last and best hope for the world. As the "salt of the earth," Christians preserved the nation from destruction through prayer and faith. Here again, Wesley cast love as a force for action in the responsibility Christians maintained to care for "your contentious brethren" by seeking God's forgiveness for their sins. Peacemaking, motivated by love for all people, became the privileged role for Christians, who, as "the great means of saving a divided kingdom," had within their power the ability to change the course of the world by staving off its annihilation.[48]

But when Wesley again moved away from shared sin as the cause of the conflict to seeing only the Americans as unlawful, and more importantly as immoral and unrighteous sinners who undermined the divinely established sovereign, overthrew religious and civil liberties, and carried out murderous plots against the innocent, he could not only justify war as the obligation of a responsible monarch and loyal citizenry, but he could also cast it as part and parcel of the greater battle against sin and unrighteousness. This process depended on the British moving from shared guilt for the hostilities to righteous victims of American aggression, bearers of divine blessing, and the defender of divine order and religious and civil liberty. These conclusions turned particularly violent when they intersected with Wesley's understanding of government as established by God and divinely empowered to utilize the sword to punish wickedness. Unlike the individual Christian who might gain righteousness by passively suffering the aggression of others, God required the government to call forth the full force of its military power as a defensive act to suppress rebellion against the king and, more importantly, a righteous act to punish sinners and further God's aims for the eradication of evil. By intersecting the spiritual warfare against sin and evil with political struggle, Wesley's concerns that the war might hinder the Christian's pursuit of holiness all but disappeared. Wesley transformed the war into a righteous battle. He even argued that religion prospered through such warfare.[49]

Wesley's shifting views of the colonial rebellion offer a fascinating example of the permeability of the boundaries between the spiritual battle for salvation and social violence. By characterizing the Revolution as a sacred battle with cosmic significance, Wesley cast the Christian as both a temporal and spiritual warrior. The king's soldiers might not literally save their souls by killing their enemies, but they could be sure that theirs was a righteous battle against evil that would help make the greater battle for salvation possible. In the process, Wesley willingly joined the spiritual weapons of love to enemy and Gospel preaching with the physical weapons of war.

American Methodists and the Revolutionary War

Wesley's defense of Britain's right to war set him apart from many of his American followers. Wesley's official statement to the American preachers in 1775 called for neutrality. The leadership in America largely complied. Thomas Rankin (1738–1810), for instance, marked his time as Wesley's general assistant in America by publicly attempting to avoid war, even though he sympathized with the British.[50] Rankin even wrote the American secretary Lord Dartmouth with suggestions for diffusing tensions between the colonies and mother country.[51]

The other leading Revolution-era Methodist in America, Francis Asbury (1745–1816), expressed serious concern over participation in the war. The long-time general assistant and future bishop refused to take the Maryland oath of loyalty and went into hiding in Delaware in 1778 for the remainder of the war. Interestingly, he spent most of this time at the home of Judge Thomas White, a loyalist. Though Asbury explained that he had a "natural affection for my own [British] countrymen" during the Revolution, he also showed considerable sympathy for the Americans, lamenting that Wesley had come out against the colonists so publicly and even arguing that Wesley might have arrived at a different position had he lived in America:

> I . . . am truly sorry that the venerable man ever dipped into the politics of America. My desire is to live in love and peace with all men; to do no harm, but all the good I can. However, it discovers Mr. Wesley's conscientious attachment to the government under which he lived. Had he been a subject of America, no doubt but he would have been as zealous an advocate of the American cause.[52]

Wherever Asbury's political sympathies resided, the future bishop became an avid defender of nonviolence during the Revolution, chiding zealous proponents of war.[53] Asbury made his sentiments clear when he wrote his friend Richard Dallam to criticize his military career and express the preacher's hope that Dallam "would soon change your way."[54]

Asbury founded his opposition to the Revolution in his belief that war endangered the eternal condition of human beings. For Asbury, concern over the "defence [sic] of our bodies and property" paled in light of the expediency to "watch and fight against Sin and Satan, in defence [sic] of our souls, which are in danger of eternal damnation!"[55] If anything, war distracted people from this holy warfare.[56] In contrast, Asbury believed that conversion and the reformation of behavior that flowed from conversion would culminate in the eradication of war in ways similar to Wesley's vision of the realization of God's kingdom on earth through the proclamation of the Gospel and holy living.[57]

Asbury also celebrated preachers who were arrested for refusing to take part in the war or sign oaths of loyalty to the colonies. In one provocative reference in his diaries, Asbury suggested that God might have punished those who persecuted Methodists for their acts of conscience. In this passage, Asbury suspiciously noted that the men who had apprehended two Methodist preachers "were dangerously wounded within a few weeks after they had laid hands upon them."[58]

Of course, not everyone followed the pattern of neutrality set forth by the highest ranks of the Methodist leadership. Itinerant preacher and former British soldier Thomas Webb, influential in the establishment of Methodism in Pennsylvania, New Jersey, Maryland, and New York, drew on his military background and familiarity with the American environs to provide information to British forces on colonial attack plans. Colonial authorities later arrested Webb, but released him in a prisoner exchange. After returning to England, Webb offered to recruit Methodists to defend England if it were invaded during the war.[59]

Other Tory supporters such as layman Chauncey Clowe further tarnished Methodism's image in America. Clowe was arrested and hanged for leading a company of Tories to join with British forces.[60] Another loyalist, Martin Rodda, stirred the seas of controversy when word circulated that he distributed King George III's Proclamation of Rebellion on his circuit and then fled to England to avoid arrest.[61] To the American patriots, however, the most damning evidence of Methodist loyalty to the crown came when the English-born preachers commissioned by Wesley, save Francis Asbury, abandoned their ministries and either retreated behind British lines or returned to England for the duration of the war.

Some American Methodists assumed the polar opposite position and fought on the side of the colonies. Howell Williams, who converted to Methodism in the early 1770s, assumed the rank of colonel in the colonial armies in 1776.[62] Another convert, Green Hill, accepted a commission as major in the Fifth North Carolina Regiment of Militia.[63] James O'Kelly, an itinerant preacher who later rose to fame through his revolt against the newly formed Methodist Episcopal Church in the early 1790s, also fought on behalf of the colonies.[64]

American Methodists came to be most renowned or despised, as the case may be, not for their loyalism or rebellion, but for their acts of neutrality, which many Americans perceived as a covert form of loyalism. Methodist preachers fell into this category in large numbers. Their neutrality clearly compromised Methodism's reputation in the minds of those who believed that the Revolution was a sacred duty to which all should contribute. It did, however, reveal the independence that American Methodists could exercise from John Wesley as well as from their own native government.

Among the traveling preachers, neutrality dominated.[65] Only eight of the twenty-one preachers on Maryland's Eastern Shore in 1774 took the loyalty oath.[66] Not one of the five-member committee of preachers selected to oversee the Methodist community during the Revolution gave their blessing to the war.[67] Their position was not held only by preachers; many laypeople followed suit. In Baltimore, where almost 20 percent of all Methodists lived in 1776, William Lux, justice of the peace, wrote to the governor that all the Methodists in his jurisdiction refused to take the oath of allegiance to the colony.[68]

One of the most curious instances of Methodist resistance to the war comes from Jesse Lee (1758–1816). Lee was a Maryland native who rose to fame after the war as the first historian of American Methodism and founder of Methodism in New England. He later served as chaplain to Congress and narrowly missed election as bishop in the Methodist Episcopal Church. As hostilities with the British commenced, Lee joined the military, though he refused to carry a gun, reasoning that "as a Christian and as a preacher of the gospel I could not fight. I could not reconcile it to myself to bear arms, or to kill one of my fellow creatures." Not surprisingly, Lee's convictions ran afoul with his commanding officer, who consigned him to prison.[69]

Ultimately, Lee managed to create an intensely awkward reconciliation of his convictions and his patriotism. Lee refused to bear arms, but he rejoiced with his fellow troops when American forces "killed many of the enemy" in a victorious battle. He even attributed such success to God's orchestration.[70] Later, Lee refined his notion of permissible fighting by telling his commanding officer that although he still could not kill anyone, he would be willing to fight with a switch rather than a gun.[71] Lee's offer, as absurd as it probably sounded to his commanding officer, suggests the lengths to which some Methodists might go to define acceptable and unacceptable expressions of fighting.

The actions of Jesse Lee and his denominational compatriots raise an important question about why some Methodists reconciled themselves to fighting in the war while others did not, even when they might have sympathized with one side or the other. Many scholars have noted American Methodism's resistance to the Revolution, though surprisingly few have explored the reasons behind their decision.[72] The broader religious context in the Revolutionary War era in which other evangelical groups opposed violent action prior to the Revolution, only to shed those convictions during the war, makes this lacuna all the more significant. Rhys Isaac's monumental work on Virginia linked the common evangelical resistance to physical aggression prior to the Revolution to concerns about social control or, more specifically, to the ways evangelicals perceived culture creeping toward disorder. Southern attitudes toward violence, whether in the form of "rivalry and convivial excess" as part of entertainment, or in defense of social status in a culture of honor, reflected a dangerous lack of self-control. Thus, evangelicals instituted tight restrictions on social practices to limit disorder even as they created space for disorder in religious ceremonies, all with the effect of creating an alternative community that ultimately challenged the traditional social hierarchy.[73]

This early opposition to violence waned within most evangelical denominations during the Revolution. Methodist leaders, on the other hand, maintained their antiwar sentiments. Why did Methodists champion neutrality when so many other evangelicals differed? The nature of the literature on religion and the Revolution, much of which tends to focus on the contributions of religion to inducing and defending revolution rather than resisting it, complicates the answer to this question. Among the most well-known and highly critiqued explanation of religion and the Revolution is Alan Heimert's *Religion and the American Mind*. Heimert argued that the religious revivals of the so-called First Great Awakening fundamentally shaped the "American mind" and provided the content, inspiration, and model structures for colonists to imagine a new political entity birthed through revolution.[74] Heimert's stamp remains present in the interpretation of evangelical contributions to the Revolution, though more recent approaches have come to see a much broader religious influence on the Revolution than the Awakenings or have assigned a more indirect causation to religion. For instance, Ruth Bloch, like Heimert, located much of the popular religious support for the Revolution within groups most closely related to the Calvinist tradition, but she also resisted the attempt to characterize support for the Awakenings as the primary dividing point. Calvinist supporters and opponents of revivalism championed revolution. By looking at the connections between Revolution-era rhetoric and the Calvinist tradition, Bloch argues that Calvinists' abilities to infuse notions of civil liberty with spiritual significance, impute the fate of the nation with "transhistorical" importance, and imagine a "millennial future" for the new republic served as the more likely factor that thrust Calvinists into the heart of the Revolutionary conflict.[75]

One of Bloch's most compelling conclusions focuses on the capacity of the American patriots to imagine a millennial vision of future worldly perfection. Bloch sees this ability as "basic to the formation of American revolutionary ideology," not so much as a direct force in causing the Revolution, but in providing the framework through which many Americans "understood the ultimate meaning of the revolutionary crisis and the birth of the American nation."[76] Thus, millennialism became a kind of predisposing force that influenced Americans to fervently support the war. Bloch suggests that Methodists' tendency not to devote serious attention to millennial ideas may have been one reason they failed to support the Revolution in large numbers.[77]

Bloch's argument becomes less helpful when we consider neutrality or loyalism—the latter commanded as much as 20 percent of the colonial population—as viable options.[78] If millennialism and other theological interpretations of the war helped pave the way for colonial patriotism, it is not at all clear how differing views might have influenced the decision toward neutrality rather than loyalism, particularly when John Wesley voiced his support for the crown.

J. C. D. Clark has found the religious impulse in the Revolution in dissenting and heterodox traditions. Since Methodists remained within the Anglican Church at the time of the Revolution and espoused an orthodox theology, Clark's argument suggests that we should expect to see Methodists oppose the colonial war effort. But Clark is more apt to see conforming and orthodox traditions as loyalists rather than neutral. This approach works well for someone like John Wesley, but is less helpful for understanding American Methodist neutrality.[79]

A different approach attempts to rescue the revivalism-revolution connection by identifying indirect influences of revivalism upon the Revolution. This approach, while recognizing the dominance of Calvinist traditions in America prior to the Revolution, relies less specifically on elements within Calvinism than on the structures and spirit created by the revivals. More specifically, adherents of this approach contend that the revivals established structures and new patterns of leadership, communication, and public participation that bred and sustained resistance to traditional authority. Thus, the revivals fostered cultural and institutional forms and feelings that helped condition people to support the Revolution.[80] Gordon Wood takes a different tack on this position by arguing that both the Awakenings and the Revolution emerged from similar social forces. Changes in population and economic markets altered traditional social and religious structures, thereby creating anxiety as well as opportunity for radical change. The same forces that led religious adherents to challenge traditional clerical authority in the Awakenings would also empower the colonists to challenge traditional political authority.[81]

An exclusive reliance on any of these arguments fails to explain Methodism's resistance to the Revolution. Methodists experienced the same social transformation that Wood believes helped fuel both the Awakenings and the Revolution. They too offered similar critiques of religious authority and actively promoted most of the same methods of communication and leadership that historians have found to support Revolutionary ideology. Further, attempts to explain American Methodist neutrality theologically or ecclesiastically by connecting it to an Arminian rather than Calvinist tradition fall flat. Though Methodists shunned the doctrine of predestination, lacked a highly developed millennialism, and resisted using the language of a covenant to define their relationship with God, they did not lack other theological components that might have helped them support the war. As John Wesley's example shows, at least some Methodists imagined themselves part of a larger, providentially ordered history, infused the political realm with religious import, and cast their enemies as opponents of God's righteous plans in ways that helped them legitimate the war.

Many social and cultural factors combined to influence Methodist perspectives on the Revolution. Pragmatics may well have come into play as American Methodists found themselves in the complex position of having to negotiate a relationship with their Tory founder, John Wesley, and their kinsmen rebels in America. Neutrality may have made the most sense in the face of such a Gordian knot, though zealous American patriots often failed to appreciate the differences between neutrality and loyalism and sought retribution against all those who refused to take up arms to support the colonies. Yet when Methodists tried to explain their perspectives on the Revolution, they frequently referred to their ideas about the relationship between the Revolution and their dualistic battle between good and evil. Specifically, American Methodists, unlike Wesley, refused to imbue the political struggle with what Mark Juergensmeyer has called "cosmic significance" such that the political struggle necessarily influenced the direction and fate of the spiritual battle. In his study of contemporary religious movements, Juergensmeyer found that this identification was critical in the move toward violent action.[82] The same appears true for eighteenth-century Methodists. Those viewing the political conflict as bearing on the war against evil championed the military endeavors of the nation they saw as the best steward of the cosmic struggle. Those who could not see a connection between the political and cosmic wars not only remained on the sidelines, they used their sense of identity as warriors in a different kind of battle, one that seemed to transcend the political crisis, as a primary means for dismissing the war.

The priority Methodists gave to their spiritual wars for salvation can be further nuanced by separating those who opposed all forms of war and violence because of the cosmic struggle from those who only opposed the Revolution. Proponents of the latter did not necessarily oppose war always and everywhere, they simply did not impart cosmic significance to the Revolutionary conflict. Itinerant preacher John Young of North Carolina captured this idea beautifully in a sermon on the biblical text of Hebrews 12:14: "Follow peace with all men and be holy." Here Young reflected Wesley's theology that through redemption Christians recaptured a peace with God and fellow human beings that precluded violent action or even contentious behavior. The only possibility Young allowed for diverging from this rule was in cases where someone or something threatened "the gospel faith."[83] When this occurred, the boundaries between the spiritual and political battles broke down and the two conflicts became linked so that the believer needed to participate in the political struggle.

The difficulty, of course, was establishing whether a conflict really did undermine the "gospel faith" and as a consequence the believer's ability to successfully wage the spiritual battle. For John Wesley, the spiritual and political struggles did intersect in important ways. Believers participated in an intense war between good and evil that Wesley believed had profound effects on the temporal world. For Wesley, the political struggle emanating from the colonies became immersed in this cosmic battle insofar as sin gave birth to the American cause and undermined God's legitimately established government meant to protect religious and civil liberty. God ordained England's ruling monarchy with power. Thus, the attempt to cast off the king's authority assaulted God's order. The depths of the sin Wesley observed, and the important consequences of victory, made the war all the more significant. The war became more than just one struggle in a long battle between good and evil. Wesley used the "Late Work of God in North America" to paint the conflict as a critical chapter in God's ultimate defeat of evil. As a result, Wesley condoned Christians fighting in the temporal sphere on behalf of their ruler and in defense of God's ultimate victory over evil.

Methodists in America shared Wesley's cosmology of a universe beset by powerful forces of good and evil, agreed that sin exerted power over human beings and their society, and called their coreligionists to take part as soldiers in the battle against evil.[84] However, those Methodists who remained neutral observers failed to see a connection between the cosmic battle and either the Revolution in particular or war in general. For instance, let us return for a moment to John Young, who argued that a Christian might take action when the gospel faith fell under attack. Young apparently did not think the Revolution satisfied this criterion because he refused to fight after his conversion.[85] Other Methodists took a similar stance. William Watters argued that Methodists did not necessarily preach passive obedience and nonresistance. Methodists could challenge ruling authorities when necessary. However, he chose to avoid military service and leave "politics to those better qualified to defend and discuss them" because he believed himself called to the higher purpose of teaching "men how to live and be prepared to die."[86]

Many of the staunchest elements within the American cohort simply found it impossible to apply the cosmic struggle to the war because of their theological objections to all war. Philip Gatch, a Baltimore native who entered the itinerancy in 1773 and was appointed to the committee to oversee the Methodist community during the war, spoke for many when he insisted in his autobiography on the incompatibility of Christianity and war. Gatch postulated that participation in war could threaten one's salvation because God obligated Christians to seek peace and holiness with all people for salvation.[87] Similarly, Freeborn Garrettson reasoned that a Christian could never shed blood because vengeance belonged to God alone.[88] Instead, Garrettson argued for the primacy of the spiritual over the political struggle. When confronted by a soldier about serving in the army, Garrettson not only refused the soldier's demands to enlist, he warned the man about the eternal significance of privileging the political conflict over the cosmic battle, saying "that if he did not learn to fight with other weapons he would go to hell."[89] Likewise, Benjamin Abbott argued that he did not meddle "in the politics of the day" because his "call was to preach salvation to sinners" and "to wage war against the works of the devil" rather than fight against his fellow human beings.[90] For these preachers, the primacy of evangelism over war and the inherent link between sin and war meant that even if the cosmic struggle embroiled a temporal conflict, the bloody military efforts of nations could never solve the problem. These Methodists devalued the significance of the earthly conflict and refused to apply cosmic proportions to war by emphasizing the importance of the spiritual conflict that transcended political interest.

The testimonies of those who converted during the Revolution also make clear the power of the spiritual battle to dissuade participation in the political. Thomas Ware explained that converting to Methodism helped assuage the enmity between people created by the war and undermined the contentious spirit that led to armed struggle in the first place.[91] Ware experienced this transformation in his own life. As a young man, Ware dreamed of a career in the military. Flush with patriotism at the onset of hostilities with the British, Ware eagerly enlisted to fight for the American colonies. But under the influence of Methodist preaching, he explained that he began to sense that even if the Revolution freed the country from bondage, it had little impact on the greater battle to free human souls. Following his conversion, Ware gave up his dream of military glory to become an itinerant preacher.[92]

Similarly, to the great joy of his friends and family, Joseph Everett enlisted to fight in the Revolution. Sometime during his service, Everett converted and almost simultaneously "lost the martial spirit," finding in its stead "the spirit of humility." Everett's increasing lack of interest in the political conflict soon influenced his participation in the spiritual battle when the "Devil began to rouse his forces" against him, at least in part because of his decision to leave his military career to become a preacher.[93]

The conversions of both Ware and Everett played a critical role in their willingness to break with their longstanding political attachments. The ability of the conversion experience to facilitate social changes is often theoretically linked to Victor Turner's concepts of liminality and communitas. Donald Mathews, for instance, has utilized these concepts to argue that Methodist conversion, particularly among black followers, created a liminal sphere, what Turner defined as a "betwixt and between" state in which an individual or group moves to the peripheries of everyday life and social status. The dominant signs of social position do not apply in the liminal sphere and this often contributes to the formation of social relationships or bonds that Turner called "communitas." Such bonds are equalitarian and unstructured, thereby representing a direct opposition to dominant social relations.[94] Mathews contends that as a liminal event, conversion liberated slaves, at least psychologically, from "slavery and the subordination of race."[95] Similarly, Jean Miller Schmidt utilizes the theoretical lens of liminality to establish the mechanism by which women assumed leadership roles and became models for spiritual maturity in early Methodism.[96] Along these same lines, conversion might also have broken Methodists from their political loyalties and focused them on a spiritual struggle they then considered far more significant that political affiliation.

The value American Methodists placed on suffering violence rather than inflicting it helped mark their political reorientation. Language of defending one's rights and privileges paled when compared to the spiritual benefits of suffering for God. Philip Gatch did not resist when a crowd tarred and feathered him, believing that the privilege of ministry surpassed the pain of physical suffering.[97] Francis Asbury believed that suffering provided assurance of God's will, confessing that "the more troubles I meet with, the more convinced I am that I am doing the will of God."[98] For Asbury, as with so many others, the will of God inevitably met with opposition from "the world." By suffering, Christians could display the love of Christ and confirm among themselves that theirs was a faith tested in battle.

In their resistance to the war, American Methodists refused to intersect the political struggle with the cosmic struggle for redemption. By drawing distinctions between the two, and even imagining the political struggle to endanger the battle for salvation, Methodists avoided participation in violent warfare. The example of American Methodists suggests that we ought to resist a hasty conclusion that belief in a cosmic battle between good and evil has a direct and necessary cause-and-effect relationship in encouraging or defending warfare. Wesley and his American cohorts adhered to a cosmology of violent struggle that required the Christian to aggressively challenge evil. At the same time, Wesley and his American followers departed from one another on three points when it came to whether the cosmic struggle had any bearing on the American Revolution. First, Wesley saw the political conflict emerging out of and even threatening the very success of the Christian's warfare. Second, Wesley believed that he could clearly identify one side of the conflict as sinful and the other as a champion of God's will. This ability split the conflict into simplistic categories of good and evil rather than identifying shared responsibility for it. Third, Wesley accepted that the struggle needed to be fought with something more than spiritual weapons. The Christian soldier could legitimately take up the weapons of the state. As long as Wesley saw England and her American colonies as jointly responsible for the conflict because both had sinned, he advocated a peaceful resolution. However, when he turned from shared responsibility to envision the British as defenders of God's will and concluded that the state's right to use physical force applied to Christian behavior, Wesley justified the war and the Christian's participation in it as an important stage in God's larger quest to destroy evil. Many American Methodists, on the other hand, either could not or would not see the war in the same terms. For these Methodists, the Revolution was merely a political contest with little bearing on their war for salvation.

The priority of the spiritual over the temporal battle remained a significant factor in shaping American Methodist political involvement well after the close of the Revolutionary War. As historian Russell Richey contends, Methodists in the early republic continued to argue that "politics" was not their concern.[99] This ambivalence to politics did not translate into social ambivalence, however. Quite to the contrary, American Methodists identified a whole host of social issues from slavery to frivolous dress that they connected to sin and, by relation, the larger cosmic struggle against evil. Among the most controversial efforts included American Methodists' attempt to prevent slaveholders from holding membership in the church. The Christmas Conference of 1784 went so far as to require slaveholders to provide a legal deed promising emancipation within twelve months of the conference or face expulsion from the church.[100]

Although short-lived, the stipulations of the Christmas Conference to strike at the institution of slavery underscore the social interests of the church and the social dimensions of the cosmic struggle against sin. For many, however, the struggle for social change had to be restricted to spiritual weapons of prayer, preaching, and holy behavior rather than political legislation or, at least until the Civil War, massive armed resistance. In fact, as Frederick Norwood observed, by the early nineteenth century, Methodism's earlier goal "to reform the Continent, *and* to spread scriptural holiness over these lands" evolved into Bishop William McKendree's more hierarchical vision of the reformation of the land "*by* spreading scriptural holiness."[101] Holiness became the means for social reformation rather than a complement to it. The corresponding lack of significant social mobilization against slavery in the late eighteenth century ultimately led to Methodism's complicity in a system of terrible violence.

Even as Methodists failed to mount a significant challenge to slavery, their social engagement shifted in the 1790s through a systematic recession of Methodist political ambivalence, particularly over fears about the repercussions of the French Revolution and the power of Deism.[102] In later chapters we will have cause to explore the development of Methodist political involvement in the nineteenth century and the impact of the spiritual battle on this involvement. Over the course of the century, Methodists acceded to the cultural fascination with politics and even embraced the traditionally Puritan conception of the state as a moral entity and the role of the Christian to instill virtue among its citizenry.[103] As this change in political involvement occurred, the nature of the spiritual battle also shifted in subtle but significant ways. The most important of these changes raised questions about the relationship of the body to religious experience. The result set Methodists on a course that, though they might not have known it at the time, ultimately led to a very different expression of Methodist spirituality. The good fight for salvation would never be the same.

THREE

THE POWER TO
"KILL AND MAKE ALIVE"

*The Spiritual Battle and the Body in
Post-Revolutionary America*

In the years following the Revolutionary War, American Methodism underwent one of the most incredible numerical transformations in the history of American religion. In 1773, Methodists counted only ten preachers to minister to a meager 1,160 members. By 1776, the number of ministers had doubled and the total Methodist population more than quadrupled. Growth continued through the end of the century, with Methodists totaling nearly 64,000 in 1800. Ten years later membership had nearly tripled again, and by 1830 it stood at close to half a million.[1] At midcentury "American Methodism was nearly half again as large as any other Protestant body, and almost ten times the size of the Congregationalists, America's largest denomination in 1776."[2]

In the midst of this phenomenal growth that swelled the rolls of Methodist churches, many Methodists set a course to make subtle, but no less fundamental, alterations to the nature of the "good fight." Methodists continued to advocate the importance of both an internal and external spiritual struggle in which believers battled supernatural forces of good and evil to realize their redemption and the reform of their communities. However, while many granted a bodily component to their struggles with God and Satan in conversion, concern over the nature of those experiences mounted, particularly among influential white preachers, leading them to interpret bodily experiences in ways that placed new restrictions on the nature of the believer's participation in the "good fight" for salvation. These Methodists posed particularly important questions about whether the body could physically suffer as it conflicted with God for salvation. Methodist leaders who emerged in the post–Revolutionary War era challenged Wesley's narratives of people feeling physical pain in the throes of conversion by cordoning off the body from any sense of literal harm. They also offered different narratives of their own and others' battles with Satan. Though nearly all Methodists continued to represent Satan as a dangerous threat to their spiritual condition, it became less common for them to narrate instances of demonic forces threatening the physical body.

This limitation of God's bodily afflictions and Satan's power signifies important changes in the way significant numbers of Methodists hoped believers would engage in the Christian's warfare. In the early part of the nineteenth century, Methodists began to exert greater control over their bodies in ways that made physical harm at the hands of spiritual forces less likely for the Christian soldier. As a result, the second generation of Methodists began to draw a clear distinction between themselves and their forebears who related grave tales of physical suffering at the hands of the divine and demonic alike.

The Body, Pain, and the Fight for Salvation

In 1789, Ezekiel Cooper (1763–1847), a young itinerant preacher from Maryland, found himself in the midst of one of the most spectacular revivals he had ever seen. Thirty or forty bodies lay strewn upon the floor in front of him, their cries reaching a deafening pitch. Little order prevailed as some screamed "as under the pains of hell" while others rejoiced to God "for mercy and pardon found." The mixture of sights and sounds led Cooper to simultaneously anticipate the pleasure of heaven, where the redeemed sang praises to God, and the agonies of hell, where "the hopeless shrieks . . . of the damned . . . [plead for] a drop of water to cool their tongue."

Though Cooper relished what he witnessed as evidence of God's calling sinners to repentance and salvation, he recognized the inevitable opposition of those who would credit the bodily experiences to the natural effects of imagination, or even worse, a demonic conspiracy to deceive the ill-informed and vulnerable. In part, Cooper agreed with those who saw Satan's influence behind the shrieks and contorted bodily movements, but only because Cooper attributed these to the Evil One being "cast out" from the souls and bodies of seekers. "They were first torn by Satan, then healed by Christ; their cries were, first of sorrow, then of praise."[3]

Cooper's interpretation of the conversions that occurred at the revival meeting reflects many of the same characteristics of the inner dimensions of holy violence that Wesley found so critical to the Christian life. Satan appeared prominently in Cooper's narrative as a fearful force that believers struggled against with utmost effort. Likewise, sin proved equally powerful in preventing peace with God. Against such opposition, God dramatically intervened to strike seekers down in soul and body in order to rescue them from damnation.

Other Methodists also emphasized the importance of this internal spiritual battle for the life of the believer. Frontier preacher James B. Finley (1781–1857) explained that the obstacles to living a Christian life were so great that "I must fight" if "I would reign as a king and priest with God and the Lamb forever."[4] Such sentiments worked their way into the common discourse of many Methodists, as when John Early concluded that he felt like "fighting for my Jesus" and Joseph Pilmore called for his "feeble flock" to become "soldiers of Christ."[5] Catherine Garrettson, the daughter of a wealthy New York family and wife of itinerant preacher Freeborn Garrettson, often wrote of putting "on the whole armor of God" in order to vanquish Satan.[6] This imagery of battle and warfare as part of individual spiritual experience was so prominent in Garrettson's writings that historian Diane Lobody concluded it was "one of the governing structures of her diary."[7]

Following the pattern set forth by John Wesley, Methodists put such rhetoric to song in their hymns. The *Methodist Pocket Hymnbook* of 1803 grouped several of the "choicest" hymns under the section "The Christian's Warfare." This section included several of the militant hymns found in John Wesley's hymnals such as "Soldiers of Christ Arise," but it also expanded beyond the Wesleyan tradition to include hymns such as Isaac Watts's "Am I a Soldier of the Cross?" Just as Wesley did in his compilations, Watts underscored the significance of militant effort for salvation: "Thy saints in all this glorious war shall conquer though they die; they see the triumph from afar, by faith they bring it nigh."[8] Similarly, in 1801, Richard Allen, who later formed the African Methodist Episcopal Church, published a collection of hymns several of which contained explicitly militant imagery. Of these, "Hail the Gospel Jubilee" proclaimed:

> Rise ye heralds of the Lord
> Take the breastplate, shield, and sword
> Against the hosts of hell proclaim
> A war in Christ's all conquering name,
> Nor fear to gain the victory.[9]

As we have already seen, the war against sin and evil that these figures imagined certainly had social dimensions to it, but for the most part, American Methodists centered their battles on the changed hearts flowing from conversion that, in turn, they hoped would lead to holy living and reformed communities. Such conversions often included a bodily component, both for Wesley and his American counterparts of the late eighteenth and early nineteenth centuries. As we saw above, Ezekiel Cooper witnessed many people fall in agony as Satan tore their bodies. Philip Gatch and Bishop John Early did the same.[10] Rev. Henry Smith spoke of the "arrows of the almighty" piercing people, causing them to scream and fall to the ground.[11] Itinerant Jacob Young recorded falling to the ground during his conversion and provocatively called it his "death wound."[12]

Jesse Lee provided an extraordinary account of these bodily battles for salvation in his history of the Methodist Episcopal Church, published in 1810. Lee recalled that while in Virginia in 1787 he witnessed a group numbering in the hundreds: "some were lying and struggling as if they were in the agonies of death, others lay as if they were dead. Hundreds of the believers were so overcome with the power of God that they fell down and lay helpless on the floor, or the ground; and some of them continued in this helpless condition for a considerable time."[13]

These bodily experiences were by no means limited to men. Fanny Newell recorded one of the most memorable experiences of falling out during which she "was lost to all that was around" her. Newell's account offers the rare opportunity to learn what one might have seen or felt while on the ground. In her fallen capacity, Newell recalled hearing the "shrill voice of the enemy [Satan]" promise her damnation, a terror that she said only paled when Christ appeared and seemed to desire to kill her. To Newell's relief, Christ offered her mercy and forgiveness, which she described as "one sentenced to death and pardoned."[14] Other women related similar experiences. Mary Coy Bradley said she fell under "an awful sense of the presence of God" during which she experienced "pain" in her heart that caused her to groan and have difficulty breathing.[15] Mary Orne Tucker said she felt like "a poor worm surrounded by a circle of fire."[16]

If, as many have argued, women and men differed in the ways they related their conversion experiences, it does not appear that in the late eighteenth and early nineteenth centuries Methodist men and women disagreed that their bodies could be a site for the battle for salvation.[17] In fact, many Methodists took pains to emphasize the universality of such bodily experiences, as Jesse Lee did in 1810 when he argued that such experiences transcended race, class, and gender lines.[18]

At first glance, early American Methodist narratives written in the late eighteenth and early nineteenth centuries offer little evidence of difference with Wesley concerning the internal components of the Christian's war. The battle against sin, the world, and Satan obligated the Christian to fight, and for many, the body was a primary target in the battle with spiritual forces, both divine and demonic. However, a closer look at the post–Revolutionary War period reveals important tensions in Methodism, particularly related to bodily religious experiences. Philip Gatch explained as much in his autobiography when he noted that many complained about the appearance of people falling out in conversion.[19] Among the earliest American Methodist critiques of public displays of bodily religious experiences was *Methodist Error: Or Friendly, Christian Advice, To Those Methodists Who Indulge in Extravagant Emotions and Bodily Exercises,* published anonymously in 1814 but later identified as the hand of John Fanning Watson, a Methodist layperson from Philadelphia.[20] As the title suggests, Watson objected to "the unprofitable emotions of *screaming, hallowing and jumping*" [emphasis in original], among other experiences. The author attributed these to nothing more than the "heedless" emotions of "credulous, uninformed minds; who before their change of grace, had been of rude education and careless of those prescribed forms of good manners and refinement, of which polite education is never divested."[21] Watson contrasted the unrefined practices of what he considered to be a radical minority by tracing religious experience through the Hebrew Bible, the New Testament, and Christian history to contend that proper religion "is seated in the understanding, and felt in the heart," resulting in a "stable, meek, quiet, gentle" nature.[22]

Ann Taves has found that those Methodists, like Watson, who expressed the greatest concern about bodily religious experiences in the early nineteenth century tended to be white, middle-class men from northeastern states. Nevertheless, Taves also argues that in the early nineteenth century the Methodist community was far from agreement about the marginalization of bodily religious experiences. Taves sees Methodists drawing on European and African traditions to formulate a distinctively popular and American tradition of interactive shouting, dancing, and shaking. The popularity of these experiences ensured that efforts to control them by some white males would meet with limited success.[23] While critics such as John Fanning Watson attempted to characterize these experiences as emanating from a radical few, if the records of itinerants are accurate, those joining the church through the revivals that included bodily religious experiences outnumbered those converts who opposed them.

Methodist discussions of a new bodily movement that arose in the American South and West in the early nineteenth century reveals the tension within the Methodist community about bodily religious experiences and the implications of this tension for the nature of the Christian's "good fight" for salvation. This experience, called the jerks, first appeared sometime around 1803.[24] It entailed uncontrollable quakes of the body that many Methodists attributed to divine power. One observer explained, "I saw women, who were held by two or more strong men, throw themselves back and forward with such violence, that they threw the combs out of their hair, and then their loosened locks would crack nearly as loud as a common carriage whip."[25] Methodist chroniclers of the jerks argued that the experience did not strike any particular group of people, but affected both saint and sinner regardless of race, class, or gender.[26] The universality of the experience, at least among those in the West and South, may have contributed to the struggles many Methodists encountered in explaining it as something other than a divine act. Peter Cartwright, for instance, postulated that the jerks served as a judgment from God to bring sinners to repentance.[27] Cartwright believed that physical affliction allowed people to feel God's power and the wrath due them because of their sins.

Cartwright's assessment reflects the ways some Methodists not only extended the fight for salvation to the body, but could also envision the battle taking dangerous forms. Jacob Young explained that the jerks could be so intense that onlookers feared they would snap a person's neck.[28] Peter Cartwright claimed that a man died because he resisted the jerks until his neck broke.[29]

Those who experienced the jerks could easily place them in the context of the Christian's warfare that included bodily effects such as falling motionless to the ground, appearing as if one were choking, and so on. Amidst the destructive power of sin, God intervened and, in the case of the jerks, shook the body and soul while achieving a person's spiritual healing. Other Methodists, however, expressed a more guarded skepticism. As one preacher understated, the jerks "were not easily accounted for."[30] This same writer evinced some optimism about the divine role in the experience by denying that religious enthusiasts fabricated it or that the experience was simply a natural phenomenon, at least in every case. He claimed that people with no religious pretensions were suddenly and unwillingly struck. Yet the author also distanced himself from the experience by emphasizing that "he never felt a symptom of this strange affliction."[31] For at least this writer the jerks might have some link with the work of God, but his personal experience that did not include such bodily manifestations implied that the jerks were certainly not normative for a true conversion experience.

Similar attempts to express concern about the jerks without dismissing them altogether appear within the writings of other more notable American Methodists. Like the author just mentioned, William Capers, later bishop in the Methodist Episcopal Church, South, emphasized that the jerks struck many who were not previously religious seekers. After observing these people's testimonies, Capers concluded that their experiences were part of an authentic conversion. On the other hand, Capers took pains to underscore the brief manifestation of the jerks among Methodists—he claimed they only lasted two years—while he also emphasized the power of revival meetings that did not include the jerks.[32] Itinerant preacher and presiding elder Jacob Young went further than Capers by denying that God actually played a role in the jerks, despite some people who "often thought it [the jerks] to be the power of God unto salvation." Yet Young tolerated it among his congregants, saying that the belief "did them no kind of harm." The wise preachers, said Young, ignored the jerks and went about making converts "as though it was not in the country."[33]

The ambivalence manifest in these discussions of the jerks reveals the important legacy that bodily struggles played in the religious experiences of early Methodists and the concern among American leaders over the role of the body in religious experiences of God in the early nineteenth century. American leaders did not dismiss the jerks altogether. They inherited a tradition from Wesley and others in which a great cosmic battle between good and evil, salvation and damnation, enmeshed the body. To deny the body's place in this fight seemed to call into question the validity of those experiences that appeared so prominently in the "good fight" of the faith. Methodist history was rife with stories of bodily movements accompanying a person's deliverance from sin. In fact, many who expressed reservations about the jerks defended other bodily religious experiences like falling out.[34] Nevertheless, the preachers' guarded approach to the jerks suggests some discomfort with it. While they did not deny that God *could* accomplish the salvation of souls through the jerks, they subtly expressed their preference for an alternative.

This alternative might well have been more serious attention to the health and well-being of the body. Rather than emphasizing the body's pain in ways that reflected the death and rebirth of the person's spiritual state, Methodists subtly separated the body from harm. This concern for the well-being of the body owes much to John Wesley's own interest in medicine. Wesley published the immensely popular *Primitive Physick* as a guide to healthy living and the cure of diseases. In this work Wesley emphasized the spiritual and physical benefit arising from the control of bodily desires. The book's recommendations for bodily health received increasing attention in the nineteenth century and may have contributed to Methodist perceptions of appropriate bodily religious experiences as inducing bodily healing rather than harm. R. Marie Griffith sums up the interest in bodily health among nineteenth-century Protestants: "good health was no mere matter of luck . . . but rather a choice that could be fulfilled by attention to the scientific principles of diet and related regimes of bodily care. The messianic undertones . . . left no audience member uncertain that what health reformers believed to be at stake was the salvation of the world."[35]

A clear concern for the well-being of the body appears in the narratives of those Methodists who converted in the late eighteenth and early nineteenth centuries. These accounts continued to relate experiences such as falling out or shouting, but with more or less explicit comments that the experience did not include pain or suffering. A frightful encounter related by itinerant Billy Hibbard (1771–1844) exemplifies the anxiety that many people felt over the place of pain in religious experience. As Hibbard conducted a church service in the midst of a particularly intense thunderstorm, he took the opportunity to exploit the natural elements for divine purposes, hoping that people's association of stormy weather with divine judgment might prove useful in their conversion. Hibbard called out to God, "O Lord, thunder conviction to the sinner's heart." Almost simultaneously, "the lightning, like a sheet of fire, flashed, and an awful clap of thunder shook the house." Hibbard repeated his call and still another clap of thunder "shook the house more than the first," blowing out the candles and rendering the room dark. When the light was restored Hibbard saw two women lying on the floor "as dead." Assuming they had been struck with the common experience of falling out, the minister continued the service, and shortly one who had fallen arose and joined in prayer. But the other remained on the floor in the same condition for more than two hours as the crowd dispersed. Hibbard concluded that "it was nothing more than a powerful operation of Divine grace" and went to sleep.

Sometime in the middle of the night a parishioner awoke Hibbard and informed him that the fallen woman had died. The minister rushed to the woman's side to check her pulse and respiration, but found no signs of life. Her body was cold. Pulling off the woman's shoes and stockings, Hibbard saw that her feet were swollen, and he somehow concluded that God could not have killed her. The complaint that took her life was surely "natural." Nevertheless, Hibbard knew that "if she should be dead, the case of religion would be reproached" since everyone left the meeting believing that her condition resulted from the power of God.

Hibbard instructed those present to rub her limbs and neck with the hopes of circulating her blood while he cried to God "with all my heart" to restore the woman's life. Hibbard blew air into her lungs and finally, after several hours, she regained consciousness. Relieved, Hibbard thanked God that "no scandal arose" from the events of the preceding evening.[36]

Hibbard's fear of scandal should the local community learn that a woman died during a revival meeting reveals the concerns over associating divine action in the pursuit of salvation with bodily harm. Hibbard's parishioners might allow people to fall under God's power, but they simply would not accept that God might literally kill someone in the process of "making them alive."

If Hibbard's parishioners refused to accept that true religious experience could result in someone's death, others eliminated pain altogether. When speaking of falling out, preacher James B. Finley directly contradicted the testimony of Wesley by asserting that "I have conversed with persons who have laid in this situation for many hours, and they have uniformly testified that they had no bodily pain, and that they had the entire use of their reason and powers of mind."[37] Other preachers who emerged in the early nineteenth century such as Charles Giles (1783–1867) and William Swayze (1784–1841) emphasized the same point.[38]

While these Methodists denied that true religious experience involved pain, still others began to prove the truth of their religious experiences by their lack of pain or injury. Alfred Brunson explained that when he first saw someone fall out before he was converted he thought it the work of the devil. Even after his conversion, Brunson found it difficult to associate an experience of God during worship with death. Brunson declared, "I have seen men fall from being shot, and have stepped over the dead on the field of battle; but the idea of such a fall, and as I thought for a moment, a death in the house of God, and connected with his worship, gave me such feelings as I never had before or since." By contrast, Brunson made it very clear that no one was ever hurt during the experience even though he saw many people hit their heads as they fell to the ground. Brunson concluded "that no person could receive injury, in such an exercise, when it was from the divine influence; *for God never did, and never will hurt any body*" [emphasis added].[39]

Brunson's words speak volumes about how Methodist leaders, even those who sympathized with bodily religious experiences, began to define and even defend their religious experiences by restricting them from bodily pain. God would not, in the words of Alfred Brunson, harm a body. Rather, God protected bodies even from natural harm that might befall them during religious experience. This new interest in distinguishing between experiences on the grounds of whether or not they included bodily harm separated early nineteenth-century American Methodists from their founder John Wesley, who granted that the testimony of the spirit could be attended by actual physical pain.[40] American Methodists began to offer a very different assessment. Methodists, particularly white leaders, questioned and even eliminated physical harm from their conceptions of "true" religious experience. The result was a qualification of the nature of the fight for salvation. People might still fall to the ground "as dead" or scream in terror, but not because they were in pain. A person's "wound" became more spiritual than literal. Though hardly detectable to most around them, this change signaled a first step in the demise of the bodily component of Methodists' war with God for salvation.

Methodists' alteration of the bodily component of Christians' battle against their own sin did not occur in a social or cultural vacuum. Rather, it reflected powerful influences in American religious life. The Puritan heritage in America had long cast aspersions on seemingly uncontrolled bodily experiences. Involuntary bodily exercises appeared to many Puritans as not only undignified, but more importantly, reflective of spiritual chaos. The model Puritan saint, as Max Weber showed, strove to be a rational and orderly being.[41] The flesh, a potent source of sin, needed to be subjugated as part of every Christian's responsibility to live a holy life. Thus, Puritans observed a host of public and private fast days as ways to control the flesh, offer a symbol of humiliation before God, and as preparation for petitioning God for favor. Furthermore, because Puritans also believed that the body reflected spiritual realities, they interpreted unusual bodily markings and uncontrolled movements as bodily evidence of Satan's influence over the soul, thus providing a caution against atypical bodily experiences. Such concerns were so deeply ingrained in the culture that when bodily experiences of falling to the ground, screaming, or weeping accompanied the transatlantic revivals of the mid-eighteenth century, they drew intense criticism from formalists and skeptics, who denounced them as religious enthusiasm, despite an ingenious defense from Jonathan Edwards.[42]

The intellectual spread of the Enlightenment on American Protestantism in the late eighteenth and early nineteenth centuries further entrenched concern for bodily religious experiences. We have already noted the influence of certain Enlightenment ideals, particularly related to human progress, empiricism, and science in Methodism's founding. But the influence of the Enlightenment on Methodism, as among nearly all Protestants in America, continued to grow throughout the eighteenth and early nineteenth centuries. As Mark Noll has concluded, "during the half-century from Edwards's death [in 1758] to the founding of Andover Seminary [in 1808], American religious thinkers gradually accommodated theology to the demands of science, reason, and law."[43] The Enlightenment's most profound influence on American Protestants was its ability to instill an optimistic assessment of the natural powers of common sense, reason, and the moral sense for understanding the physical universe, embracing the truth of Christianity, and acting virtuously. The world became a more reasonable place and rational self-control became a cherished value. As more and more people assumed the broad tenets of the Enlightenment's image of humanity and the cosmos, they interpreted bodily religious experiences of falling out, uncontrollable shaking, and shouting as discordant with the value of reason and order. Not surprisingly, this emphasis on reason also helped to discredit belief in supernatural forces impinging on the natural world. Through reason and experimentation, natural explanations emerged to account for phenomena previously credited to supernatural beings.

These intellectual changes also had important political ramifications. In the early American republic, self-control, particularly over the body, was a source of intense concern. The American Revolution's dissembling of traditional forms of political control, the migration of huge numbers away from the historical centers of social refinement in the East, the evolution of a market economy that remade economic relationships, and the appearance of "upstart" religious communities that undermined established ecclesiastical authority all created anxiety regarding the sources for maintaining order and control. In this context of upheaval, Americans postulated how the newly formed United States could stave off social and cultural anarchy. One of the solutions that emerged was a commitment to self-control as a virtue; the body moved to the center of consciousness as a threat to the civic and cultural order if uncontrolled, but a site for moral virtue if properly harnessed. As a result, the body needed to be controlled by reason and vigilantly policed, if not by the individual, then by the myriad reform societies— Sabbatarians, temperance societies, antiprostitution crusades, etc.—that began to emerge.[44]

All these factors surely influenced Methodists' concern for bodily religious experience in the early nineteenth century. Most American Methodists in this period were not yet ready to release the body as a critical site for Christian experience. Bodily religious experiences of falling to the ground could even function as a form of discipline of the body by physically marking the destruction of the sinful body and the resurrection of a justified and progressively sanctified body that could adhere to moral law. In this sense, many of the Methodist preachers who emerged in the early nineteenth century resisted the larger criticism of bodily religious experiences, but also demonstrated sensitivity to this criticism by cordoning off the body from harm. The body continued to be an important site for contestation in the struggle for salvation, but Methodists began to ensure that it would not suffer pain at the hands of God. The divine *only* healed the body in salvation.

The Body and the Fight with Satan

Methodist depictions of Satan's role and power reflect an even deeper concern about the body's harm in spiritual experiences than the questions Methodists raised about the body's relation to God. Methodists considered Satan's relation to the body more problematic than God's because Satan based his work on a desire for destruction whereas God intended benefit. In chapter 1, we saw that John Wesley made a very real and tangible struggle against evil spiritual forces a central part of Methodist spirituality. To deny the reality and power of Satan and the providential interventions of God to thwart evil sapped religion of its vitality and, more dangerously, lulled humans into a false sense of security about their eternal condition. When it came to Satan and his minions of evil, Wesley warned his listeners that Satan and demons could destroy both body and soul. Mental distress, physical illness, bodily possession, even death, all served as Satan's means to prevent the redemption of those under his command.

The only periodical of the Methodist Episcopal Church in the late eighteenth century, the *Methodist Magazine,* attests to the first American Methodists' agreement with Wesley's admonitions about the dangers of evil and Satan. The second edition for that year began a multi-issue reprint of Wesley's sermon "Of Evil Angels" taken from Ephesians 6:12: "We wrestle not against flesh and blood, but against the rulers, against the authorities, against the powers of this dark world and against the spiritual forces of evil in the heavenly realms."[45] The June edition of the periodical also included a story of a man who believed he was "spiritually" taken to hell, "where he was seized by many devils, who rejoiced over me, and dragged me away." The man explained that he struggled against his persecutors as they attempted to push him "into the fire." Interestingly, though the author earlier claimed the experience was purely "spiritual," he later added a physical component to the narrative when he confessed that he felt such tremendous physical pain that "had I been in possession of the whole world; I would have given it for a moment's ease."[46]

Early Methodists also published autobiographies in which individual struggles against Satan appeared prominently. Among the most popular was the journal of Freeborn Garrettson. Born in 1752 to a wealthy Maryland family, Garrettson rose to distinction as one of the early American-born Methodist leaders. Despite the refinement that came from a privileged background, Garrettson vividly recounted numerous struggles with Satan in his journals, first published in 1790. He recalled that Satan met his early efforts at conviction with "powerful darts" meant to derail his pursuit of salvation. As Garrettson groped for redemption, "the devil strove hard to drive away all my good desires." Persevering, Garrettson attempted to overcome the temptations and trials by continuing his "secret devotions" meant to stir the fires of redemption even when his pursuits were "cold enough." But "the grand enemy" would not release him that easily and "began to exercise my mind" in other ways that eventually led Garrettson to leave off his pursuit of salvation.[47]

Fortunately for Garrettson, God strove with him as eagerly as Satan worked against him, and his conviction returned. But "the devil . . . seemed to rise higher and higher" causing Garrettson to became so "opprest [sic] that I was scarce able to support under my burden." He fled to the woods to pray, where he "sensibly felt two spirits, one on each hand" contending with him. While the good spirit encouraged him toward salvation, "the enemy" would "rise up on the other hand, and dress religion in as odious a garb as possible." Garrettson initially gave in to the evil spirit, only to respond once again to the beckons of the good spirit and "submit to the Lord." At once, he "saw a beauty in the perfections of the Deity and felt that power of faith and love that I had ever been a stranger to before."[48]

Though Garrettson credited the experience as the conversion for which he longed, Satan did not give up. Garrettson recorded frequent "assaults" and "afflictions" from Satan in the days following his conversion, eventually becoming so unbearable that Garrettson hoped his "horse might throw me, and put an end to my life; or maim me so that I might not be able to go on."[49] Again, the young man fought off the devil's attacks, but these would be lifelong struggles. The preacher even explained that later in life he became "deranged" because of the assaults of Satan.[50]

Garrettson limited most of his encounters with Satan to mental temptations that caused doubt and fear, but the preacher's wish that his horse would throw him and end his life suggests that mental temptations could have dangerous bodily implications. For Garrettson, as for Wesley, the body and mind were both sites for Satanic attack. Garrettson did not record accounts of literal possession, but he did describe physical appearances of Satan. Most notably, the preacher recalled one evening when the devil assumed a physical form before him: "The devil made his appearance upon it [the bed]: first he felt like a cat, he then got hold of my pillow, and both pulled at it; I cried out, get behind me Satan. And immediately he vanished."[51]

Garrettson argued that other Methodists of his generation had similar experiences of Satan in bodily form. One man claimed that "for a long time the devil had followed him, and that he had frequently seen him with his bodily eyes."[52] In another instance, Garrettson told of a man who confessed to him that Satan appeared "in his bodily shape" while he worked a field.[53] Other Methodists, such as the famous itinerant preacher Benjamin Abbott, confirmed these experiences. Before his conversion, Abbott locked himself in his house and refused to leave because he feared that the devil would apprehend him.[54]

As they did when responding to narratives of bodily harm in divine encounters, many skeptics challenged the authenticity of narratives of physical encounters with Satan. We noted in chapter 1 that eighteenth-century European Protestants raised questions about the reality of Satan, let alone Satan's ability to appear in physical form. Andrew Delbanco has argued that in America, Satan, while still imagined as the source of sin and damnation, was more "maddeningly elusive" than easily identified as a physical figure in this period.[55] Eighteenth-century Methodists in England and America were less convinced that Satan no longer represented a threat to their bodies. The relative absence of possession narratives among the earliest American Methodist writings might signal a difference with Wesley from the start, but the first generation of Methodists in America demonstrate more similarities with Wesley's demonology than differences. Like Wesley, eighteenth-century American Methodists emphasized the mental, spiritual, social, and even bodily manifestations and dangers of Satan. In so doing, they challenged the century-long trend of restricting Satan to attacks of the mind rather than the body.

The ways early Methodists negotiated and questioned the boundaries of Satan's power in the post–Revolutionary War era appears in the denomination's dealings with one of its early leaders, William Glendinning. A Scottish immigrant, Glendinning rapidly rose through the ranks of early Methodism in Maryland and Virginia, culminating in his appointment to the committee to oversee the Methodist community during the Revolutionary War.[56] Despite his success, Glendinning ceased preaching in 1786 after "all spiritual comforts" departed from him and he began to doubt his salvation. The depths of his suffering were palpable:

My whole nature, as I apprehended, had now undergone an entire change, I became stripped of all, but entire enmity against the Most High, and all that appeared sacred. All consciousness was taken wholly from me, while I became divested of every passion of the human mind, and all the feelings of human nature—and though I was upon earth, yet I felt as if I was shut up in eternity, and laid in the regions of the damned, and as if the very bars of eternity had shut me in. The very miseries of the damned did I feel, passing through every part of my frame. Here I cannot describe my feelings, it was, as if whole spears of fire were darting into every part of me.—Had I been tearing piece by piece, I could not have felt more misery than I then frequently did, while the flames of misery were sensibly burning within me.[57]

Glendinning's travails only deepened when he began to suspect that Satan caused his suffering. One evening "a loud rap at the door" confirmed his deepest fears. "I opened it, and saw his [the devil's] face: it was black as any coal—his eyes and mouth as red as blood, and long white teeth gnashing together."[58] Although Satan disappeared almost immediately, Glendinning explained that his demonic persecutor appeared in bodily form "two or three times a week" throughout the winter of 1786:

He appeared upward of five feet high, -round the top of his head there seemed a ridge; some distance under the top of his head, there seemed a bulk, like a body, but bigger than any person; about 15 or 18 inches from the ground, there appeared something like legs, and, under them, feet; but no arms or thighs. The whole as black as any coal; only his mouth and eyes as red as blood. When he moved, it was [like] an armful of chains rattling together.[59]

Glendinning labored in this condition for five years. During this time, Glendinning never claimed that Satan possessed his body, though he did admit to feeling physical pain "as if whole spears of fire were darting into every part of me" and at other times that his head felt as if it "would be torn from my shoulders." Just as serious, Satan afflicted Glendinning through mental anguish by placing his impending damnation before him in visions of hell.

At night, when I would lie down in my cabin, the place provided for me, I would feel as if I were thrust under the very pillars of the earth, and laid over the very gulf of misery. The flaming pit would be laid open to my view, burning all around me: only the small spot of earth, on which I lay, appeared to be all that broke the flaming gulf from me.

Such fearsome experiences were so horrifying that Glendinning twice attempted to kill himself.[60]

The first signs of restoration came, according to Glendinning, when the demonically inspired phrase "away thou damned spirit" disappeared from his mind and "some rays of divine light" shone upon him.[61] Glendinning began praying again and shortly thereafter the devil's appearances waned until Glendinning mustered the courage to confront his demonic persecutor. "I then spoke, and told him, that he could not hurt me, and that I was not afraid of him,—and that his power was limited. Then in the name of the adorable and ever-blessed Jehovah, I commanded him to depart. At which he shrunk back, and went toward the other fallen angels—in a little time, they all departed, and I saw him no more."[62]

After being tried with the presence of Satan for five years, Glendinning finally enjoyed a vision of God and claimed that he received verbal instructions from God to return to preaching, though with a very specific restriction to avoid sectarianism. He complied with God's directions and refused to formally identify with any particular denomination, especially the Methodists, whom he said had strayed from their course of simplicity in their form of church government that began to emerge in the 1780s. Nevertheless, Glendinning began preaching at regular Methodist meeting places and even had his preaching appointments set by the local Methodist presiding elder.[63]

Glendinning's return to preaching posed a challenge for Methodist leaders at the end of the eighteenth century. Glendinning's account of his struggles with Satan was in most instances no different than the tales Wesley told. Both Glendinning and Wesley offered horrifying accounts of Satan's mental and physical attacks, and both could attest to the power of God to triumph over those attacks. However, the church eventually barred Glendinning from preaching. The process through which the denomination arrived at this decision and its motivations for doing so reveal the first inklings of a church deeply ambivalent about Satan's power. Asbury sent a curt letter to Glendinning in December 1791 after ministers at a quarterly conference in Virginia refused to recognize him as a member of the itinerancy. However, the letter did not explain why the conference decided as it did.[64] The leadership clarified itself when Glendinning submitted a formal request for readmission to the itinerancy at the General Conference meeting in 1792. Glendinning's application requested that his association with the denomination be limited to the oversight of his moral conduct and doctrine, explaining that he did not seek "church office" because "I see things in your government [of the church], since the revolution, that I do not approve of."[65] The conference's response focused on Glendinning's opposition to the discipline of the church: "After mature deliberation, it was concluded, 1st, That you cannot be considered as one of us, *unless you come under the discipline of our Church;* 2d, That you are not to expect the use of our houses for public worship; and 3d, That our preachers are not to make your appointments, nor countenance your proceedings, *while you pursue your present plan*" [emphasis added].[66]

Although the official comments of the leadership focused on Glendinning's refusal to submit to discipline, Glendinning suspected his experiences with Satan were the real problem. According to Glendinning, bishops Francis Asbury and Thomas Coke expressed their disapproval of Glendinning's penchant for publicly relating his tales of Satan's attacks. Glendinning recalled that at the quarterly conference held in Petersburg, Georgia, in 1791, Thomas Coke told him that "all such accounts of creatures having any intercourse with beings from eternity, were only imaginary."[67] Glendinning further claimed that Asbury warned him not to tell others about his encounter with Satan and that when the preacher refused to comply, Coke intervened and forbade him from re-entering the itinerancy.[68]

Asbury made his opinions about Satan in general and Glendinning's case in particular far less clear. On the one hand, the bishop contemplated Glendinning's sanity in his diaries, saying, "I am clear he is not right in his head or heart, and am therefore resolved he shall speak no more at my appointments."[69] On the other hand, Asbury did admit that Satan exercised some influence over Glendinning. In a letter Asbury wrote to his friend and fellow Methodist Edward Dromgoole, Asbury confessed, "I believe Satan is in him and will never come out."[70]

If Glendinning's experience with Satan influenced his expulsion from the church, it is likely that the central issue was not the existence of Satan or even the idea that Satan represented a threat against which the Christian must struggle. Asbury filled his diaries with references to the dangers of Satan. Take Asbury's words of April 22, 1777: "On Tuesday Satan raged against my soul as if he would immediately destroy [it]." Two days later Satan again confronted the would-be bishop by casting "several darts" at him.[71] In addition to this, Asbury often suffered from periods of what he called "heaviness" or "dejection." He called this a "constitutional weakness," but explained that Satan took advantage of this in order to undermine his "peace" by calling his ministry into question.[72] As a result,

Asbury believed it incumbent on himself to "fight" Satan or "die" trying.[73] The most effective weapon in this fight was prayer, which Asbury called the believer's sword to become "the terror of hell and the devil's plague."[74]

Asbury evinced a greater reservation about Satan's direct threat to the body. Take for instance a passage in Asbury's journals in which Asbury told of a disgruntled man who went to a church to curse a preacher "in his heart." Asbury explained that the man suddenly died after his arrival at the church. The people concluded that the man died because "the devil pulled his heart out." However, the only commentary Asbury offered on the matter was that he was "at a loss" to know how to interpret the incident.[75] Likewise, Asbury described an account of a girl possessed by "a dumb spirit." Asbury claimed that God "cast out" the spirit after Methodists held a three-day prayer service. But the lack of drama in the story—Satan did not tear the girl's body, she did not perform unusual feats, nor did she need to be restrained for fear she would harm herself or others—clearly distinguishes this account from Wesley's narratives.[76] Asbury's tolerance of the people's beliefs in Satan's bodily assaults prove he was no enemy of claims of Satan's power to harm the body, but his tendency to avoid commentary and the scarcity of occasions in which he featured such experiences in his journals suggest he was also no zealot.

To Asbury's guarded opinions, Glendinning's account of Satan's bodily appearance must have seemed all too vivid. Many within the itinerant ranks agreed with Asbury's suspicion that Glendinning might be insane.[77] So too did the famous physician Benjamin Rush, who noted as much in his journals.[78] This resort to a pathological explanation of Glendinning's experience reflected the emerging intellectual and scientific currents that medicalized visionary experiences. But pathologizing Glendinning presented a problem for Methodists at the end of the eighteenth century in that doing so seemed to contradict John Wesley's testimony regarding Satan's power. It also seemed to challenge the leadership's indulgence of Glendinning's contemporary, Freeborn Garrettson, who offered similar, though admittedly more tempered, experiences of Satan's physical appearances. In such a dilemma, Glendinning's newly formed views of church discipline might have provided a more solid basis for expelling him.

A connection between church discipline and claims to supernatural experiences may have run deeper than first meets the eye. Since at least the early eighteenth century, Protestants evaluated the validity of claims to supernatural experiences based on whether or not they called into question the existing social, political, and/or ecclesiastical order. Protestants frequently deemed false those experiences that encouraged the overturning of traditional authority.[79] In the same way, Glendinning's claim that his experiences confirmed his opposition to Methodist discipline may well have been the evidence Methodists needed to distinguish his experience from Garrettson's and those Wesley chronicled in his journals. Glendinning used his experience to challenge the church's authority, whereas Garrettson and Wesley did not. If this argument is correct, the decision to bar Glendinning probably had less to do with whether Satan could harm the body than with discerning true and false claims of Satan's bodily attacks.

If Asbury and other early leaders of the Methodist community in America dealt with claims to Satan's power with a significant degree of caution, many among the new crop of preachers who emerged in the early years of the nineteenth century clarified any ambiguity by eliminating Satan's power over the body altogether. Preachers not only more frequently omitted bodily manifestations of Satan from their writings, they also tried to eliminate references to Satan's harming the body. Of course, this rule was not without exceptions. Peter Cartwright explained that he felt "the power of the devil physically and mentally" that caused him to go temporarily blind.[80] Satan not only tempted Jarena Lee to kill herself, but also physically appeared to her in the shape of a dog.[81] Most others, while continuing to speak of Satan's "assaults" and "attacks" that required militant resistance, no longer communicated the same bodily component to those attacks that so long attached themselves to ideas about Satan's power. Benjamin Lakin (1767–1848) illustrates both the enduring commitment to the idea of a battle with Satan and the preference of more Methodist preachers to limit that battle to the spiritual realm. Lakin, who converted while living in Kentucky, pursued a successful though at times troubled career as an itinerant preacher. On one occasion he described a dream in which he confronted the powers of evil. In his journal, Lakin recalled that he dreamt he was in a place in which "evil Spirits" were "preparing a place of destruction of the children of men." Lakin thus attempted to "counter" these designs by entering into a "circle" and praying in the direction of the spirits. Unfortunately, his voice failed and he feared his efforts would fall short. Suddenly, "the Lord appeared to me in human shape. I began to pray again, an evil spirit appeared in the shape of a red Bird, and calling to his companions, but none appeared. I reached out my right hand toward them and cried, Lord Jesus look there, in a moment the evil Spirit took his flight toward the place where they intended to destroy mankind[.] They were all vanqu[i]shed."[82]

The depth and detail of Lakin's account make it a fascinating example of the enduring popularity of Methodist belief in spiritual battles with Satan. However, the fact that the struggle was a dream is also significant. Even if Lakin had intended to convey that his dream prophesied some future event, his writings do not provide evidence that this or any other bodily struggle between Jesus and demons ever took place. Nevertheless, Lakin did fill his journal with waking spiritual fights with demonic forces. Early in his ministry, Lakin recorded almost daily bouts in which he believed Satan tormented him in ways that caused him to suffer serious doubts about his salvation and question his abilities as a minister. Even worse, Lakin experienced periods of sleeplessness, ineffective preaching, and even suicidal inclinations.[83] In none of the battles, though, did Satan assume bodily form or directly attack the body; Lakin limited Satan's attacks to mental temptations.

Similarly, Bishop John Early frequently chronicled Satan's attacks, writing of the devil "roaring" for prey and tempting him to abandon his call to ministry, but he never wrote of physical encounters with Satan or cases of possession.[84] The same is true of itinerant preachers Henry Smith and Henry Boehm, both of whom refer to struggles with Satan, but never in bodily form.[85] The most common exception to this rule was when preachers allowed Satan an indirect power over the body by associating evil temptations with leading people to harm themselves or others. For instance, Methodists commonly attributed their physical persecution to Satan's prompting sinners to assault them.[86] Others like James B. Finley recalled that Satan tempted him to kill himself.[87] Nevertheless, it was not Satan who harmed the body, but a human who responded to Satan's direction.

This new generation of Methodists also rarely related occasions of Satan's possessing a human being. Peter Cartwright referred to casting out "at least a legion of very dirty little devils" from a man, but this is one of the few possible references to possession in literature written by Methodists who emerged in the early nineteenth century, and even this, as we will see, could be interpreted in a way other than literal possession. More often Methodists distinguished their encounters from actual possession. Charles Giles spoke of Satan's expulsion from the soul of a woman rather than from her body.[88] William Swayze wrote about a man with a "wicked spirit" in him that caused him to curse and blaspheme.

Although Swayze said the man fought the devil, Swayze did not call him possessed but a "lunatic."[89] Similarly, James B. Finley hesitated in identifying a case of possession saying only that it "seemed" that a man at one of his meetings was possessed.[90] Billy Hibbard explained that he believed "the Devil in some Deist had come into the meeting." However, the only adverse activity the man displayed was that he stared, "grinding and twisting his mouth," while Hibbard preached. Hibbard did not suggest that the devil tore the person to pieces in the way Wesley often described possession. He did not even try to free the man from the devil's presence, but simply sent him out of the meeting.[91]

Hibbard's reference to the devil's being in someone may have become a way to refer to an act of bad manners or immoral conduct rather than an actual case of possession. In this sense, the devil's getting into someone meant the person followed an inclination that originated with the devil's temptation rather than with God. A story that circulated about Francis Asbury demonstrates this point. After a fight broke out at a revival meeting, Asbury warned other potential troublemakers that not all Methodists were sanctified. Therefore if "you get them angry and the devil should get in them, they are the strongest and hardest men to fight and conquer in the world."[92] Since the men were Methodists it is hardly likely that Asbury intended his reference to the devil's getting in them to mean that Satan literally possessed them. Rather, he meant that Satan would influence them to do something unbecoming of a Methodist.

The fact that men composed most of the available accounts of Satan's attacks raises the prospect that these changes were gendered. Some historians have argued that eighteenth- and early nineteenth-century women's conversion narratives included more vivid accounts of struggles with Satan than those of their male counterparts.[93] However, there is no evidence in Methodist conversion narratives in this period to suggest that women imagined Satan as any more of a direct threat to the body than men did. Nancy Caldwell, Fanny Newell, Mary Coy Bradley, Zilpha Elaw, and Jarena Lee all chronicled profound struggles with Satan in their writings, but none related occasions of bodily possession or Satan's directly harming their bodies. Likewise, men who chronicled women's conversions also did not commonly offer accounts of Satan's possessing women or physically harming them. If Methodist women struggled in more intense ways with Satan than men did, those differences did not extend to the body.

In this new reticence to acknowledge the power of Satan to directly harm the body, American Methodists moved away from the tradition established by John

Wesley and conformed to a larger and increasingly pervasive cultural movement skeptical about the figure of Satan. As we have already seen, beginning in the seventeenth century, the end of the wars of religion, the advance of reason, economic growth, and developments in science and technology encouraged many western Europeans "to view this life with less tragic resignation than during the previous decades of fire and blood." This deeper optimism about life and the embrace of a more rationalized world forced a reconceptualization of the nature of Satan within Western Christendom, at first limited to the intelligentsia but widening over the course of the eighteenth and nineteenth centuries. Once viewed as a nearly all-powerful being and terror of the human body and soul, Satan became increasingly limited by Christians to a mental influence, and by the nineteenth century some even referred to Satan as simply a metaphor for the evil within the human person.[94] Still others could only find entertainment in Satan, "drawn in the outlines of caricature, with the inner detail of his malice washed out; squat and inelegant, this new devil was closer to a dybbuk or leprechaun than to the old grandmaster of hell."[95]

If by the Revolutionary War era the process of removing Satan from relevance in the world was still incomplete such that Americans were divided between the "skeptics and seekers," as Andrew Delbanco has put it, Methodists were certainly not skeptics.[96] Methodists underwent something of a transformation in the early nineteenth century. Most did not go so far as to render Satan a metaphor or form of literary amusement. Even one of the more radical Methodist writings of the early nineteenth century, John Fanning Watson's *Methodist Error,* mentioned earlier, assumed a far more subtle position on Satan. While asserting in principle that demonically influenced practices like witchcraft remained real threats to body and soul, Watson doubted whether such practices endured in America, saying that such powers "seem now to have been banished from among us" at least in part because of "the light of the gospel and the increase of prayers, have greatly increased over our land."[97] Satan might still exercise power in some places, but Watson sought to clarify that America had already been freed from the demonic stranglehold.

The rank-and-file Methodists found in this chapter are certainly more representative of the common beliefs among Methodists than is Watson. These Methodists maintained a belief in Satan and the importance of the struggle against him. However, more and more agreed with the cultural cynicism about Satan's power over the body. Methodists continued to see Satan as a force to be reckoned with, but they nevertheless rested more easily knowing that at least they could protect their bodies from the Evil One's harm.

While Methodists in the early nineteenth century tried to preserve the reality of a spiritual fight for their own salvation, many devalued the bodily nature of that fight. To speak of God slaying the sinner less commonly included feeling some kind of bodily pain. At the same time, Methodists increasingly refused to allow Satan the power to assault them bodily and restricted his attacks to mental temptations. Methodists were beginning to seize control of their bodies from spiritual powers. Even so, the body's role in a cosmic struggle between good and evil did not come to an end. Methodists identified other opponents to contend with as they associated the battle against evil with political figures and events. In the process, Methodists found grounds to commit acts of bodily harm in the name of a divinely sanctioned battle. As Methodists limited the power of God and Satan to harm their bodies, they assumed the power to harm others, and they often justified this power theologically. Even the traditionally peaceful Asbury bowed under the pressures of the "Wild West" and succumbed to the possibility of violent action. "If reports be true, there is danger in journeying through the wilderness; but I do not fear—we go armed. If God suffers Satan to drive the Indians on us; if it be his will, he will teach our hands to war, and our fingers to fight and conquer."[98]

FOUR

BEATING THEIR PLOWSHARES INTO SWORDS

*Methodists and Violence in
Antebellum America*

In 1819, the *Methodist Magazine* began printing a series of articles on Methodism in the West. The first article in this series included the story of Samuel Tucker, a local Methodist preacher who was attacked by a group of Indians while traveling by boat down the Ohio River in 1790. Tucker's foes fired several rounds at the preacher's boat, at least one of which struck Tucker and mortally wounded him. Fearing that his traveling companions would suffer the same fate, Tucker returned fire. In the ensuing battle Tucker killed several of his foes and caused the others to flee. The article's author praised the preacher for his "bravery and presence of mind" that led to the rescue of the women and children who accompanied him. That Tucker died from his wounds made the story quite symbolic.

The courageous preacher gave his life to save those under his care, a parallel to Christ that the magazine's readers surely appreciated.[1]

In the years that followed the publication of this story, Methodists retold Tucker's battle with his Indian foes countless times, turning it into something of a legend in Methodist circles. James B. Finley cast Tucker as a "noble . . . hero-missionary" who fought "manfully" to defend women and children.[2] Jacob Young's account also valorized Tucker, calling him the "wisest and best" of his siblings. To Young, Tucker "bore a very active and successful part, in trying to civilize and Christianize the people," a claim made all the more interesting because we have no record of Tucker ever converting anyone or successfully establishing a mission. Tucker's intrepid protection of his companions during the assault that took his life impressed Young the most. Young described Tucker as a great general who assumed the role of "commander" in order to orchestrate the party's defense. In these last moments of Tucker's life, Young found a model piety as Tucker issued religious instruction to his "soldiers" and then "kneeled down, made his last prayer and expired."[3]

Although it is hard to know whether any of the accounts of Samuel Tucker's life and death are accurate, the narratives strike a powerfully discordant tone from earlier American Methodist prohibitions against the use of violence.[4] The Tucker narratives not only depict a preacher using violence to defend himself and others, the narratives also celebrate this violence. The authors do not raise questions about whether a preacher could carry a weapon; they do not offer regret that Tucker would be placed in the unenviable position of having to take the life of another human being; they do not question the appropriateness of using violence to defend others; nor do they struggle with whether violence is a sin—all issues that earlier Methodists debated.

What accounts for this different perspective on violence? How did Methodists come to see a story of a Methodist preacher who kills his Indian assailants as worthy of celebration in the pages of the denomination's flagship periodical, the *Methodist Magazine*? And how do we understand this celebration of bodily violence within the very same context in which Methodists expressed concern about the body's harm in salvific battles with God and Satan? If Methodists took action to protect the body from physical harm from spiritual forces, why would they extol the virtues of bodily harm in the temporal realm?

The increasing involvement of Methodists in the evolving economic, social, and political structures of the new republic plays a significant role in answering these questions. As Methodists entrenched themselves in these structures, they found their fair share of enemies and much to defend. However, changing economic, social, or political standing only tells part of the story. The religious significance Methodists attached to these emerging structures is also critical to understanding Methodists' willingness to celebrate the use of social violence against Native peoples. In the early decades of the nineteenth century, Methodists joined with other Protestant Christians in articulating the importance of Christianity to the health and preservation of the republic, and the importance of the republic for the future of Christianity. More specifically, Methodists began to embrace the evolving civic theology of the nation as birthed by God and providentially chosen for spreading national moral, economic, and political values to the world. As the nation assumed religious attributes, and Methodists entrusted Christians with an essential role in supporting the nation, political and social enemies assumed greater significance as part of the cosmic battle between good and evil. If God willed the creation of the nation and blessed its ideals as sacred, by extension the nation's enemies became enemies of God and God's moral law, which had been integrated into the country's laws and values. As members of the body politic and church militant, Methodists found themselves fighting the powers of sin and evil on two fronts, the spiritual realm through prayer, scripture reading, and holy living, and on the temporal battlefields with swords, guns, and cannon.

Party Politics and the Legacy of Eighteenth-Century Methodism

I explained in chapter 2 that American Methodists in the Revolutionary War era frequently argued against political involvement because they feared it might compromise their quest for salvation and their spiritual identity, which transcended national boundaries. Methodists repeatedly reminded themselves and others of the trivialness, and even danger, of political identification. Methodists negotiated the pitfalls of public life by emphasizing the importance of citizenship in God's kingdom, which transcended political identity. Followers intended the Christian identity to break the corrupting bonds of the fallen world and the power of sin and Satan that entrapped humans in a false sense of economic or political security. In turn, the Christian joined a community of saints bound by the new birth rather than racial, gender, or national boundaries. The dangers and difficulty of the break with "the world" meant that the true Christian worked militantly to focus her or his attention on matters of spiritual import. Insofar as many early American Methodists considered their battles for salvation to supersede the political controversy of the Revolution, they found little reason to compromise their place in the cosmic battle by participating in the American colonies' war with England.

In the years following the Revolution, Methodism's Protestant peers continued their tendency to sacralize the nation by drenching their discourse with declarations of America as God's chosen people.[5] However, as Russell Richey has shown, Methodist leadership in the post–Revolutionary War era more often focused themselves on notions of the continent and its salvation than on envisioning the land they traveled as a nation. Richey summarized this as an interest in "geography" rather than "civitas," place rather than nation. Most Methodists at the turn of the century spiritualized their language of citizenship by viewing themselves as citizens of two nations, a lesser earthly nation and a greater spiritual Zion.[6] This otherworldly interest helped keep Methodists from heavily investing themselves in political activity that seemed to them to pose too great a distraction from the essential work of conversion. Of course, Methodists were not the only ones who failed to fix upon a national identity or produce a ready answer to the question of the role of religion in the republic. These tasks fell to those who came of age in the late eighteenth and early nineteenth centuries.[7] Methodists lagged behind most of their denominational peers in the speed with which they attached a unique religious destiny to the American republic, but they lost little time catching up in the nineteenth century.

Methodism's first strides into serious political involvement took place within a broader social context that wrestled with the meaning of government and the significance of the nation. Many in the early republic fashioned a civic theology that saw Christianity girding republican virtue and thus serving a necessary role in civic life. Quite simply, Christianity was thought to foster good citizens. In addition, civic theology rooted the foundation, values, and mission of the nation in God's redemptive plan for the world. America became, in the words of the Congregationalist pastor and Yale president Ezra Stiles (1727–1795), "elevated to glory and honor" by God. In this exalted position, the United States, "God's American Israel" as Stiles termed the nation, had a divine obligation to spread religious and civil liberty at home and abroad.[8]

Although most Methodists at the turn of the nineteenth century could not be counted among those who had already fashioned a singular or pre-eminent role for America in God's dealings with the world, they slowly articulated what it meant to be a Methodist and a citizen. In the famous Christmas Conference of 1784 in which the Methodist Episcopal Church was born, the refashioned Articles of Religion clearly commanded Methodist loyalty to the United States.[9] American Methodists followed Wesley in making obedience to the nation a religious obligation and in so doing they not only signaled the authority of the government over civil affairs, but they also acknowledged their willingness to make that obedience religiously significant.

Methodists symbolically reinforced these obligations in various pronouncements throughout the 1780s and 1790s. In October 1796, for instance, with the French Revolution's "Reign of Terror" still fresh in the minds of many Americans, the Methodist General Conference declared a day of General Thanksgiving, in part "to take into remembrance the goodness and wisdom of God displayed toward America, by making it an asylum for those who are distressed in Europe with war and want, and oppressed with ecclesiastical and civil tyranny; and the rapid settlement and wonderful government, that they may be kept pure and permanent; for the admirable Revolution, obtained and established at so small a price of blood and treasure."[10] This complex statement expressed several important sentiments. It distinguished America as a land of liberty, identified a divine intention for the nation in making it an asylum for those experiencing tyranny abroad—a typical image of American empire in the early republic—and reflected the willingness of Methodist preachers to seek divine favor for the nation.[11]

Such ways of imagining the nation and promoting its welfare reflect a set of common political assumptions that historian Richard Carwardine observes among American Methodists in the early decades of the nineteenth century. Carwardine finds that Methodists were generally willing to envision the government as sanctioned by scripture, founded on Christian principles, a defender of religious liberty, and a beacon used by God to shine upon the world. Hence, the principal political obligation for Methodists was to engage in prayer for rulers. But Christians were also expected to vote, consider candidates who promoted the common good, and represent Christian morals and faith in the public sphere.[12]

Perhaps the most pressing concern that brought Methodists into the political realm in the early years of the republic was the issue of disestablishment. British preacher George Shadford asserted in 1776 that Methodists favored the establishment of the Anglican Church in Virginia. Yet Methodists did not follow this trajectory after the war.[13] Methodists made official statements opposing the establishment of a national religion as early as 1784.[14] A general consensus took root among Methodists that the disestablishment of religion in the new states was crucial, not only for religious tolerance, but also to successfully carry out the denomination's evangelistic endeavors. In 1789, Methodists took to the public stage to defend disestablishment by publishing in the New York press an address to President Washington that called for "the preservation of those civil and religious liberties which have been transmitted to us by the providence of God and the glorious revolution." In this same year they also attacked the Episcopal Church for seeking to establish a national religion, "which we abhor as the great bane of truth and holiness, and . . . a great impediment to the progress of vital Christianity."[15]

Richard Carwardine finds two other basic factors that encouraged Methodist political involvement in the early republic. First, widespread interest in politics among the populace in the early nineteenth century pressured Methodists to fashion their own political identities. Second, many Methodists feared that not participating in politics, particularly in the wake of the radicalism of the French Revolution, would create a moral void in the national political life that would ultimately compromise religious and civic liberty.[16]

This burgeoning sense of political responsibility did not translate into a single party identity, however. Methodists counted a strong Federalist presence in Maryland in the 1790s, including the governor, secretary of state, and a justice on the Court of Common Pleas. In New England and the West, Methodists often aligned themselves with the Republican Party.[17] Many Republicans then became Jacksonian Democrats under the Second Party System, most notably Peter Cartwright, who unsuccessfully ran against Abraham Lincoln for a seat in the Unites States Congress. However, Carwardine finds that the largest number of Methodists in the Second Party System identified as Whigs.[18]

If by the late eighteenth and early nineteenth centuries Methodists showed a greater proclivity to participate in partisan politics and at times even valorize the nation as born of God, they were still a long way from the fully developed civic theology of Christian republicanism popular among other American Protestants. Many of Methodism's peers, including Presbyterians, Congregationalists, Baptists, and Episcopalians, had already identified Christians as the essential cog in the formation and preservation of a nation that possessed a millennial role in global transformation. By contrast, Methodists typically avoided the association of the United States with the millennium, opting to see the country in much less theologically exceptional ways. In keeping with their theology of providence, Methodists recognized God's role in the nation. However, at the close of the first decade of the nineteenth century most Methodists simply had not yet announced a unique theological mission for the nation in the culmination of history. Rather, the church continued to appropriate much of the popular political rhetoric and redefine it in spiritual ways, as adherents did with the language of liberty, which they more often located in the freedom that came from conversion or an empowerment for effective gospel preaching than any relation to republican government. Likewise, they more often found their communal identity rooted and nurtured in the church's love feasts, camp meetings, and classes than in national origins.[19]

Mark Noll observes that by the 1820s, however, Methodists were conforming to American Protestantism's republican discourse. By the 1830s, nearly all the preachers "were wholehearted promoters of the commonplace Christian republican vision."[20] The War of 1812 made an essential contribution to this transformation. The war provided Methodists the impetus to fashion a more fully developed sense for the unique religious significance of the nation's mission, the role of Christians in the nation's preservation, and the rights of believers to go to war to defend their newfound values.[21] Methodist claims to full participation in the national identity did not necessarily replace the spiritual communion early Methodists found in the church, but their ecclesial and national identities became far more mingled than ever before.

The War of 1812 and the Sacred Significance of the United States

Concern over the implications of European political strife for U.S. political and economic interests abroad and Great Britain's continued influence in North America helped lead the United States to declare war against Great Britain on June 12, 1812. Many hawks in Congress and their various constituents at home declared the war with England an attempt to assert the strength of republicanism over monarchy. Their rhetoric, which included fighting a noble cause to resist the illegal impressment of American citizens into the British navy and the removal of the lingering presence of the British military standing in the way of American expansion in North America, resonated in very different ways among Methodists.

The war drew its most ardent support from Americans in the South and Northwest. In the Northeast, despite the apparent threats to New England's shipping industry caused by British maritime restrictions, including the impressment of American sailors, zeal for the war was low. Citizens in the Northeast felt a greater sense of cultural and ideological identity with England, particularly in crediting Britain with a critical role in opposing the radicalism of Napoleonic France. In fact, northeasterners did not focus their economic ire on the British, whose policies may actually have served as an economic boon for New England's shipping industry, but on Jefferson and Madison's embargo with Britain and France. Northeasterners also feared that an invasion of Canada would prompt a British invasion of the Northeast.[22]

If opposition to the war was strongest in the Northeast, then the American Northwest and South became the site for the war's staunchest support. Inhabitants of both regions complained that the British violation of American neutral trading rights assailed national honor and undermined the U.S. position abroad. Britain's challenge to American trade with the European continent also aroused economic concern from farmers who faced restricted markets for their crops. Even more, northwesterners feared an alliance between Native Americans and the British that would halt American geographic expansion.[23]

Word of the declaration of war against the British had already reached Methodists as the New England Annual Conference commenced its meeting on June 20. At once, the question of the propriety of Christian participation in warfare captivated the proceedings. One partisan chronicler of the conference explained: "Many of them [delegates to the conference] regarded war as utterly and irreconcilably opposed to the gospel of peace; and others were in danger of drinking in the spirit of the times to a degree that would seriously peril their Christian character."[24]

Among those present at this conference, E. F. Newell championed a position similar to that of earlier American Methodists when he refused to see Christianity as in any way compatible with war. "WAR and GOSPEL!! O how unlike! Astonishment filled my mind, while in silent wonder my soul cried out, 'how can one man lift a destructive weapon against another! How can any man, or company of men, kneel down and pray for each other and then rise and shoot one another!'" War, for Newell, flowed not from a desire for justice, but from sin manifest as the "thirst for power and self-aggrandizement."[25] The Christian's responsibility to overcome sin and display love to friend and foe made participation in war unthinkable.

The aged leader Francis Asbury, as he had in the Revolution, urged neutrality. In fact, Asbury could not help but interpret the war ominously. He confessed in his journals, "I feel a deep concern for the Old and New World. Calamity and suffering are coming upon them both: I shall make but few remarks on this unhappy subject; it is one on which the prudent will be silent; but I must needs say it is an evil day."[26]

Charles Giles recorded a similar aversion to war. Giles enlisted in the military in the early part of the nineteenth century, but refused to bear arms, calling the army a "school of death." After only a brief exposure to military life, Giles concluded that the entire enterprise was immoral and denied even the possibility of a defensive war. In a statement reminiscent of his forebears, Giles focused on martial service of another kind. "I held myself a soldier, nevertheless, a soldier under Jesus Christ, the great Captain over the army of saints, with whom I was marshaled, and moving slowly on to final conquest." Giles limited his enemies to his own sinful nature and evil spiritual beings, against which "all the powers of my soul were roused to activity, urging me on to battle."[27]

This strong distinction between the spiritual and political, and the association of the war with sin, by no means enjoyed the dominance it had among American Methodists during the Revolution. Methodists who came of age in the years immediately following the Revolution shared a very different perspective on the Revolution and the intersection of religion and politics. They celebrated those who fought in the first war with England as heroes, and proudly claimed a lineage of familial participation in the conflict.[28] These Methodists did not see the war as inherently sinful or a dangerous distraction from the spiritual life. Rather, under the influence of a nationalist discourse, the Revolution became the heroic event that birthed a nation they considered the purveyor of sacred and civil liberty. In keeping with this different perspective on war, these Methodists grew up dreaming of their own future military glories and the contribution those battles might make to the nation. Take, for instance, the missionary preacher Alfred Brunson, who as a child during the war played military games meant to display his courage. As Brunson grew older, he explained that he longed for a military career that included attending West Point.[29]

Following the declaration of war with England in 1812, many Methodists sought to legitimate the cause theologically while others enlisted to rid America of her British occupiers. Dr. Henry Wilkins wrote Bishop McKendree that the Methodists in Baltimore, the same city where colonial officials complained during the Revolution that the Methodists refused to sign the loyalty oath, stood united in their support for the American cause.[30] Even granting a measure of exaggeration, the sentiments expressed by Wilkins suggest a profound transformation in sentiment.

Although Methodists who supported the war differed considerably over the meaning of war, many, as we have already seen, had begun to fashion a commitment to participating in the political realm, and this helped rally them to the nation's defense. Moderates expressed sympathy for the traditional view of separating Christianity from political life even as they argued that this separation need not be so extreme as to foreclose occasions when Christians' spiritual and political interests might intersect. Such was the position of David Lewis, a member of the New York Conference. Lewis admitted that the tradition of maintaining a distance from politics had value, saying that preachers "should not become entangled with the partyisms that prevail."[31] When it came to war, Lewis contended that it was "antagonistic to the Gospel" because it "authorizes robbery, oppression, and violence; and . . . weakens the tenure by which we hold our property, our liberty, and our lives." By contrast, the Christian enlisted in a greater spiritual battle fought "with weapons which are not carnal, but mighty, through God, to the pulling down of strongholds." This battle had Christ as the "captain" who empowered humans to "withstand all the assaults of the devil."[32]

Despite sounding every bit the traditional American Methodist, Lewis tempered such positions by arguing that even while Christians did well to maintain a distance from politics, they should not be prevented from "the exercise of their rights" as citizens. Like everyone else, Christians must "render unto Caesar what is Caesar's." In this, they will:

> find it necessary to give the weight of their influence in favor of that form of civil government which, to them, appears best calculated to promote the interests and happiness of the people. In a country where the people are the sovereigns, no man can innocently stand aloof, and allow the elections to go by default, so as to raise to offices of trust and power corrupt, time-serving politicians, when by attending to his privilege and duty he can contribute to hinder such unworthy elevations, and promote the election of men at least a little better fitted for the responsible positions. We owe it to ourselves, to the country, and to posterity, to vote, and to vote understandingly, with an eye single to the best interests of the whole country.[33]

Lewis's statement made little distinction between Christian participation in politics and the participation of other citizens. The responsibility of citizens to elect public officials who were concerned with the common good was sufficient in its own right. However, Lewis went on to identify a benefit from a closer integration of religion and politics. "The fact is, politics have been separated too far from religion; men are coming to think it possible to be, at the same time, religious saints, and political knaves; and, on the other hand, some are looked upon, through party prejudices, as being perfect paragons of political purity, while they are known to be morally and religiously corrupt."[34] Lewis used this argument to make clear that Christians provided a moral foundation to political life.

As the nation approached war in 1812, Lewis continued to maintain that war was sinful, but he also argued that, like other forms of sin, God "permitted" nations to go to war and then providentially ordered the conflict to bring about good. In particular, Lewis saw war as the "means to punish wicked nations." Moreover, he referred to particular political issues that might warrant war as a last resort, including "to throw off oppression" and to "maintain the rights of our manhood," as well as more spiritual concerns, namely the "evangelization of the world" and the "freedom to worship God."[35]

Lewis applied such reasoning to the controversy with Britain in 1812. By identifying and intersecting secular and religious motivations for the war, Lewis imagined the war to cast off British oppression as bearing spiritual significance. The nation's conflict assumed religious ends in his defense of war as punishment of the "wicked," extension of religious freedom, and the promotion of evangelism. In fact, Lewis read the present conflict as a continuation of the Revolution, itself a sacred battle in which "the noble blood of patriot martyrs consecrated this whole land to freedom." Lewis reflected this connection between the Revolution and the War of 1812 when he sought God's blessing of American troops by asking that "the God of power, who sustained our fathers in the Revolutionary struggle, would give us the victory."[36] Thus, despite what he saw as the regrettably violent implications of war, Lewis invested the conflict with spiritual implications by recognizing the war as a defense of divine values and arguing that the war might result in greater good for the Gospel.

While Lewis tried to establish the conditions that might justify a nation, and a Christian, to go to war, others were more assertive about the importance of Christian participation. Citizenship, they argued, obligated Christians to fight.

Peter Cartwright summed up the opinions of many of this new breed of Methodist when he proclaimed that any man who refused to take up arms in support of his country was unworthy of protection.[37] Against those who argued war was a sin and therefore inappropriate for Christians, whether loyal citizens or not, Methodists such as Alfred Brunson pointed to the endurance of their faith while enlisted in the military. Brunson insisted on the possibility of a Christian soldier, one who not only fought without compromising his faith, but fought in obedience to God's decree. When challenged on this point, Brunson simply queried, "Are we not engaged in a lawful and honorable war? And why cannot a man enjoy religion in the army, in such a case, as well as any where else?"[38]

The real concern for Methodists like Brunson was not whether a Christian could bear arms (they had already decided that much), but how the Christian ought to conduct himself on the battlefield. Thus, Billy Hibbard instructed a group of soldiers on proper behavior so that they would not "violate the decorum of christian [sic] soldiers."[39] The *Western Christian Advocate* provided an idea of just what this decorum might look like in its celebration of Peter Black, a layman from Ohio. Exemplifying what the periodical called Black's motto of "God and his country," Black prayed with and exhorted his fellow soldiers during the war.[40] In so doing, Black brought his piety into the camp and influenced his comrades to convert and conduct themselves with dignity on and off the battlefield. By defining a place for Christians in war, these Methodists deliberately undermined claims of the inherent connection between sin and war. The Christian soldier could not only preserve his faith in battle, he could contribute to the health and well-being of the nation and the soldiers who defended it.

These ideas about the right to go to war and the importance of the Christian's participation in war came together most clearly in the New England preacher and holiness leader Timothy Merritt. Merritt rooted the war in the defense of ideals that he defined as sacred. To accomplish this task, he turned to the Hebrew Bible for historical and theological precedent. Merritt compared the biblical patriarch Abraham going to war to deliver Lot from his captors in the book of Genesis to the United States going to war against Britain in 1812. In fact, Merritt explained that the heroes of the Hebrew Bible, like Abraham and Joshua, fought for the very same ideals that Merritt attributed to the current crisis.

> When you come to the fight you will remember that Abraham and David, Moses and Joshua, fought before you. Did they contend for national character and independence? So do you. Did they contend for the lives and liberty

of their brethren? So do you. Did they contend under the favor and approbation of God? They certainly did, and so I believe do you. Did they return victorious from the sanguinary field? They generally did, and so I believe will you. Let your trust, therefore, be in the God of battles, and fear not.[41]

More than simply establishing the foundations of a just war by referencing biblical proof-texts, Merritt's attempt to locate the roots of American ideals in the history of Israel sacralized those ideals. Contending for "national character and independence" no longer represented a temporal quest for political liberation that had little connection with the larger spiritual battle. The fight for political independence became part of the divine plan of the "God of battles." As such, God honored the nation's efforts through supernatural empowerment. Because Merritt identified the ideals as sacred, he could justify Methodists taking up arms for what he saw as a "righteous" war. Indeed, Merritt warned, "we shall provoke Heaven by lightly esteeming real national character and blessings."[42]

Merritt's unwavering call to arms surely differed from that of many moderates, who carefully balanced their political and religious interests. Nevertheless, the support given to the war by Methodist preachers and laypeople signaled their serious doubts about Methodism's former resistance to war. By 1812, Methodists who accepted the importance of Christian involvement in the political life of the nation began to employ a republican rhetoric that equated the ideals of the nation with the sacred. This moved them beyond their earlier view of the nation falling under the providence of God to a view of the nation as privileged by God to serve a unique role in the battle against sin and evil. The new perspective not only helped them to justify the nation's war and the Christian's participation in it, but also to define the battle as a sacred struggle. Violence itself became a usable tool for American Methodists to achieve divine purposes.

Methodists continued to develop their ideas of the religious aspects of the nation and the spiritual threat posed by its enemies in the years after the war. Their reflections on westward expansion and the evangelization of the West played a central role in this process. Methodists not only repeated earlier statements about the sacred origins and mission of the nation, but they also expanded those statements by closely associating concepts of western expansion, Anglo civilization, and Christian mission. Encounters with Native populations in the West gave American Methodists the opportunity to fully integrate the nation's political and economic interest in civilizing Native Americans with the church's interest in Christianizing them. These developments contributed in important ways to Methodists' ability to valorize violence against Native Americans, whom they perceived as standing in the way of the nation's ambitions.

Methodists, the West, and National Identity

As many as one hundred thousand people lived west of the Appalachian Mountains at the close of the Revolutionary War.[43] Peace with Great Britain in 1783 substantially increased the western population through sustained, though contested, American migration across the mountains and into areas we now recognize as the states of Kentucky, Tennessee, Mississippi, Alabama, Ohio, Indiana, Illinois, and Michigan. Flush with imperial prospects of cheap land, economic gain, and what they perceived to be a divine blessing, Anglo Americans spread west to build what they imagined as a new mighty empire.

Many of these early pioneers had little regard for the Native populations that inhabited the territory whites craved. The resulting hostilities, themselves often violent, led to formal military engagement on the part of the nascent United States government and, upon victory, the signing of treaties that granted white inhabitants the freedom to "settle" areas west of the Appalachians and east of the Mississippi. In the Old Northwest, treaties with the Delaware, Miami, Shawnee, Wyandot, Seneca, Ottawa, Chippewa, and Potawatomi in 1795 and 1815 allowed unfettered migration to the Ohio, Indiana, and Illinois territories. In the Southwest, the Treaty of Fort Jackson, signed in 1814 after Andrew Jackson's defeat of the Muskogee (Creek), opened up large tracts of that region for white settlement.

Anglo migration into these territories fueled a mythology of the West that quickly assumed a prominent role in American empire ideology.[44] Timothy Dwight, Congregationalist minister and president of Yale College, expressed the significance of western expansion for American empire in his celebrated poem "Greenfield Hill" (1794):

> All hail, thou western world! By heaven design'd
> Th' example bright, to renovate mankind.
> Soon shall thy sons across the mainland roam;
> And claim, on far Pacific shores, their home;
> Their rule, religion, manners, arts, convey,
> And spread their freedom to the Asian sea.
> Where erst six thousand suns have roll'd the year
> O'er plains of slaughter, and o'er wilds of fear,

Towns, cities, fanes, shall lift their towery pride;
The village bloom, on every streamlet's side;
Proud Commerce' mole the western surges lave;
The long, white spire lie imag'd on the wave;
O'er morn's pellucid main expand their sails,
And the starr'd ensign court Korean gales.[45]

Dwight's assertion of the West as "heaven design'd" identified the region as more than land to be traversed in an inevitable march of humankind. Something about the West itself prompted Anglo Americans to imagine it as a place that would give birth to a bourgeoning empire.

Just what this something was became the fodder for Anglo myths about the West. One of the most important of these myths depicted the West as a wilderness in need of mastery. The myth assumed a contentious relationship between the untamed West and the civilized Anglo. Anglos entered the West to subdue both the land they imagined as a dark and dangerous wilderness and the Native inhabitants, whom they described as inherently sinful. This taming of the West allowed a new paradise to emerge. More significantly, by drawing on images of darkness and light, sin and redemption, Anglos imputed the conquering of the West with religious significance as part of the Christian triumph over evil.[46]

A twist on this notion of struggle against wilderness, as Richard Slotkin's classic work on frontier mythology notes, began to emerge at the end of the eighteenth century. Slotkin argues that Americans, influenced by John Filson's 1784 promotional tract *The Discovery, Settlement, and Present State of Kentucke* [sic] and its appendix, "The Adventures of Col. Daniel Boone," began to develop a "national myth" of the frontier that posited it as the means to perfect civilization. Anglo Americans became particularly attracted to a vision of the ideal frontier settler as a "hunter hero" who entered the harsh evils of the frontier wilderness in order to be stripped of the excesses of civilization and recreated as "the perfect stoic—patient as an Indian, indifferent to danger, fearless, and content to live as the wilderness demands, by hunting and hiding in solitude." Settlers took the best of both worlds—"civilized" Anglo culture with its value of self-reliance and self-restraint, and Native culture that valued personal freedom and combat—in order to "realize, through agrarian cultivation, nature's inherent power to sustain civilization." In this sense, the wilderness, while inevitably giving way to civilization, contributed to the upward progress of Anglos by removing the excesses of urbane culture and imposing higher ideals of freedom and power.[47]

Still another myth of the West replaced the image of wilderness with that of a garden. Into the fruitful West, the farmer moved to tend an earthly paradise. As Henry Nash describes this view, "the master symbol of the garden embraced a cluster of metaphors expressing fecundity, growth, increase, and blissful labor in the earth, all centering on the heroic figure of the idealized frontier farmer armed with that supreme agrarian weapon, the sacred plow."[48] The agrarian lifestyle, according to this image, encouraged economic prosperity, moral virtue, and civic responsibility by infusing social equality, simplicity, and an ethic of hard work.[49] The garden of the West promised regeneration of the individual and society.

Both the wilderness and garden metaphors shared the image of the West as bestowing opportunity for personal as well as social renewal. Pioneers nurtured personal moral virtue by conquering wilderness and creating a garden paradise. Likewise, social benefit accrued through the growth of a virtuous and industrious citizenry that worked to preserve the civic order and promote economic prosperity.

As much as any religious community did, Methodists became enamored with the West. The denomination established a small number of circuits west of the Alleghenies by the mid-1780s, particularly in areas in western Pennsylvania, Virginia, and Tennessee. The growth in church membership in the region during the early nineteenth century was nothing short of astounding. Whereas membership in the church as a whole increased by an impressive 184 percent between 1800 and 1811, membership in circuits west of the Alleghenies increased nearly 1,000 percent over this period.[50] William Warren Sweet noted in his classic work on Methodism in the West: "The number of circuits . . . increased from nine in 1800 to sixty-nine in 1811. In 1800 Bishop Asbury . . . assigned fourteen preachers to travel these western circuits; in 1811 Bishop McKendree stationed one hundred preachers within the bounds of the Western Conference."[51] If, as Russell Richey contends, Methodism developed a southern accent in the early nineteenth century, these numbers suggest that Methodists mixed that accent with a heavy western dialect.

Three notions about the West dominated Methodist discourse in the early nineteenth century: the largely unquestioned acceptance of the western spread of the American empire, the importance of Anglos developing the territory and civilizing its inhabitants, and the moral and social benefits of the West. Like Anglo Americans in general, Methodists drew on images of the West as both a wilderness in need of development and a garden paradise. The Minutes of the Annual Conferences in 1812 remarked on the transformation of the western wilderness, "which but a few years past was only inhabited by the tawny savage and prowling wild beast; but now this wilderness has budded, blossometh as the rose."[52] James B. Finley captured this idea even more starkly when he recalled in 1854 that the same territory that pioneers settled and populated in the early nineteenth century was, during the Revolution, nothing more than "a waste, wilderness, untenanted except by the savages."[53]

Other Methodists focused on the image of the West as a lush garden. When Philip Gatch wrote his friend and fellow Methodist stalwart Edward Dromgoole about life in Ohio in 1802, much of his attention focused on the area's natural resources that Gatch believed could more than support a host of industries.

> The Countree [sic] is Beautiful in its situation and promices [sic] every advantage I believe any Country in this Wourld [sic] can do[.] The L[ittle] Miami is a Beautiful stream[.] It [i]s clear summer and winter Flush and swift and the best stream for Mills I ever saw not excepting the Brandywine[.] There is about near a Dowzen [sic] Mills on this stream and is sufficient for mills in a straight direction about sixty miles up [it]. . . . There was three Sea vessals [sic] Built on the Ohio and went down Loaded last year, great numbers of Boats also went down the River Loaded with Flower [sic] Bacon . . . I believe we shall not want for trade in this Countrey [sic]. Pumpkins and potatoes in abundance[.] In short our Countrey is good for every kind of produce that Virginia and Maryland, Pennsylvania and the Jersies take in. The land is in common Rich and a great deal of it richer I expect than you ever saw.[54]

Gatch also clearly expressed one of the moral benefits of the West, at least in the Old Northwest after 1787, the absence of slavery.[55] Many discovered that moving to a non-slaveholding territory assuaged their conscience and helped avoid persecution that arose because of their antislavery stance. Frederick Bonner (1759–1827) found the absence of slavery in Ohio particularly reflective of the land's theological significance, calling Ohio the "Land of Liberty and Equality" and, more significantly, the "American Canaan." Bonner likened Methodists to the Israelites of old and called them to flee the "country of oppression & wrong" and cross "our Jordan (I mean the Ohio [River])."[56]

Bonner's use of biblical typologies indicates how the frontier took on religious meaning for many Methodists. By situating Anglo settlement of the West in the sacred history of God's settlement of a chosen people, Methodists intertwined their spiritual pursuits with political and national interests. Using language drawn from the Israelite's experience chronicled in the Hebrew Bible, Methodists applied biblical typologies to the land, calling the frontier their "Canaan" created by God for the deliverance and prosperity of God's people. Some called the land the "Garden of God," while still others described the West as "Zion," as when James Haw, a preacher in Kentucky, wrote Francis Asbury "with good news from Zion; the work of God is going on rapidly in this new world."[57] These ways of speaking marked the geographic spread west as part of the spiritual pilgrimage toward the fulfillment of the divine plan for God's people. It also drew Methodists closer to the language of their Protestant peers, particularly Congregationalists, Presbyterians, and Baptists, who had already applied these biblical typologies to the country in ways that reinforced the evolving civic theology of America as a chosen nation.[58]

The first systematic treatment of the social and religious values of the West in Methodist literature appears in the writings of Thomas Hinde. Hinde was the son of a physician who served as Patrick Henry's chief surgeon in Virginia. After the Revolution, the elder Hinde was granted ten thousand acres in Clark County, Kentucky, where he moved his family in 1797. The home became a stopping point for Methodist preachers, including Francis Asbury, who stayed there in 1803. Later, Thomas Hinde found his way to Ohio, where he served as a local preacher before moving to Illinois.[59]

Contemporary scholars have overlooked Hinde and the important role he played in defining a vision of the West for Methodists. Along with the publication of a moderately successful hymnal, Hinde's articles published in Methodist periodicals, often under the pseudonym "Theophilus Arminius," became his most important contribution to early Methodism.[60] The May through November 1819 issues of the *Methodist Magazine* published his "Account of the Rise and Progress of the Work of God in the Western Country," the first history of Methodism that focused solely on the western territories. The work set the tone for Methodist writing on the West for the next fifty years. Hinde charted the development of evangelical religion, particularly Methodism, against the backdrop of what he imagined as its ideal geographic setting. In the midst of the dangerous and unsettled frontier, the first churches arose and, more importantly for Hinde, the religious camp meeting flourished. Hinde cast the camp meeting—what he called a place "in the wilderness" where "thousands and tens of thousands, of almost every nation" came to remove themselves from temporal concerns in order for "their hearts to become the temples of God"—as the critical tool for the spread of the Gospel in the West.[61]

Hinde proved the significance of the camp meetings by emphasizing the great numbers that attended and the extraordinary conversions that he believed helped Christianize the West. Huge crowds falling "as though they were dead," screaming for mercy, and praising God in loud song gave evidence of a peculiar act of divine grace. Interestingly, Hinde animated the camp meetings with activity that embodied at a communal level the Methodist tradition of casting the pursuit of salvation as a violent struggle. His narratives of camp meeting revivals climaxed in a battle with God in which sinners "were struck down like men in battle." Others, who Hinde explained became terrified at the sight of their friends and family falling under the power of God, tried to flee the struggle. "Like those who are closely pursued by an army in time of war," they were "overtaken by the invisible power, under which they would be struck down, and constrained to cry out in anguish, and confess their wickedness in persecuting the work of God . . ."[62] The wayward sinners became soldiers in God's holy army.

The conversions made at the camp meeting not only ushered scores into the ranks of the saved, Hinde argued, but they also radically democratized western social relations. Those persons traditionally excluded from public authority— children, slaves, the unlearned, and women—claimed spiritual authority over men of power and standing. The effect of the anointing of these typically marginalized on the traditionally powerful symbolized something profound for Hinde. Cases when the "bold and courageous Kentuckian (undaunted by the horrors of war)" might "turn pale and tremble at the reproof of a weak woman, a little boy, or a poor African" confirmed God's powerful blessing of the West.[63]

Hinde observed yet another important consequence of the camp meeting for the West: the unification of Protestant denominations. Hinde remarked with satisfaction that worshippers found it difficult to distinguish members of different denominations at the meetings. Hinde hoped that this providential work of the "spirit of the Lord" would create a "general communion of all Christians." Alternatively, Hinde's narrative marked the loss of this unity in the earliest camp meetings in Kentucky as, at the very least, a missed opportunity for the West to seize upon an eschatological vision of Christian unity, and, at worst, a dissolution into heresy.[64] Yet Hinde found the redemption of God's plan for the West in the transferal of the camp meetings from Kentucky to the Northwest territory. For

Hinde, "a spirit of enchantment" incited the pious to escape Kentucky's infidelity and flee to Ohio, "a blessed asylum for the Church in the wilderness."[65]

This shift from Kentucky to Ohio created the opportunity for Hinde to focus his full energy on the redemptive place of the West. The "new countries" allowed pioneers to escape the vices of settled regions in order to pursue a pure worship of God:

> Here the slanderous tongue does not reach him: The watchings against the devices of a subtle enemy are past. Here all have sufficient employ in attention to their own concerns. . . . Here in tranquility he reviews his life; reflects on the fleeting moments of infancy, childhood and youth, gathers up the fragments of past experience, and solemnly lays the whole to heart. In humble devotion with his companion and children, he falls to his knees, morning and evening before the Almighty Being that created him, and adores his God. . . . He in fact begins to live anew.[66]

By linking the West, particularly Ohio, to the revival of religion, Hinde connected the territory to religious prosperity. Geographic space and religious vitality became nearly synonymous. Even those who professed religion while living in settled territories became more fervent Christians in Hinde's vision of the West.[67] This religious vitality revealed the eschatological role for the West that Hinde found in his reading of the biblical prophecy of Isaiah: "The wilderness and the solitary place shall be glad for them; and the desert shall rejoice and blossom as the rose."[68] For Hinde, the revival of religion in the West marked a critical stage in the final redemptive transformation of the world. The desert bore fruit and the wilderness transformed to support a vibrant Christian community.

It is important to note Hinde's initially narrow vision of the fulfillment of this prophecy for social and religious transformation. Hinde did not feature the development of agriculture, trade, or commerce. Rather, in 1819, Hinde restricted his vision to an inner spiritual transformation fashioned in the tranquility, freedom, and innocence of the West that reformed social behavior and reconstituted social relations along new lines of spiritual authority. The untamed and dangerous wilderness was subdued not by the hands of the trader, farmer, or entrepreneur, but by the missionary, the local preacher, and the itinerant minister. Thus, Hinde celebrated the Methodist preachers whose deeds in spreading the Gospel "will be held . . . in everlasting remembrance." These figures instituted the transformation of the wilderness through the introduction of Christianity. Through the proclamation of saving faith, Christians transformed "the very mounds where the yelling red savages pinioned the unfortunate and suffering prisoner to the stake" and "the very spot . . . where the equally barbarous white savages murdered and burned the Christian Moravian Indians" into sacred sites for the worship of God.[69]

As he did in narrating the camp meetings, Hinde turned to the Methodist tradition of military struggle to define the transformation of the West. Hinde portrayed Methodists as soldiers "who did not shrink from the attack" of infidels in the West. These soldiers engaged in a "violent contest" to overcome their opponents. The obvious parallel with the ancient Israelites allowed Hinde to cast Methodists as the people of Israel fighting for victory in Canaan. In the same way God enabled the ancient Israelites to remove their enemies from the land, God empowered Anglos to defeat those who stood in their way of inhabiting their Canaan. Through these "battles," Christians secured the West from both the red savage and white infidel and marked the land "for the kingdom of the blessed Jesus."[70]

Hinde continued to contribute his history of the triumph of Christianity in the West to Methodist periodicals throughout the 1820s. In 1827, Hinde resuscitated his historical series "Short Sketches of Revivals of Religion Among the Methodists in the Western Country" that he had begun in 1822. In this series Hinde expanded his vision of the distinctions and transformation of the West: "never was a region of the earth more suitable and better calculated to sustain a rapid and flowing population, than this region. Its conquest and settlement border on the romantic."[71] Hinde also used the articles to shift from an image of the West as a place of quiet escape to one emphasizing the region's bounty that supported prosperous cities and industry. The wilderness to which the pioneer retreated for spiritual transformation amidst the pristine countryside succumbed to settlement: "Behold the rolling population, they go forth rejoicing. . . . Do you see the rising towns, cities in embryo? See every where the spires and steeples of temples of mercy or justice." This development, impressive in its own right, had a greater theological meaning for Hinde. The erection of the mighty western economic empire in cooperation with the spread of the Gospel, "even among our American Indians," indicated "the last struggles of Christianity to *girt* the earth" for the coming millennium. "Dost thou not know the order of grace and of providence? The 'best wine is kept to the last.' Here are the displays of heaven's favours. And when the glad tidings of 'great joy' which shall be sounded through all the earth, shall have passed this great theater, it will return in swelling waves of glory from the west to the east." The millennial age was about to dawn, with the West its crowning glory.[72]

Hinde's history represents an important phase in Methodist articulation of the nation as integral to God's plan for the world. Christianity followed the spread of the pioneers to create a new empire bathed in vital religion. These connections between religious growth and geographic expansion continued as Anglo Americans developed their notion of what John O'Sullivan formally named in 1845 as the nation's "manifest destiny" to control the continent of North America. Methodists not only embraced these ideals in their celebrations of the West, they fueled them, as they did in the pages of the *Western Christian Advocate* in proclaiming the "high destiny" of the West eleven years before John O'Sullivan did the same.[73] Thomas Hinde made the intersection of the destinies of church and nation clear in his writings of the late 1810s and early 1820s. Methodism's association of its mission to convert "the heathen" in the West with its responsibility to civilize Native peoples in the customs of Anglo culture further integrated church and nation in an intricate web of power.

Methodism, Spiritual Expansionism, and Civilization

The emergence of American Methodist missions is critical to the story of Methodist engagement with national political and economic ambitions and, concomitantly, Methodist perspectives on violence against Native Americans. Methodists trailed many of their Protestant peers in the formation of mission societies by nearly a decade. The American Board of Commissioners for Foreign Missions, an organization dominated by Congregationalists and Presbyterians, emerged in 1810, and the American Baptist Missionary Union arose in 1814. Methodists began establishing local missionary societies about 1819 at the same time that several notable Methodists, including Nathan Bangs, Freeborn Garrettson, Joshua Soule, Laban Clark, and Thomas Mason created the Bible and Missionary Society of the Methodist Episcopal Church. The society hoped to promote interest in missions within the church and increase efficiency by supporting the various Annual Conferences that extended their work to the "unchurched settlements." Although the Missionary Society imagined undertaking international missions, its early focus, along with that of the conference missionary societies, was clearly domestic.[74]

Weak support within the denomination, poor finances, and a lack of authority to appoint and oversee missionaries hampered the society's early efforts.[75]

Despite these problems, the *Methodist Magazine* undertook a concerted effort to promote the organization's grand optimism about the ultimate conversion of the world:

> And if every one will become a cheerful giver, "according to the ability which God giveth," we shall soon witness the rising glory of the Church; "the solitary places shall be glad for them"—the messengers of Zion—"and the wilderness shall blossom as a rose[,]" the pagan nations, which inhabit the wilds of America, and the desolate inhabitants of our new States and Territories, shall hail the effects of your bounty; -nations unborn shall rise up and call you blessed—Let, then, all hearts be warm, and all hands active, until the "ends of the earth see the salvation of our God."[76]

The early reports of the Missionary Society underscored this hope of a universal spread of the Gospel that would lead to the "complete triumph of Christianity" and the "conquering of the world to Christ."[77] The first fruits of the organization's labors—if not always measurable in successful conversions, the commissioning of large numbers of missionaries, or even the establishment of a single overseas mission until 1833—indicated, at least to supporters, enough progress that the Sixth Annual Report of the Missionary Society proclaimed the beginning of "a new era." The "triumph of Christian principles" seemed within their reach, and, although masses remained to be converted, the report announced that the Gospel moved ever forward in an inevitable path toward global conversion.[78]

With its ambitions for foreign missions still unfulfilled in the 1820s, the Methodist Church followed the geographic spread of the United States with the creation of missions to settlers and Native peoples in western territories. As one writer proudly proclaimed in the *Methodist Magazine,* the Missionary Society enabled Christians to erect the church meeting house nearly simultaneous with the establishment of each new settlement.[79] The formation of Indian missions that accompanied this spread became a source of particular pride. Methodists established missions to the Wyandot, Cherokee, Choctaw, Mohawk, Creek, Potawatomi, and Oneida all within a ten-year period in the 1820s, though several of these missions counted precious few converts.[80] Nevertheless, the notion that Methodists had begun to make inroads among "the terror of the day," as one Methodist writer described Native peoples, was a particularly potent symbol of divine blessing.[81]

The geographic expansion of the borders of the United States and the spiritual expansion of Christianity through evangelical missions intersected in ways that had important implications for Methodism's involvement in the nation. One of the central points of contact in this intersection was Methodism's inculcation of its missionary activities with a responsibility to civilize its converts. An active interest in civilizing converts is particularly curious given that the language of civilization is notably absent from the earliest Methodist writings on missions, and only begins to appear shortly after the formation of the missionary societies in 1819. This absence cannot be explained by a lack of attention within American missionary discourse. New England Puritans had long established a pattern of inculcating civility among Indians, in many cases as a precursor to evangelization. As early as 1633, Puritans argued for the need to "civill" the Indians in addition to Christianizing them, a goal that John Eliot famously systematized in his efforts to establish praying towns in the 1650s. For Eliot, proper dress, morals, and economy not only reflected the fruits of conversion, they also served to facilitate salvation.[82] These ideas continued to hold sway among Congregationalists and Presbyterians for at least another 150 years. As William Hutchinson has shown, by the Revolutionary War era Anglos' notion that they held a responsibility to civilize alongside Christianization had evolved from an earlier pragmatic measure to facilitate conversion to a virtue that furthered their millennial vision of the improvement of society coterminous with world salvation.[83] By 1816, Samuel Worcester, the corresponding secretary of the leading mission board in America, the American Board of Commissioners for Foreign Missions, could define the missionary's role as "'civilizing and christianizing,' in that order."[84]

These same commitments to civilizing activity evident in seventeenth- and eighteenth-century missionary discourse do not appear in the founding documents of the Methodist missionary societies on either side of the Atlantic. In 1786, for instance, the central figure in British Methodist missions, Thomas Coke, led British Methodists to approve a framework for conducting overseas missions, though the document made no explicit reference to civilizing as a goal of missions.[85] A similar failure to give attention to civilizing work also appears in Coke's record of his missionary journeys, which, while including offhand comments about the extent to which natives exhibited civilized behavior and customs, focused on the growth of the community through Gospel preaching and conversion.[86] Coke's missionary endeavors certainly included civilizing activities, however. According to Zachary Macauley's plan for the creation of a mission in Sierra Leone, of which Coke was a supporter and principal recruiter, Coke's missionaries would not only preach the Gospel to indigenous Africans and freed slaves, but also civilize them through personal example and instruction in "the improvements in Agriculture and other useful Arts . . . [and] the erection of Schools."[87] Similarly, George Davidson described Coke's mission on the Island of St. Vincent as playing an important role in civilizing the natives.

It is striking, then, that Coke did not use the word "civilization" when describing the goals of his missions. In fact, he edited from his journal George Davidson's argument that the "grand point" of Methodist missions in the Caribbean was the civilization of natives.[88] Although it is difficult to argue from silence, Coke and other early Methodists' desire to prioritize the spiritual endeavor of conversion undoubtedly helps explain the lack of explicit attention to civilizing endeavors.[89] While Coke acknowledged that Christian missions might contribute to the work of civilization, he avoided highlighting those efforts for fear that they might distract from the ultimate goal of conversion. Conversion remained the priority, though Coke surely believed it paved the way for civilization. This is exactly what Coke concluded in 1789 when he remarked in his journals on the history of European colonization: "if Missions for the establishment of the gospel among them [native peoples] were set on foot, and through the blessing of God succeeded, as [sic] would probably make any benevolent scheme of a civil or political kind, not only feasible, but easy."[90]

In America, neither the word civilization nor the idea that the work of the missionary should involve the intentional promotion of Euro-American civilization appeared in the founding charter of the Missionary Society of the Methodist Episcopal Church in 1819. Rather, the organization stated that its "primary intention" was evangelization through preaching and the circulation of Bibles. "Send, therefore, the living messenger of God, with the Bible in his hands, and let that finally decide the controversy between the sinner and the truths delivered. This method, we believe, will be the most effectual to convey the glad tidings of salvation to those who are *perishing for lack of knowledge*" [emphasis in original].[91] The authors omitted any reference to the traditional civilizing endeavors of English education, vocational training, and behavior modification.

It did not take long for Methodists to remedy the absence of civilizing activity. The first mention of the responsibility to carry out the work of civilization appears in the 1820 General Conference that approved the Missionary Society's charter, drafted the previous year. The evangelization of Native Americans in the western territories was the main impetus. The conference established a direct connection between Native evangelization and civilization by asserting that evangelization enabled Natives "to perceive and to appreciate the blessings" of Euro-American civilization, by which members meant "civil and domestic economy, and finally to attend to farming and mechanical pursuits."[92] Members of the General Conference insisted on the primacy of Christianization, but they firmly believed that conversion would be the primary point of entrance to civilization.

Monetary support for the civilizing activity of the Methodist Episcopal Church flowed from the United States Congress's passage of the Civilization Fund Act in 1819. This act empowered President Monroe to award $10,000 a year to "persons of good moral character" who were willing to instruct Native Americans in "the mode of agriculture suited to their situation; and for teaching their children in reading, writing, and arithmetic."[93] Monroe opted to disburse this money to benevolent societies and church mission boards. Among these, Methodists stepped forward to accept government funds to support their missionary efforts and thus formally embarked on a dual responsibility of promoting the religious good of Christianization and the civic good of civilization. In 1822, William Capers reflected on the denomination's rationale for integrating the two efforts: "the government wished to better the condition of the Indians, by having their children instructed; and the Churches felt it their sacred duty to go forward in this good work. We sought not their lands; nor desired their money; but we wished to do them good."[94] Similarly, the Missionary Society idealized what it saw as the progress of science that followed the spread of Christianity when the society proclaimed that the missionary strove to "bestow the blessings of civilization and pure religion on all who dwell on earth."[95]

While those who carried out this civilizing work often expressed an intention to help Native peoples, they imbued the deeply interconnected relations between civilizing work and nationalist power. Robert Berkhofer summarized the dominant notion of "civilization" for Anglo Americans in the early nineteenth century as:

> an upward unilinear development of human society with the United States near the pinnacle. Comprising civilization was a cluster of institutional arrangements that Americans sought to achieve between the Revolution and the Civil War. Economically, they moved toward allowing economic individualism free rein under the liberal state. Politically, they first realized repub-

licanism, then democracy. Lastly, the liberty of the individual was foremost in their minds; hence all social institutions were assumed to exist solely for the benefit of the individual (white) members of society.

Anglos also prioritized a belief in the inevitable progress of Western civilization that contributed to the articulation of a national mission "to spread their superior institutions into the western wilderness and even beyond their country's boundaries."[96]

In practice, Methodists carried out their civilizing responsibility among the Native populations through a policy of intentional assimilation, particularly in the founding of schools to teach English reading and writing and the promotion of the "useful arts": sewing and cooking for women and agriculture and craftsmanship for men. Occasionally, Methodists established "itinerating schools," in which a traveling preacher organized a temporary school for instruction along the circuit where he taught basic skills of reading, writing, and arithmetic. After a period of six months or so the preacher would close the school and create another in a different location on the circuit.[97]

Whether in a fixed or temporary location, Methodist schools "tried to shape Native Americans into productive individuals whose value and life-style would support the republic."[98] Missionaries supported this work by modeling piety and industriousness and modifying the conduct and traditions of students by cutting their hair, requiring Western dress, changing their names, redefining gender roles, and emphasizing respect for private property. In the case of the initially successful Wyandot mission, Methodist missionaries also encouraged written laws that in 1827 signaled to Methodist preacher James Gilruth that "their entire civilization will be completed in time."[99] The most famous missionary to the Wyandot, James B. Finley, added yet another feature of civilizing work beyond education and written laws: the division of tribal land among individual tribal members.[100]

In fact, the Wyandot became the earliest model for Methodists of the possibility of civilizing Indians. The precursor to this mission in the upper Sandusky region of Ohio was established by a lay person, John Stewart, himself part Indian and part African, who began preaching to the Wyandot around 1814–1815. At the urging of Stewart, who received his license to preach in the Methodist Episcopal Church in 1818, the Ohio Annual Conference formally approved a mission to the Wyandot, with Stewart serving with another missionary until Stewart's

untimely death in 1823. James B. Finley became the full-time resident missionary in 1821 and quickly established a school and church. The following year, the
conference appointed Charles Elliott as missionary and teacher and made Finley
superintendent and presiding elder.[101]

The missionaries' successes among the Wyandot became a sensation. In
January 1825, Bishop Joshua Soule celebrated the contrast between the "deplor-
able" moral, economic, and religious state that nurtured the tribe's "ignorance
and stupidity" prior to the mission with the profound transformation wrought
by the advance of Christianity. "Their former superstitions have almost entirely
yielded to the force and simplicity of truth. The wandering manner of life is
greatly changed, and the chase is rapidly giving place to agriculture, and the
various necessary employments of civilized life. The tomahawk, and the scalp-
ing knife, and the rifle, and the destructive bow, are yielding the palm to the
axe, the plough, the hoe and the sickle." The change, Soule asserted, proved the
wisdom and necessity of the confluence of the missionary effort to convert and
the government's interest to civilize.[102] Similarly, John Leib confidently wrote
the War Department in 1827 that he considered the civilization of the Wyandot
complete. Leib praised the work of the Methodist missionary James B. Finley
as the essential cog in fashioning this "model of a colony."[103] Even more, David
Lewis used a portion of his memoirs to contrast the Christian Wyandot's "sobriety, order and devotion" with the rest of the "heathen" Native population.
One comparison in particular struck Lewis: a prideful young chief covered with
rings and beads similar to the "wild sons" of the forest and the converted Wyandot's humble appearance and simple lifestyle. Lewis continued: "the marks of
improvement in their condition, attributable to their having received the Gospel,
were not confined to the camp-ground, or their solemn assemblies." Rather, as
he passed into their country he beheld "their neat, well-furnished houses and
barns, their clean yards, high fences, well-cultivated fields, and luxuriant corn."
Lewis left convinced that Methodists could convert Natives and in the process
civilize them.[104]

While most Methodist missionaries distinguished at least certain aspects of
their Christianizing and civilizing work, and in almost every case prioritized the
former over the latter, they clearly came to see the two as complementary. The
mutuality of the two led Methodists down the well-trod path of their Congregationalist and Presbyterian peers, who had, as so many historians have shown,
integrated Christianity and civilization much earlier. The religious identity they

forged became part of an imperialist mentality that justified geographic expansionism and the eradication of Native peoples perceived as "savage" barriers to the providential extension of the United States.[105] Methodists might not have been conscious of all these implications, but the zeal to transform Native culture and traditions, even if motivated by compassion for Native peoples, wrapped Methodist missionaries into a culturally imperialist mindset from which they found it nearly impossible to extricate themselves. Their embrace of the dominance and universality of Anglo civilization, and their acceptance of a providentially controlled national mission to extend this civilization, fully ensconced Methodists in the civic identity of the nation.

This process of enculturation into a national identity and civic theology played a central role in the transformation of Methodist views on the use of violence, in this case against Native Americans. No longer could Methodists claim disinterest in political controversy as they had in the Revolution. A sizeable and influential number of white Methodists accepted the nation as providentially established, recognized the values of liberty and democracy as sacred, made obedience to the nation a religious obligation, and made the work of Christianization a necessary precondition for civilization. These changes allowed Methodists to become major players in defining the national interest and to announce their willingness to violently defend those interests as part of God's battle against evil. Methodists who came of age in the years immediately following the Revolution repeatedly confirmed their acceptance of the use of violence, whether by the government or by themselves, to defend these ideals. As in the narrative that opened this chapter, the Indian proved the most common object of Methodism's newfound willingness to defend and even celebrate the use of violence.

National Mission, Civilization, and Social Violence

Methodist literature, including Annual Conference Minutes, denominational histories, periodicals, and autobiographies, regularly chronicled violence against Native Americans in the antebellum era. While pro-slavery Methodists in both the North and South sought to defend the violent system of slavery in the antebellum era, their writings rarely celebrated bodily violence against slaves like Methodist narratives of Native peoples did. Most often, Methodists embedded these narratives in their accounts of the settlement of the West that, like the account that opened this chapter, featured stories of hardy pioneers killing their

Indian attackers. Take, for instance, the article "Early Scenes in the West," which appeared in seven installments of the *Western Christian Advocate* in 1834. The author, identified only as "F. B.," used her or his family's migration to the West as the backdrop for providing an episodic history of Anglo settlement of the West in the years immediately following the Revolutionary War.[106] The narrative opens in 1788 with the author's father partaking in the Anglo "desire to inherit its [the West's] rich land, and enjoy the advantages of its wide spreading cane-brakes." But, the author lamented, terrible opposition loomed from the "jealous" Indians, who were "wrought up to fury" and who, the author dutifully informed readers, had recently employed treacherous methods to murder pioneers by feigning injury to lure the immigrants' boats to shore. The author's father and his traveling companions thought they encountered the very same deceptions when they observed "a long and continued effort . . . to persuade them to land, by a person that appeared to be in great distress." The travelers, sure the person contrived the situation in order to attack them, ignored the pleas and continued safely to their destination.

The author used this narrative to establish something essential about the context of the frontier. The West was a land of danger, not because of anything the pioneer did, but because of the bloodthirsty Indian. The author made the pioneer an innocent victim of Native aggression. The violent response of the settlers— armed men, women, and children with guns and with assigned "port holes" in their homes from which they shot their Native enemies when attacked—became defensive acts. The author also stretched this image of the innocent pioneer who acted in self-defense to include more pre-emptive attacks, as in the author's narration of one "S. D.," who shot and killed an Indian for the crime of making an appearance on a river bank.[107]

Following the settlers' own bloody battles, the author moved to celebrate General Anthony Wayne's heroic victories against Native warriors on behalf of the United States government. Only after the military's defeat of the Indian menace did the author paint the true blossoming of the fertile land under the direction of God. The "most perfect garden all planted and watered by the hand of the Almighty" gave rise to a vibrant population numbering in the millions and commerce that appeared "more like magic than reality." The West could finally realize its providential destiny. The author made the defeat of the uncivilized savage essential to the story.[108]

This account shared a formulaic quality with other narratives of Methodist settlement of the West. The innocent pioneer, often a preacher or missionary, moves west in search of fertile land and the expansion of God's kingdom. The narrator prepares the reader for conflict by briefly chronicling the Indian's murderous and savage history in the region the pioneer is entering. Without fail, the Indians attack, often by surprise or through despicable trickery. The immigrants repeatedly defend themselves, their families, and fellow travelers in heroic fashion at the expense of Native lives. These battles finally cease, generally through the intervention of government forces, and give rise to the development of the land's rich resources as well as the conversion of its population to Christianity under the direction of God's care and blessing.

We cannot read these accounts apart from Anglo assumptions about the superiority of their civilization, their rights to western land, and their ability to enforce their rights and culture through violence, whether on the part of the government or the individual pioneer. The authors' sense of the legitimacy of western expansion, even in the years prior to the signing of treaties granting the United States legal right to the land, is integral. Methodists justified their migration, whether before or after the treaties, by continually referencing the divine blessing of the land, its growth, and, most importantly, its Christianization. Anglo presence in the West contributed to the fulfillment of God's providential plan. Methodists believed that they helped confirm the expansion of the nation under God's care by bringing Christianity to the region as well as the arts and sciences of civilized culture they believed were closely associated with Christianity. Natives, as savage beasts who sought to kill the pioneer, represented the antithesis of this perfect plan.

For these writers, the unrestrained violence of Natives, or at least the prospect of such violence, against the innocent, pious, and patriotic Anglo pioneer required its own violent response. Francis Asbury uttered as much during the War of 1812 when he predicted the intervention of government forces against Native peoples: "the Creek nation have taken up the hatchet: unhappy people! The whites will take vengeance, cruel vengeance on them for their barbarian warfare on unoffending women and children. O God, save thy people from rage of the heathen!"[109]

Methodists also justified individual acts of violence by characterizing the acts of the earliest pioneers, who set off for the frontier beyond the protection of the government, as defensive. Recalling the "heroes" of old, James B. Finley described the necessary defense that uncivilized Native aggression required. The settlers "stood, with gun and tomahawk in hand, between our mothers and their children and the incensed and revengeful rage of the red man. They were our guardians from savage barbarity; their names were precious then, and still are to those for whom they ventured their lives and their all." Such wonders were not just the prerogative of men, but also women and children. "In those days of blood and carnage all were warriors. Our mothers, like the women of Amazonia, were trained to war, and could handle the rifle with great dexterity, and the children were trained up to be soldiers from childhood. A boy of ten years old was counted able to carry arms, and fight; and at sixteen would enter the regular service."[110]

In these celebratory narratives, authors attempted to portray civilization as resting in the hands of the pioneers who fought against Native peoples. James B. Finley took pains to illustrate this to his readers when he asserted that settlers and soldiers fought not out of lust for that which another possessed, but because the superiority of their systems necessitated expansion. "We conquered them [Native tribes] on the field not to usurp territory but to place them in a condition to observe how much more their interest and permanent prosperity would be, and have ever been, promoted by the plow rather than the sword."[111] The military victories the United States enjoyed over Native Americans during the late 1780s and early 1790s proved to Finley and others the value of their cause as well as the final humiliation of Native Americans.[112] In fact, Finley believed that the continued existence of Native Americans depended on their embrace of Anglo culture. "A few only will probably escape this doom, by attaining to a higher civilization, and intermingling with the white race, which even now is flowing all around their forest home."[113]

Of course, Methodists did not all share the same views on the use of violence, particularly against Native peoples. Some adherents offered important critiques of Anglo expansion, as when Methodist preacher Samuel Doughty addressed the Female Missionary Society of New York in 1826 and proclaimed that "the Indian is the rightful owner of the soil on which we tread." Even more, Doughty criticized the violent manner whites used to wrest the land. "Might, alas! Triumphed over right; and the conqueror's title to the red man's land was written with the red man's blood."[114] Likewise, Stephen Olin directly contradicted dominant notions of the settlement of the United States as a response to a divine calling when he declared that the Europeans who first came to America were "unbidden and unauthorized" invaders of Indian territory. Native people, not Anglos, insisted Olin, had been "planted . . . in this fair continent" by God, only to be denied the land by war and "the contaminating vices of civilized life, unaccompanied by a single safeguard or one redeeming principle, which education and religion have invented to counteract their destructive influences."[115]

The Methodist tradition of noninterference with the government entered in important ways into the conversation about the treatment of Native peoples. I have already shown how Methodists drew upon this philosophy in the Revolutionary War era to support their argument against participating in the war. By reducing the conflict to a "political" matter that had little to do with the Christian's eternal state, many Methodists argued that they would not fight in the war. Methodists moved away from this tradition in the late eighteenth and early nineteenth centuries as they established a divine sanction for the government and defined a critical role for the Christian in the republic by infusing morality and accountability within political life. Nevertheless, some Methodists continued to turn to political noninvolvement to circumscribe the lengths to which they allowed Methodists to involve themselves in "political" matters such as slavery or Indian removal. Methodists who took an active role in defusing Methodist opposition to Cherokee removal in the 1830s did so just to prevent social action on behalf of the Cherokee. As William McLoughlin observed of the Methodist mission to the Cherokee, "the sweeping of Methodism through the Cherokee Nation was the prelude to sweeping the Indians out of the valley. The miracle of Christianity (the missionaries believed) was that this would all take place painlessly."[116] We now know just how wrong the missionaries were. The story of Methodism's involvement with Cherokee removal has been told many times. However, it is important to consider the ways some Methodists negotiated the tradition of noninterference during removal and how this influenced Methodists' abilities to engage social issues and challenge violent action.

Methodists established their mission to the Cherokee in 1822 and quickly met with success. After only a year, the mission reported more than a hundred members. By 1830, the mission claimed over a thousand members.[117] Unfortunately for the Cherokee, gold was discovered in Georgia in 1828. Anglos' interest in the land intensified while their support for the missions declined precipitously. The Georgia legislature passed laws to effectively deny the Cherokee their right to the land and their ability to testify against whites in court. The state also made it a crime for whites to live among Indians without a license.

In 1830, eight Methodist missionaries signed a resolution seeking support for the Cherokee. The resolution celebrated the progress of the Cherokee toward civilization and firmly opposed removal. "It is unanimously resolved, by this missionary connection, that the present aggrieved condition of the Cherokees, in this nation, loudly calls for the sympathy and religious interposition of the Christian community in these United States, together with all the true and faithful friends of humanity and justice."[118] The resolution placed a moral responsibility on Anglo Christians to take action on behalf of the Cherokee. Methodists in the East rallied around the resolution, particularly the editor of the *Christian Advocate,* who published the resolution and who had already spoken out against removal.

However, the Tennessee Annual Conference, which directed the mission, saw the issue as less a matter of morality and more a matter of politics.[119] The conference rejected the missionaries' appeals and expressed "regret" for the missionaries' action, which they saw as "depart[ing] from the principle of our Church in carefully refraining from all such interference with political affairs."[120]

When the state of Georgia required all missionaries to leave Cherokee territory or risk imprisonment, most Methodists complied, though James J. Trott, who had earlier signed the resolution against removal, refused to leave. Trott and his fellow missionary Dickson McLeod were arrested. Government troops force-marched Trott, who was married to a Cherokee woman, 110 miles out of the state. His removal from Georgia eclipsed the remaining support for the Cherokee within the Tennessee Conference. Henceforth, Methodists "restricted their work to preaching and teaching school."[121] Active political engagement effectively ceased.

The refusal of the Tennessee Conference to take formal action to oppose removal, and, even more, their embrace of the traditional stance of noninvolvement in politics, not only proved to be the death knell for the effectiveness of the mission, but it also blocked Methodists in the Tennessee Conference from challenging the horrendous violence that accompanied Cherokee removal.[122] In 1834, the United States government signed a series of treaties with a minority of the Cherokee to convey seven million acres to the Cherokee in exchange for the land east of the Mississippi. The government obligated the Cherokee to move by 1838. Only two thousand did. Another fourteen thousand were forcibly removed from their homes and marched on what is now called the Trail of Tears. Four thousand Cherokee died along the way. The Tennessee Conference fell silent.

When Methodists directly engaged the question of violence against Native peoples, most tried to distinguish between what they deemed to be appropriate violence used in the establishment of Anglo settlements and egregious violence used by traders who plied Natives with alcohol or by the government that violated treaties in order to remove Indians further west. James B. Finley, the most prolific Methodist writer on the West in the mid-nineteenth century and one of the most ardent supporters of Anglo expansion, encouraged these distinctions. Finley's popularity as a successful missionary and frequent contributor to Methodist periodicals helped fuel Methodist images of the West as a sacred place that God ordained for the development of Western civilization and Christianity. He also chronicled battles against Native peoples that he considered the heroic deeds of fearless pioneers. Yet Finley also excoriated Anglos for their slaughter of peaceful Indians and he railed against traders who robbed Natives of their possessions and stole their property. Following the forced removal of Indians in the 1830s, Finley grew particularly angry, promising that "God will, in a coming day, settle the accounts of the Government and her agents and traders, for their conduct and treatment to the poor Indian; and eternal Justice will punish the worst and the most inhuman of all our race."[123]

So how did Finley distinguish legitimate battles that required violent action on the part of settlers from the sinful use of violence against Native peoples? The answer to this question is important for our understanding of the conditions in which Methodists in the antebellum era thought it appropriate to use violence. It is also critical for understanding the limits Methodists placed on violence. Finley's writings offer several important clues. First, his justification of pioneer violence relied on his characterization of pioneers as acting in purely defensive ways against Natives. Because Finley imagined pioneers migrating west as part of a divine calling for the church and nation, he characterized Native attacks as acts of aggression and pioneer violence as simply a matter of self-defense. Second, Finley constructed a moral distinction between the two groups by depicting Natives as brutal and deceitful tricksters and the early pioneers as pious immigrants who aimed to civilize and Christianize the West. With a divine right to inhabit the land and a sacred calling to Christianize it, Finley described the violence of the early pioneers as defensive acts to protect a sacred aim.

On the other hand, Finley had more trouble characterizing Native removal as a defensive action of pious individuals. Removal seemed to jeopardize the Indian missions that symbolized God's plan for the Christianization and civilization of the West and the faith these missions nurtured among Native converts. In such circumstances, Finley imagined the Native inhabitant as the innocent victim of American aggression. Here again, a moral distinction appears as Finley characterized removal efforts as arising purely from an interest to expand the nation's economic growth with no concern for the spiritual or economic well-being of the Native population. In such cases, the forced removal of Natives became a sinful act of American aggression.

This justification of violence on the basis of whether the person or group acted in defense of self or others undermined the community's earlier valuation of suffering violence. As shown in previous chapters, both John Wesley and Revolutionary War–era American Methodists used their personal experiences of suffering violence as a way to display their conformity to Christ's sacrifice. They also used the theological value of suffering violence as an argument for renouncing violent action. The writings of American Methodists that began to appear in the first three decades of the nineteenth century emphasized the moral value of defending the self and others. These Methodists not only argued they could justify violence when they thought it defensive in nature, they also imagined this form of violence as a religious obligation.

Cultural changes surely influenced Methodists' defense of violent action. The Revolution represented a powerful symbol of the benefits that came through violence. Even more, dominant images of masculinity and the cultural fascination with violence in the West and South also made it easier to justify the use of violence as a reasonable and even necessary responsibility.[124] But Methodists' intersection of their political, cultural, economic, and religious interests also helps explain their acceptance of violence. By enmeshing spiritual interests and national identity, Methodists justified the exercise of the government's right to use violence against Native peoples in terms of a larger divine plan for the nation and its people. In keeping with this right to use violence, in cases where Methodist geographic spread outpaced the reach of civil law and U.S. military might, Methodists employed their own sense of moral law to enforce what they considered God's destiny for themselves and their nation. Methodist narratives made clear that they fought for and on behalf of the nation's interest and God's interest.

Negotiating the Limits of Bodily Harm

If Methodists assumed new, if regrettable, responsibilities to violently harm others, how do we understand Methodists' growing acceptance of the use of social violence at the same time as they challenged the powers of spiritual beings to harm the body? While it might be tempting to think that Methodists separated the body from religious life and limited it to the control of political and social powers, this argument would only be partially correct. The discipline of the body continued to have religious import for Methodists and they expressed this value in their participation in a host of reform movements that sought to control the body's excesses. Methodists did not necessarily recast the role of the body in religious life, but the nature of the involvement of God and Satan over the body. While Methodists vehemently defended the reality and influence of spiritual forces for good and evil, they limited the extent of this involvement to a mental and spiritual influence over people rather than direct control over individual bodies. More and more Methodists doubted that Satan might appear in physical form to torment humans or possess the body. Satan's ultimate power rested in the temptations placed before the hearts and minds of believers and unbelievers. Likewise, though believers continued to narrate intense struggles for their salvation, as we saw in chapter 3, they rarely related experiences that included physical pain.

Methodists offset this limitation of the powers of spiritual beings by extending the powers of human beings. As Methodists became more involved in the political and social life of the nation, they accepted the civil responsibility to punish the wicked and defend the innocent. Even more, Methodists religiously justified human control over the body in the late eighteenth and early nineteenth centuries by asserting that God had established the government, given it a sacred mission, and empowered the ruling authorities to protect civil and religious liberty. In this sense, Methodists employed a rationale similar to that of John Wesley, who fifty years earlier had defended the responsibilities of Christians and their rulers in times of war. This intersection between the interests of the church and the nation legitimated war by making the subjugation of the enemy part of the promotion of divine order and providence.

Although American Methodists' rationale for violence reflected Wesley's defense of the Christian's right to participate in war, this rationale diverged from Wesley in the value Methodists placed in the individual's responsibility to defend the self and others. In cases when the civil authorities evinced an unwillingness or inability to maintain control, some Methodists took it upon themselves to enforce God's moral laws to Christianize and civilize the West by arming themselves and killing their attackers. The battle might belong to the Lord, but these

FIVE

METHODIST RESPECTABILITY
AND THE DECLINE OF THE
GOOD FIGHT FOR SALVATION

In 1878, Julia Tevis, a schoolteacher and minister's wife, penned her autobiography, *Sixty Years in a School-Room*. As was common to the period, Tevis paid special attention to her religious formation and conversion. Like many before her, a camp meeting—which had taken place fifty-five years earlier in 1823—proved integral to Tevis's conversion. The site was nestled in "a beautiful grove of grand old trees in a lovely mountain gorge" in Smyth County, Virginia. Prior to the meeting, the twenty-two-year-old Tevis had already experienced religious impressions that convinced her of her need for salvation. She arrived at the camp meeting with great expectations for spiritual transformation and what she called the "sweet communion" with devoted Christians that the remote surroundings promised. What Tevis found did not disappoint her.

One evening, on her return from preaching, Tevis and her friends discovered a woman "lying on the couch, in a state of total insensibility." Tevis indicated that the woman suffered in this condition for several hours and "the icy touch of her folded hands" suggested to those present that the woman was near death. As onlookers began to mourn the impending loss of a beloved friend, the woman surprised everyone by waking. The woman's explanation of her condition led the shocked onlookers, including Tevis, to agree that the woman had undergone a bodily religious experience of God.

If a religious experience that took on the appearance of death signals a similarity to the camp meetings of old, Tevis described this event and, in fact, the entire camp meeting very differently. Methodists had long spoken of camp meetings as virtual hotbeds of religious zeal, with tens and even hundreds of penitents under conviction of sin screaming for mercy and shouting for pardon. The bodies of others quaked uncontrollably and some even fell as though dead. Methodists described the campground as a battleground in which God slew the forces of evil and raised up an army of saints. Yet Tevis described a very different scene. She replaced the rough-hewn preachers of Methodist lore with what she remembered as "reverend, good-looking men, whose very appearance inspired confidence." Like their ministerial authorities, the people conducted themselves with great respectability and dignity, so much so that Tevis declared, "I never saw more perfect order, more attention to politeness and decorum, in any assemblage of people."[1]

If the camp meeting took on a more respectable air, how might we understand Tevis's account of the woman she found on the couch? The woman's symptoms—lying unconscious for hours, a frigid body, and weak vital signs—would seem to signal that she had fallen out or at the very least entered into some form of trance. Either way, the experience symbolized the kinds of bodily religious experiences that Methodism's opponents, and even some of its adherents, singled out as evidence of Methodism's flirtation with enthusiasm. Tevis likely had such controversy in mind, for her narrative seems contrived to avoid connections with the past. Tevis certainly never said that the woman fell under God's power. Conveniently, Tevis entered the room to find the woman lying on a couch. How she got there is anyone's guess. What is more significant is Tevis's account of what happened when the woman awoke. Tevis recalled that the woman "opened her eyes and softly whispered,—'This sweet calm within my breast / Is the best pledge of heavenly rest.'" The woman then simply closed her eyes and we learn no more about the experience, though Tevis takes pains to inform us that the woman never referred to it as something remarkable. What we can tell is that there was no conflict, no bitter struggle between Satan and God, no vision of Christ crucified. The experience puzzled Tevis and we presume her readers as well, for Tevis made sure to note that the woman was no religious fanatic. She was "well known, and loved and respected, as a model of unpretending piety." Tevis asks: "had she heard unutterable things, and seen visions that were ineffable?" The woman reduces the question to a rhetorical one by refusing to speak of the experience, and Tevis compounds the mystery by insisting that she would "have no comment to make upon it." Tevis leaves readers with only the words of calm whispered by one filled with "melody and love." Tevis's description of the people, the ministers, the religious experiences, even the grounds themselves conjured images of peace and serenity rather than war and battle.[2] This camp meeting certainly did not have the look and feel of those that came before it.

Tevis's narrative reflected important changes within mid-nineteenth-century Methodism. Fundamental shifts in Methodist theology and practice marginalized the idea of a battle as necessary to the individual's path to salvation. Whereas Wesley and many of his early followers emphasized that Christian peace required fighting the good fight, thereby rooting much of the religious life in conflict, many midcentury American Methodists envisioned religious experience very differently. Rather than the "continual warfare" Wesley described, these Methodists emphasized the passivity of the inner religious life. Christian piety became more of a repose from a tumultuous world than a militant struggle in itself.

Methodists responded to these changes by describing their conversions in new ways. If a significant and influential number within the generation of American Methodists that emerged after the Revolution distanced themselves from a bodily connection between their spiritual "wounding" and redemption, another generation of Methodists in the 1820s and beyond tried to strip conversion narratives of references to warfare altogether. The conversion accounts that dominated Methodist periodicals and monographs in the mid-nineteenth century no longer compared conversions to God's slaying, shooting, wounding, or killing them. Instead, they referred to a still and soft calling from God, a quiet and peaceful retreat to the tender arms of a loving savior.

This is not to say that Methodists lost all connections between fighting and their spiritual lives or that all Methodists cast aside warfare as a useful image for Christian living. In fact, many still adhered to the notion of a battle between good and evil, and this commitment led some Methodists to continue to call for an aggressive battle against spiritual forces. However, it became more common for Methodists to rely on a sentimental understanding of religion, especially in practitioners' understanding of and relation to the divine, in ways that marginalized the cosmic battle from the everyday experience of the Christian life. By the middle of the nineteenth century, the dominant discourse in Methodism found affection rather than conflict a far more useful path toward spiritual formation. In the process, Methodists separated the ongoing war between good and evil from the daily experiences of Christians. Methodists still believed the war existed, but many doubted whether it had much bearing on the Christian's path to salvation and holiness.

This chapter explains the changes Methodists made to their religious lives in the Civil War era and the cultural forces that contributed to these changes. It will also pay particular attention to the relation of these changes to Methodist interpretations of the Civil War. As a gulf emerged between the way Methodists described their devotional lives and the cosmic battle that they continued to believe occurred around them, the onset of the Civil War in 1861 attested to the ongoing importance of the cosmic battle for Methodists' interpretation of social and political events. Methodists, inspired by rhetoric that cast the war as a part of, if not the climax to, the great cosmic battle, armed themselves for war and mutilated one another on the battlefield. The path to salvation might have been sweetened by God's love and peace, but as citizens of warring nations that identified themselves as divinely blessed, American Methodists knew that God called them to fight and that their fight would have profound implications for the future of Christianity.

Methodism and the Dominance of Middle-Class Culture

Beginning in the 1820s, Methodism responded to important cultural and economic changes in America. A set of middle-class ideals emerged, at first largely in northern cities, but in the ensuing decades across the United States. These values emphasized refined sensibilities, genteel behavior, and relational bonds of affection. They were also largely antithetical to the experiences and discourses that supported the "good fight" that Wesley and his early American followers advocated. These new cultural norms dominated the periodical and biographical literature published by the Methodist Episcopal Church and, after the denomination split in 1844, the Methodist Episcopal Church, South as well. Popular Methodist periodicals such as the *Christian Advocate and Journal,* the *Methodist Quarterly Review,* the *Western Christian Advocate,* and the *Ladies' Repository and Gatherings of the West,* biographical literature, and sermons all marginalized fighting sin, the world, and Satan as a spiritually beneficial part of the practice of the Christian life.

A character of restraint, sobriety, and self-control established itself as among the most cherished of cultural ideals in the nineteenth century. Republican rhetoric insisted that the public good depended on these traits lest the very liberties won during the Revolution devolve into destructive anarchy. Justified at least in part by a traditional Puritan ethic of frugality and a reformed republicanism that balanced millennial interpretations of America's divine calling with a belief in religion's role in instilling virtue in the nation's citizens, these ideals also had important religious connections. In fact, the commitment to restraint weighed heavily upon religious expression. Experiences like falling out appeared antithetical to restraint and therefore dangerous to good order and right religion. The *Christian Advocate and Journal* lamented in 1833 of the "growing evil" of "loud shouting, horrid, unnatural screaming, repeating the same words twenty or thirty times, jumping two or three feet high, and throwing about the arms and legs . . . in a manner shocking not only to religion, but to common decency." The *Advocate* deemed these experiences the result of excited passions rather than the work of the Holy Spirit as part of the battle against sin. In response, the periodical urged proper restraint to bring this natural disorder into subjection. The editorial garnered such a favorable reaction from readers that the magazine reprinted the article in an expanded form the very next month.[3]

Americans recognized that model citizens were not born, they were made. As Nancy Cott and Mary Ryan have shown in their classic histories, the cult of domesticity emerged in the early republic to charge mothers with an essential role in creating good citizens. As this task implies, domesticity's significance expanded beyond the home to include an organizing principle for society in general. Briefly stated, domestic ideology placed the mother at the head of the household and posited the home as the sanctuary from the sinful and fallen world. Supporters described the ideal mother as inherently moral and religious, traits she needed to communicate to her children with the intention of instilling virtue in them. This process of moral and social formation called for the relations in the home, whether between husband and wife or parent and children, to be based on affection. Through nurturing bonds of love and pious example, mothers formed their children for productive lives in the community and nation. Of course, middle-class Americans did not always live out the ideals of domesticity. The ideals did, however, become powerful models for the family and society among white middle-class Americans in the nineteenth century.[4]

Methodists certainly lent their support to domesticity. A. Gregory Schneider has argued that an evangelically based domestic ideology that emphasized separation from the world, self-restraint, and relations with others based on love and affection was a logical extension of Methodist thought and practice.[5] Reflecting this quality, the popular Methodist periodicals like the *Ladies' Repository* championed a domestic ideology such as that contained in the following essay:

> Those women who are not blinded by pride or a misled patriotism, have said, and ever will say, "Public life is not our sphere; ours is in the retired family circle; and though this task is a less brightening one, it is still important enough; for while we live unknown and retired, we have in our hands the means to do much good to our beloved country. Is it not to our sex that, to a great extent, was confided the education of children; and do we not know, by the history of illustrious men, of those who were most distinguished in Church and state, what influences have exercised on the development of their minds the example and the words of a faithful and enlightened mother?" If we are convinced that order and obedience in the family are the ground of all prosperity in the state, we shall no longer think slightly of the task of women.[6]

While middle-class values stressed domesticity, restraint, and self-control, they also called for refined taste in houses, clothing, and manners. Over the course of the first half of the nineteenth century, middle-class Americans increasingly believed that a dignified presentation in behavior, décor, and dress reflected a civilized morality and intellect. In fact, in his groundbreaking work on refinement, Richard Bushman argued that refinement intersected with domesticity and religion in important ways in the nineteenth century. "Gentility exercised a powerful influence on religion; in certain circles good taste became virtually a principle of Christian morality. Gentility also took over more and more of the house and yard, attempting to refine all of the domestic activities in those spaces and setting the tone of respectable home life." At the same time, domesticity and religion influenced middle-class gentility by making it less aristocratic and more "homely." "The refined Christian home with its parlors, books and well-mannered children combined the highest forms of piety and gentility under the superintendence of a tasteful, devout, and well-read mother."[7]

Although Methodists, like their Baptist competitors, entered the race toward refinement later than other mainstream religious groups, they charted an intentional course toward gentility by the 1820s.[8] Charles Elliott's biography of Methodist bishop Robert Roberts (1778–1843), printed in 1848, offers one of the clearest examples of Methodism's commitment to gentility. In this work, Elliott painted Roberts's character as every bit the refined ideal.

> As a *man,* his personal appearance was peculiarly dignified, and commanded immediate respect from almost every observer. There was something so noble in his countenance, his manly form, his gait, that he was an object of respect wherever he went. His presence seemed to enlist the regard of observers at once.
>
> His *manners,* too, were remarkably simple and dignified. In the habitation of the poor, or the wigwam of the Indian, he was at home; and all the inmates felt that their guest was one who could mingle with them at their fire-side, and be a fellow-partner in such things as they had. In the palaces of the rich, too, he was entirely at ease and passed through the highest circles of life, when his lot was cast there, as one possessed of the most accomplished manners, yet without a shred of ostentation, or even without aiming at a single rule of politeness, except what flowed from the kindness of his heart, and his own good judgment of what was befitting in regard to time, place, persons and circumstances.[9]

Indeed, Roberts becomes the very model of refinement through Elliott's description of his actions and attitudes as emerging naturally from his character rather than contrived to suit his surroundings.

Methodism's quest for refinement led adherents to seek intellectual respectability as a means to win adherents a place among the nation's respectable elite. In an 1836 editorial in the *Christian Advocate and Journal,* for instance, the Rev. C. Richardson offered a biting critique of ministers who "with deep piety, and a small share of intelligence" had grossly limited the effectiveness of the ministry. Richardson called for preachers possessing "thorough knowledge and exposition of the Holy Scriptures," supplemented by "extensive" command of grammar, philosophy, history, and the physical sciences.[10]

This concern for education helped renew interest in the formation of Methodist colleges. American Methodist higher education stretches back to the formation of Cokesbury College in 1787. However, the school's successive failures, culminating in a fire that leveled the institution in 1795, signaled to many at the time, including the school's namesakes Francis Asbury and Thomas Coke, that Methodist concerns lay with evangelism rather than education.[11] This sentiment helped discourage the creation of schools and colleges for the next several decades. However, as Methodism's numbers and wealth increased, and with it the desire to extend its influence, higher education became a priority. Several additional factors also influenced the shift. In particular, the general population increasingly emphasized education as vital to good citizenship and morality. As Americans came to see education as essential to the preservation and growth of the nation, the common charge of ignorance and illiteracy waged against Methodists proved a powerful motivator for change. Second, as the number of Methodists expanded, particularly among more prosperous persons in the Northeast, congregants who themselves were educated came to expect an educated ministry. Third, theological concerns also influenced Methodist educational efforts. Methodists argued that education would help form students in the theological and moral tenets of the faith.[12]

Methodists' burgeoning interest in education led to several important initiatives. In 1816, the Methodist General Conference formalized a required course of study for those preparing for ministry, and in 1820 the conference recommended that all annual conferences establish "literary institutions, under their own control, in such a way and manner as they may think proper."[13] The response, though slow at first, was nevertheless significant. Between 1830 and 1860 Methodists established more than two hundred schools and colleges.[14] Although these schools were different, they all sought to offer their students a broadly Christian education from a particularly Methodist perspective. In this sense, Methodist schools reflected the larger interests of nineteenth-century evangelicalism "to maintain their distinctiveness and their wish to testify to the unity of the evangelical faith."[15]

In addition to increasing opportunities for formal education, the desire for intellectual respectability also led Methodists to experiment with efforts to deepen the intellectual sophistication of followers through the publication of popular periodicals. In the first edition of the *Methodist Magazine* in 1818, editors Thomas Mason and Joshua Soule contrasted their new periodical with its defunct predecessor and explained their plan to disappoint those readers expecting "curious tales, wonderful narratives, or miraculous phenomenon."[16] Reason, the editors contended, not superstition would govern the pages of the magazine, and hopefully the lives of its readers as well. "If the Governor of the universe recognizes man as a subject of reason, it follows that faith must be grounded in evidence; and therefore we should consider it as an intrusion upon the rights of an intelligent being, to publish a narrative of any wonderful occurrence without the support of competent testimony." Actually, readers might have wondered just what constituted "competent testimony" since the editors essentially denied even the possibility of such wonders, asserting that "the age of miracles is past."[17]

Later Methodist periodicals carried the emphasis on intellectual rigor even further. The *Methodist Magazine* evolved into the *Methodist Magazine and Quarterly Review* in 1830, with the explicit desire to defeat "the danger . . . of satisfying ourselves, on one hand, with light and transient reading, and, on the other with light and transient writing." By contrast, the editors meant this periodical to draw upon "our best writers" to occupy "ampler and more precise discussions" of theology, ecclesiology, and polity.[18] In 1841, the periodical underwent yet another transformation, becoming *The Methodist Quarterly Review*. Once again the editors expressed their commitment to the strengthening of the denomination's intellect, though stated in negative terms: "But those whose morbid appetites can only be satisfied with the creations of a disordered imagination can have little to hope from our labors, or those of our correspondents. The Review will deal in sober realities. And though all due pains will be taken to gratify a well disciplined taste, its great object will be to make its readers *wiser* and *better*" [emphasis in original].[19]

Though not as pessimistic about popular literature's failure to contribute to the intellectual vigor of its readers, the Methodist Episcopal Church, South published its *Quarterly Review* with scholarly objectives similar to its northern counterpart. The editors explained in their first volume in 1847 that they intended "not only to improve the popular taste, but to turn it in other directions, and prepare the millions of its readers, the better to appreciate publications of standard merit, in all various departments of literary production."[20]

Such comments represented a significant shift away from the experiential emphasis of early Methodism that gave life to the inner dimensions of the Christian's warfare and indicated a move toward an immersion in the leading intellectual positions of the period—commonsense realism in the earlier part of the century, moral philosophy in the middle decades, and eventually higher criticism in the last quarter of the century. As Mark Noll has recently explained, Methodism's early history in America offered little evidence that its followers placed a high value on the life of the mind or engaging dominant intellectual theories. Instead of theological formulations, Methodists emphasized experience. As a result, Methodist publishers produced experiential literature such as hymnals, biographies, and journals. Only after Methodists began to realize considerable evangelistic success and the great defender of the old ways, Francis Asbury, died in 1816 did Methodists begin to pursue a more intellectually rigorous path.[21]

This new concern to display intellectual respectability included casting past leaders as monuments to mental lucidity in the voluminous biographies and histories of Methodism spilling off the presses in the second half of the nineteenth century. In his biography of western preacher Valentine Cook (1765?–1820), Edward Stevenson carefully traced the formation of Cook's "strong and vigorous intellect" enhanced by a college education at Cokesbury College, which enabled Cook to mature into a man possessing "the highest order of talents and literary attainment." Stevenson boasted that "in literary, scientific, and useful attainments, he was equaled by few, while in biblical learning and practical piety he was surpassed, perhaps, by none."[22] Despite such accolades, Cook never sustained a career in education nor did he produce a formidable or creative theological text. Even in Cook's pursuit of a hunter's life, an endeavor many of the preacher's contemporaries saw as antithetical to intellectual development, Stevenson emphasized Cook's intellectual predilections by noting that Cook daily took time out to read and study, thereby never losing "sight of the improvement of his mind."[23]

Of course, refinement meant more than displaying greater intellectual sophistication. It also had everyday implications for such things as one's hygiene and manners. The pages of the popular Methodist periodical *Ladies' Repository*, for instance, regularly featured articles that called for more concerted efforts at politeness toward others and emphasized "neatness" at home.[24] Similar articles in another leading Methodist periodical, the *Christian Advocate and Journal*, included an essay advocating regular baths. "The two great considerations which recommend the bath are its influence, first on cleanliness, and next, on health; and the latter is in a great degree dependent on the former." In fact, drawing clear allusions to the spiritual benefits of cleanliness, the author reminded readers that "such is the connection between outward and inward purity, that in all religions, the one has been the symbol of the other."[25]

Methodist periodicals published in the West made clear that Methodists in that region shared similar values. In addition to the work of the *Ladies' Repository* mentioned above, which was published in Cincinnati and at its height commanded forty thousand readers, the *Western Christian Advocate* frequently featured articles and editorials that reinforced the cult of domesticity and admonished readers to adhere to refined and genteel conduct. Articles continually reinforced women's role as a moral authority and nurturer and called young men to protect their character from corruption. This was done by enriching the mind by reading books and cultivating an "amiable" heart by examining the beauties of nature.[26] The periodicals also urged husbands and wives to found their marriages on mutual affection.[27] Outside the home, writers instructed merchants and shopkeepers in the operation of moral and respectable businesses and ordered churchgoers to preserve "neatness, cleanliness, and order in the house of God."[28]

Refinement certainly had its opponents among Methodists who expressed concern that the church's transformation signaled conformity to "the world," which beckoned spiritual decline. John Wigger contends that the entire genre of itinerant autobiographies published in the mid-nineteenth century "can be seen as a series of jeremiads, calling the church back to the zeal of its earlier, less refined days."[29] Though certainly overstated, Wigger's claim reflects a good deal of truth. Among the most prominent and vociferous of those who criticized the church because of its conformity to codes of respectability was the aging Peter Cartwright. Cartwright's larger-than-life personality and tales of pioneer life catapulted him to fame within Methodist circles in the mid-nineteenth century. Toward the end of his life, Cartwright contrasted the state of the church at midcentury with what he believed prevailed in his youth, a strict devotion to simplicity that resulted from deep experiences of God.

> We had no Missionary Societies; no Sunday-school Society; no Church papers; no Bible or Tract Societies; no colleges, seminaries, academies, or universities; all the efforts to get up colleges under the patronage of the Methodist Episcopal Church were signal failures. We had no pewed churches, no choirs, no organs. . . . The Methodists in that early day dressed plain; attended their meetings faithfully, especially preaching, prayer and class meetings; they wore no jewelry, no ruffles. . . . Parents did not allow their

children to go to balls or plays; they did not send them to dancing schools. ... If the Methodists had dressed in the same "superfluity of naughtiness" then as they do now, there were very few even out of the Church that would have any confidence in their religion.[30]

The pursuit of refinement and respectability cost the church, according to Cartwright, divine power and effectiveness. Cartwright saw this most clearly in the education of clergy, whom he believed substituted a seminary education for divine calling and empowerment. "When God wants great and learned men in the ministry, how easy it is for him to overtake a learned sinner, and, as Saul of Tarsus, shake him a while over hell, then knock the scales from his eyes, and, without any previous theological training, send him straightway to preach Jesus and the resurrection."[31] Cartwright insisted that "I do firmly believe that if the ministers of the present day had more of the unction or baptismal fire of the Holy Ghost promoting their ministerial efforts, we should succeed much better than we do, and be more successful in winning souls to Christ than we are." In fact, if preachers "depend less on the learned theological knowledge of Biblical institutes, it is my opinion they would do vastly more good than they are likely to do."[32]

Among Cartwright's colleagues, James Quinn echoed Cartwright's assessment of the dangers of education, declaring that "what we gain in learning we lose in power."[33] Charles Giles made a more sweeping remark when he lamented the loss of an earlier commitment to the strict observance of the Methodist Discipline. "In those days," explained Giles, "our Discipline was observed with great punctuality by preachers and people. Class meetings were held in due form; and love-feasts were Christian love-feasts indeed." Even more, "the members of our community were also conformed to rule in their apparel, which punctuality comported well with their holy profession." Giles concluded that though the Methodist rule might have been strict, people adhered to it because they acknowledged that "such self-defying acts were necessary to constitute a real Christian."[34]

These figures, and others like them, bemoaned the newly dominant expression of Methodist spirituality and practice, but even opponents of respectability made accommodations, though perhaps unconsciously, to dominant middle-class social customs. Charles Giles criticized the growing laxity of the church, but he also encouraged Methodists to obtain a formal education.[35] Peter Cartwright based much of his narrative around the "civilizing" transformation of the untamed wild through the introduction of law, religion, and traditional social distinctions. While Cartwright possessed an idealized respect for frontier pioneers and the rugged life that accompanied them, he balanced this with a commitment to the idea that the expansion of Methodism helped to civilize the frontier by instilling proper ethics, including temperance, Sabbath observance, and the abolition of slavery, as well as inculcating appropriate social relations such as the preservation of gender and age distinctions.

Methodist popular literature produced in the mid-nineteenth century reveals the value that followers found in refinement, respectability, and domesticity. Discourse centered on controlled behavior, good manners, and sound reason, offering little space for the language of warfare and battle. But how did these new ideals influence the religious experiences that once rested at the center of the Christian's warfare? In what follows, we will see that Methodists recast their conversions and sanctification experiences as peaceful retreats toward a God of love rather than violent struggles with spiritual forces.

Fighting's Retreat from Religious Experience

In 1848, Methodist historian Abel Stevens reflected on what he considered to be the fundamental characteristics of a Methodist. Stevens emphasized an "experimentally known" salvation characterized by the direct testimony of the Holy Spirit that a person's sins had been forgiven as the central pillar of the Methodist church, both historically and in his own age.[36] Stevens's assurance that experiential religion remained essential for mid-nineteenth-century Methodists testifies to the enduring importance of conversion. Apart from an "experimentally" known conversion, Methodists could not legitimately claim a Christian identity.

Yet Stevens also questioned the nature of the conversion experience in ways that reflect an important shift in the ways many middle-class Methodists understood how conversion occurred. Stevens appealed to scientific reasoning to dismiss many of the experiences that so powerfully cast conversion as a spiritual struggle. Recalling a conversation he had with a British Methodist who saw some of the "stoutest men fall to the earth as suddenly as if shot through the heart," Stevens made clear that such experiences "seldom appear now-a-days" and agreed with his conversation partner that the only way to explain such phenomena was "some yet undiscovered law of the nervous system" rather than an act of God.[37]

By naturalizing falling out and related experiences, Stevens and other like-minded Methodists denied the authenticity of one of the traditional components of the Methodist's warfare: the bodily enactment of God's wounding of penitents in order to heal them of their sins. This shift occurred as part of a much more extensive effort to recast conversion and sanctification in terms of passivity rather than militant struggle. Take itinerant preacher Lorenzo Waugh's (1808–1900) recollection of an influential sermon that led to his conversion. In traditional language, Waugh recounted how a preacher told him he could never obtain salvation on his own merits, but that he could still hope for redemption from his sins. The preacher countered that "there is a balm in Gilead . . . Christ Jesus the Saviour, by the voluntary sacrifice of himself once offered, has paid all the debt and satisfied Divine Justice, and made the way open and sure by which all may come and be saved." Although the preacher's attempt to direct Waugh and his fellow congregants to the work Christ achieved on their behalf might have been quite traditional Methodist theology, what followed reveals the importance of this sermon for the changes besetting Methodist expressions of conversion. In explaining how his listeners could obtain salvation, the preacher insisted that the path to salvation was not difficult. God made an "easy condition" for people: accept Christ through faith by "simply" repenting and confessing their sins and recognizing "the efficiency of the Saviour's merit and love and power." The path to salvation set forth by this preacher did not take the form of a battle in which one fought the self's evil inclinations and Satan's vicious hold, nor did God need to wound the person either bodily or spiritually. Any hint of Wesley's warning that only one who fought and conquered sin, the world, and Satan could truly count themselves a Christian is impossible to detect. The process was, in the preacher's words, "easy," a simple act of repentance.[38]

Others specified what this easy path to salvation included, or, more specifically, what it did not include—the struggles and sufferings that characterized almost every early Methodist conversion account. Missionary bishop of Africa William Taylor (1821–1902) made this clear when he related the advice he received during his conversion. Taylor recalled that as a child he tried "to scream and pray my way in" rather than simply surrender to God. While at a prayer meeting, during which he was "praying and crying at the top of my voice," a man "soothed [him] down" by suggesting that salvation came much easier. The boy only needed to "believe on the Lord Jesus Christ and thou shalt be saved." The man reasoned, "[Y]ou do believe on the Lord Jesus Christ; therefore you are saved." Still resolute, William demanded more tangible evidence, perhaps hoping for the kind of dramatic bodily experience made famous by his Methodist forebears. His adviser challenged him with a very different image of God than the warrior who killed his enemies. God, said his adviser, called to people in a "gentle voice of mercy" through "the touch of his loving hand."[39]

Some converts indicated that their conversion experience did not proceed as smoothly, but downplayed that fact in order to conform to the new rhetorical approach. The Rev. Nicholas Vansant noted that he experienced moments of despair prior to his conversion. However, unlike earlier Methodists, he not only failed to describe his despair in any detail, he also softened it by emphasizing that his conversion proceeded "gradually and *gently*" [emphasis added]. Likewise, an article in the *Christian Advocate and Journal* confessed that true conversion originated in "a troubled state of mind arising from conscious guilt and dread of condign punishment," but the article passed quickly over this state to focus on a new life evidenced by "love, joy, peace, gratitude, and all the fruits of righteousness."[40] Even some of those who sought to defend the old ways came to interpret conversion experiences in terms different than a great struggle. One writer, seeking to restore what he considered the lost power of the Methodist ministry, admitted that the "sympathetic emotions producing trembling and weeping" that accompanied so many "violent" conversions earlier in the century likely resulted from natural psychological effects rather than the supernatural working of the Holy Spirit.[41]

These "gentle" and "natural" conversions depended on an image of God different than the warrior who killed sinners in order to heal them. In the mid-nineteenth century, middle-class evangelicals across the spectrum of denominational affiliations began to speak of God in more benevolent ways. As Richard Rubenstein has observed of New England piety, "the notion of divine majesty, omnipotence, immutability, or even infinitude, was irrelevant. The beauty of God, because it could be felt, was more vital to . . . [Christian] saints than his power."[42] In keeping with this trend, when most mid-nineteenth-century Methodists contemplated how best to speak of God, their first inclination did not lead them to describe God as the warrior who slew incorrigible sinners in order to save them, nor did they resort to the vengeful figure that literally killed those wandering from the divine will. More commonly, they referred to God and the divine nature in terms of love and kindness. In fact, love became the fundamental divine characteristic and the lens through which Methodists began to refract all other attributes. As one writer explained, "what is his [God's] omnipotence but the arm of his love? What is his omniscience but the medium through which he contemplates the objects of his love? What is his wisdom but the scheme of his love? What are the offers of the Gospel but the invitations of his love?"[43]

The centrality of love in Methodist conceptions of the divine required followers to recast aspects of God's nature that appeared discordant with love. In an article written for the *Ladies' Repository,* for instance, one of the leading American Methodist theologians of the nineteenth century, Thomas O. Summers, attempted to describe God's punishment of human beings in ways consistent with divine love. "The divine benevolence or love, is as really . . . displayed in the chastisements which are administered to the people of God, and the fiery vengeance which is poured upon his enemies, as it is in the undisguised and positive blessings which are lavished upon saints on earth or seraphs in heaven."[44] The punishment of the disobedient, for Summers, actually represented the expression of love to the obedient in two ways. First, it safeguarded the obedient from the terrible influence of the disobedient. Second, the punishment of the disobedient presented a motivation for free human agents to obey the law necessary for the right ordering of the universe and, ultimately, salvation itself. God's love for humankind, expressed through a desire for human salvation, necessitated divine punishment of transgressors.[45]

The focus on a God of love also had important implications for how Methodists described God's relation to the world. In some cases, Methodists created a dichotomy between God and the world, positioning the struggles of life or the cruelties of the world in opposition to God's love, to which believers fled for protection. The following poet opined in the *Ladies' Repository*: "O earth! Thy cup is bitterness / And poison taints thy gales / And vipers creep among the flowers / That blossom in thy vale!" This disgust for the world led the author to God, whom he described in filial ways: "Then let me turn to thee, O God! Sole Friend that mortal knows / And on the bosom of thy love / My soul shall find repose."[46] Similarly, another poet explained in the *Christian Advocate and Journal,* "So turns my weary soul to thee / My faithful and unerring Guide! Ah! Let me to my refuge fly / And in his shadow safe abide!"[47] These Methodists preserved the traditional conceptions of a contentious relationship with the world, but they described the nature of the religious life as a flight from this contention to rest and comfort in a God defined almost purely in terms of love.

In other cases, Methodists evinced a less conflicted relationship with the world, viewing nature as a means of understanding God's love. Writing for the *Ladies' Repository,* W. F. Lowrie composed a multipart essay, "Deity and Nature," that appeared over the course of eight months. In it, Lowrie argued that the examination of nature, whether the solar system or the workings of planet Earth, showed that divine benevolence was God's fundamental character trait.[48] Similarly, an interpreter of Psalm 125:2, which likened God to the mountains surrounding Jerusalem, drew his readers to contemplate how these mountains communicated God's nature: "we must recollect that these mountains were generally beautiful and fruitful, producing olives, vines and pasturage. . . . What striking emblems were they of the power and mercy of Him whose arm is our defense, and whose paths drop fatness, to all who put their trust in him!"[49]

Access to God's love could also come through nature. One writer, reflecting on the beauties of spring, declared that "surely the naturalist, the botanist, the Christian cannot fail at this lovely season, in wandering through fields of flowers, to have the great and beneficent Creator in all his thoughts."[50] Others set such sentiments to poetry: "God's spirit smiles in flowers / And in soft summer showers."[51] Another explained that the divine "mingles with the pale light, when the moon in her chaste beauty, shines from her blue course."[52]

The closeness with which midcentury Methodists wanted to experience this more personal and loving God translated into a larger role for the figure of Jesus as the incarnation of God in human flesh. Historian Stephen Prothero argues that evangelical interest in Jesus ultimately led to a redirection of emphasis away from God the Father.[53] Not surprisingly, the image of Jesus that emerged centered on love and friendship.[54] This focus on the love of Jesus led Methodists like the Rev. William Thompson to write of his late daughter's Christian life as a romance with Christ. "A few years past the Prince of heaven [Jesus] wooed my youthful Sarah. She fell in love with him, and consented to a union. She had his kind embraces, tokens of his love, and frequent visits to her Father's house." Their union, Thompson contended, came at death when Sarah "gave her full consent to leave her all below, and go and be forever with her love."[55]

Because love dominated God's nature, God did not call people to salvation in ways that might seem discordant with this nature, especially in awesome displays of power that caused people to fall to the ground or scream out in horror. Rather, God worked more subtly on the person. As noted above, William Taylor's exhorter spoke of the touch of God's loving hand. Others spoke of hearing God's call as a "small voice."[56] Older leaders like Billy Hibbard complained that midcentury Methodists simply refused to believe that God could act any other way.[57]

The influence of God's loving nature on the narration of Methodist conversion comes into clear view in what the *Christian Advocate* said were the last words of advice a dying soldier gave his children. The soldier rejected images of a distant God in favor of identifying the divine as a "parent" who drew him to salvation not through a slaying, but through "the sweet attractions of his grace." The soldier gave force to such leadings through the recognition of "the amazing love of God in giving his Son Jesus Christ to bleed and die for mankind," which resulted in God's "speak[ing] peace to my soul." As if deliberately attempting to counter any thoughts that God might withhold salvation to the earnest because of a lack of effort or struggle, the soldier closed his brief essay with an exhortation to his children to "seek him," being assured that if they did "he will be found of you" since the divine "is every where present, and we have every where free access to him."[58]

If many joined with this soldier to suggest that the path to salvation was marked by outpourings of God's love rather than militant struggle, others insisted that the actual moment of conversion was also more peaceful. Bishop Erastus Haven did not cry out or fall to the ground, smote by either God or Satan. Rather, Haven recalled, "I made no demonstration, uttered no word, nor was anything said to me." Silently, Haven left the meeting without anyone present knowing he was converted.[59] Another spoke of conversion as simply finding "rest to his soul," which did not result in a loud shout or a fall to the earth, but a "subdued spirit" and a soul that "glowed with love to God and man." The man could not even express the precise moment of his conversion.[60] Amanda Smith, a member of the African Methodist Episcopal Church, expressed similar experiences of peacefulness in her description of sanctification. Smith explained that sanctification did not include a violent strike by God, but a gentle push on the forehead that brought joyous feelings of peace.[61]

The move to a more peaceful encounter with God presented certain problems for Methodists. For those who expected great drama or struggle, a less martial experience raised questions about the reality of the experience. E. H. Stokes recalled that he doubted the authenticity of his conversion because it seemed to lack the bodily and emotional intensity of others. The lack of outward signs led him to "look within" in the hopes of finding an internal change. This inner analysis caused him to believe that peace and joy replaced his earlier fears. He therefore concluded that his conversion was authentic. Stokes marked this realization with the behavior that characterized so many Methodists at midcentury and differed so dramatically from earlier generations: "and so, without a word, and almost without an emotion . . . I lay down to profound and peaceful slumber."[62]

Holiness advocates within the Methodist Church evinced the most ambivalence about these refined spiritual experiences. Timothy Merritt's hugely popular *The Christian's Manual: A Treatise on Christian Perfection* (1854) drew heavily on John Wesley and John Fletcher to provide specific "directions for such Christians . . . desirous to obtain" perfection. Merritt recognized with Wesley that God wrought sanctification "on condition of our seeking and striving for it," and therefore that the Christian needed to "be willing to make every sacrifice to get it." Yet unlike Fletcher and Wesley, Merritt resisted using any forms of martial imagery to describe what this striving entailed.[63] God demanded human effort, to be sure, but readers of the *Christian's Manual* could never conclude that their effort might somehow be grueling, painful, or even terribly difficult.

In contrast to Merritt, Phoebe Palmer (1807–1874), whose Tuesday meeting became one of the most widely known purveyors of holiness teachings, relied on military images to describe the person's responsibility to pursue the blessings of conversion and sanctification. Palmer also highlighted the opposition that such pursuits might entail. Humans participated in "warfare" against "the world, the flesh and Satan" and therefore needed to employ "that holy violence which the kingdom of heaven suffereth" to overcome such obstacles and finally enter the kingdom of God.[64] She noted in her own life that Satan "assaulted" her through temptations that exhausted her mind and body.[65] Taking up arms against her spiritual foe, she also described her victories. "The feeling that possessed my soul was, that of defying Satan in the name of *Christ*; the enemy every moment saying that my state of grace did not warrant the testimony that I had given . . . I felt such conscious victory over the powers of darkness that my soul was filled with triumph" [emphasis in original].[66]

While Palmer's theology drew upon images of warfare, Palmer did not establish warfare as the dominant metaphor for describing the Christian life. Rather, she more commonly spoke of sacrifice. Palmer called Christians to place themselves upon a metaphorical altar by sacrificing the desires of the world in order to obtain the blessing of deliverance from sin. "By the right of purchase, God demands, and beseeches, that we present our bodies a *living* sacrifice. We present the offering, and are cleansed. . . . It is then and only then, that we can fully mingle in song with the spirits of the just made perfect around the throne" [emphasis in original].[67]

The centrality of Palmer's "altar theology" to her broader theological understanding and her evocative imagery of sacrifice has drawn the attention of many of Palmer's biographers. Charles Edward White argues that Palmer's altar theology systemized sanctification by providing a "shorter way" to holiness than the patient but militant action that attended Wesley's characterization of the path to sanctification. As long as the person placed herself on the altar and exhibited faith that God willed and accomplished every Christian's sanctification, then Palmer insisted that God would sanctify the person. There was no need to wait, no need to undergo a particularly emotional experience or bitterly strive with violent effort.[68] Palmer made sanctification an instantaneous act accomplished through the exercise of faith. Another biographer summarized this same feature of Palmer's theology: "The instantaneous nature of entire sanctification was strongly underscored, pivoting on the act of a free human agent in the 'crisis' of entire consecration. Process, or growth in holiness, though not denied, took a decided backseat to immediacy."[69]

Palmer's conception of sanctification relied heavily on the initiative of the person to place himself or herself on the altar. This active role for the individual, compounded with Palmer's resistance to associating sanctification with particular emotional or physical experiences, worked to undermine the importance of the battle in Palmer's theology. Palmer feared that connecting justification and sanctification with a necessary set of feelings or bodily reactions created artificial barriers to conversion and holiness. She confessed that her own experience of sanctification occurred "apart from any excitement of feeling, other than the sacred awe inspired by the solemnity of the act."[70] She therefore discouraged her followers from comparing their experience with others, arguing that differences in experience resulted from variations in people's natures. As a result, Christians could not rely on such differences to prove the presence of divine grace.[71]

Palmer also took issue with those whose experience suggested that God withheld spiritual blessings from someone until he or she proved their seriousness through intense struggle. The key to obtaining justification and sanctification, argued Palmer, rested with faith that God would deliver a person from sin *immediately.* People did not have to wait on God but could pursue their deliverance from sin with faith that God would respond. Palmer wrote to an inquirer, "I do not think we have any Scripture ground for the supposition, that God ever withholds the power to exercise faith from the sincere inquirer." She continued, "[I]f you will now make confession of your sin . . . he will *now* receive you" [emphasis in original].[72] Further, God's willingness to forgive the person did not require great effort on the person's part. "How truly it is not according to the tears shed, nor the length of time spent in the pursuit, nor according to anything else, other than, 'according to our faith it is done unto us!'"[73]

Some older Methodists, especially Palmer's friend Nathan Bangs (1776–1862), perceived Palmer's emphasis on the responsibility of the person to exercise faith apart from intense struggle as a serious departure from the historic Methodist formulation of the limited role of the individual in salvation. As editor of the *Christian Advocate,* one of the founders of the Missionary Society of the Methodist Episcopal Church, president of Wesleyan College, and one of the first historians of the Methodist Episcopal Church, Bangs exercised perhaps the most influential role over Methodist thought in the first half of the nineteenth century. In 1857, the aged Bangs criticized Palmer because he believed her emphasis on faith detracted from the traditional Methodist teaching of the pre-eminent role of the divine in salvation expressed through the testimony of the Holy Spirit.[74]

Such critiques were simply not sufficient to convince Palmer or her followers. Palmer continued to emphasize the responsibility of humans to sacrifice themselves to God and stressed sanctification as the immediate result of this action. Palmer's unyielding focus on God's willingness to bless the seeker and to do so without significant bodily effects or emotions obscured her references to fighting.[75] Salvation and sanctification became blessings from God that did not require pain, suffering, or any other work of the Spirit. People did not need God to "slay" them for their salvation. Deliverance from sin required faith in the divine work and a gracious God. This emphasis caused Palmer to cut off her use of martial language for the Christian life from her theological understanding of justification and sanctification and in the process essentially reduce war imagery to colorful metaphor.

Other holiness proponents shared Palmer's belief in the Christian life as a battle, but also attested to her concern that martial efforts were not necessary to achieve forgiveness and holiness. In 1844, an article advocating holiness teachings in the *Ladies' Repository* made clear that "the Christian's state on earth is militant" and that the battle not only preceded sanctification, it followed it as well. The sanctified, argued the author, "above all Christians, should look for sharp conflicts. They are detailed to commence assaults on Satan, and lead the sacramental hosts in holy onset against his legions."[76] However, like Palmer, A. C. Morehouse expressed concern that persons make a decision for salvation and sanctification rather than waiting for a particular experience marked by struggle or emotion. During his own conversion, Morehouse blamed Satan for his thoughts that his conviction was inauthentic because it was not accompanied by tears. Morehouse recalled that though he realized he was a sinner and went forward for prayer as one seeking salvation, he could not achieve a terribly profound sense of his sinfulness. Morehouse responded to this dilemma by concluding that salvation did not depend on emotional experiences or physical displays, but occurred because of the person's expression of "faith . . . now."[77]

In their preaching and writing, holiness proponents like Palmer, Morehouse, and Merritt acknowledged the need to "fight the good fight" for salvation, but they helped spread a theology that diminished the importance of martial struggle to the spiritual life. Their concern to remove what they saw as artificial barriers to a person's salvation led them to emphasize the exercise of faith without reference to certain bodily experiences or emotions. In so doing, they undermined the presence of conflict in conversion and sanctification insofar as it originated in God. The divine did not withhold spiritual blessing or make access to that blessing difficult. One simply needed, through an act of faith, to accept God's promises.

At the same time, although imagining Christian spirituality as a sacrifice created an alternative to the view of life as a battle, sacrifice did share some important features with earlier Methodist assumptions about redemption and Christian discipleship. Like the battle imagery of being wounded or even killed in order to be healed, sacrifice assumed that the believer must in some sense suffer and die in order to gain spiritual deliverance. Through this sense of sacrifice, holiness advocates retained violent discourse, though their sacrificial language had little relation to a person's bodily experiences. Christians needed to sacrifice their sinful cravings for the world and their misdirected will, not their bodies.

This different sense of violence within the Christian life, one of self-sacrifice, relied on a popular theology that emphasized human ability.[78] Recall that Wesley described the human person as utterly depraved. Under the aid of prevenient grace, human beings could progress toward salvation. This established a conflictual theology in which the depth of human sinfulness meant that humans had to ardently struggle to challenge the power of sin in their life, while the power to do this came from God's grace.[79] By midcentury, however, Methodists placed greater emphasis on the ability of the human to realize salvation. This reflected much of the work of Methodist theologians at midcentury, particularly Daniel Whedon. Whedon served as editor of the *Methodist Quarterly Review* from 1856 to 1884 and is seen by many as the leading American Methodist theologian of his time. Whedon offered a subtle but important alteration to Methodist understanding of the human person by emphasizing free will over depravity. Whedon defined the will as "the power of the soul by which it is the conscious author of an intentional act."[80] His stress on the consciousness and intentionality of the will comes into important focus in his understanding of freedom, which must include the ability "both *to* [perform] and [refrain] *from* the act" [emphasis in original].[81] Unless both of these powers applied, God could not hold humans morally responsible for their actions.[82] God would be unjust to punish those who lacked the power to obey the law.[83]

Whedon applied this understanding to the traditional Methodist doctrines of human depravity and redemption. Whedon admitted that humans inherited a depraved, sinful nature from Adam because the "law of descent" requires that "the nature of the primogenitor is the nature of all his generations," but, in effect, he dismissed the relevance of human depravity in soteriology on two grounds. First, he argued that humans lacked moral responsibility for their nature because their nature prevented them from acting otherwise. Whedon explained that "there can be no guilt for not obeying a motive which was never in the agent's reach; nor can there be any guilt for the existence of the nature which excludes, the power of the volition and the motive. . . . The man no more made himself than he made Satan; and he is no more responsible for his own nature than for Satan's nature."[84]

Second, and more importantly, Whedon focused his attention on the restoration of moral accountability through Christ's redemptive work, which permitted "the return of the Holy Spirit to every soul of man as soon as born." This brought "the revelation of the system of divine truth to his developed intellect" that transforms the sinful nature of all humans and restores their free agency.[85] By emphasizing the elimination of the effects of depravity in the process of recreating human freedom, particularly in the process of salvation, Whedon left human depravity only a symbolic place in Methodist theology. Humans did in the divine decree: "Hath not he [God] who placed Moses in Mount Sinai to utter law over the wilderness, placed us on this continent to shout the Gospel over two oceans? Will he suffer the mission to be confounded? Hath not he who bound us in one language, laws, and religion, also riveted our states together by the mountains, and cemented them by the streams?" Most northern Methodists answered this line of questioning with an unequivocal yes.[91]

Against northern arguments for the preservation of the Union, southerners countered that the defense of their rights denied them by the North obligated their government to go to war. The Rev. Robert Newton Sledd argued as much when he preached before a group of Confederate cadets that because God intended their happiness, "if a state of independence be most conducive to our happiness and to our accomplishment of the objects of life, then have we an inalienable moral right to that state, and to the unmolested fruition of its advantages." The North's denial of that right, urged Sledd, not only necessitated war, it also prompted God's blessing of the South: "God, by His providence, if not by his word, bid us buckle on our armour, and 'behave ourselves valiantly for our people, and for the cities of our God.'"[92]

As these arguments about states' rights and the preservation of the Union imply, the war symbolized far more than the defense of political values. Methodists integrated the war into the greater cosmic battle between good and evil. Such sentiment appeared commonly in the pages of the *Christian Advocate and Journal,* where, for instance, the following writer envisioned the war as perhaps the last and greatest battle in the process of restoring God's dominion through the final conquering of sin and Satan.

> What we see to-day is but an extraordinary, perhaps a final, outbreaking of a warfare that has raged nearly six thousand years; sometimes secretly, often openly; an irrepressible conflict between good and evil, right and wrong, truth and error; God and all heaven on one side, Satan and all hell on the other. . . . Today it would seem the powers of hell are marshaled on the plains of the earth for what may prove to be a more terrible conflict than ever before convulsed the moral universe of God. But just as sure as there is a God in heaven truth will gain the victory on earth.[93]

Similarly, another Union supporter viewed all of America's wars as unambiguous battles between good and evil. The American Revolution, he declared, wrested liberty from the clutches of Satan. With the Civil War, Americans once

ual theology in which the depth of human sinfulness meant that humans had to ardently struggle to challenge the power of sin in their life, while the power to do this came from God's grace.[79] By midcentury, however, Methodists placed greater emphasis on the ability of the human to realize salvation. This reflected much of the work of Methodist theologians at midcentury, particularly Daniel Whedon. Whedon served as editor of the *Methodist Quarterly Review* from 1856 to 1884 and is seen by many as the leading American Methodist theologian of his time. Whedon offered a subtle but important alteration to Methodist understanding of the human person by emphasizing free will over depravity. Whedon defined the will as "the power of the soul by which it is the conscious author of an intentional act."[80] His stress on the consciousness and intentionality of the will comes into important focus in his understanding of freedom, which must include the ability "both *to* [perform] and [refrain] *from* the act" [emphasis in original].[81] Unless both of these powers applied, God could not hold humans morally responsible for their actions.[82] God would be unjust to punish those who lacked the power to obey the law.[83]

Whedon applied this understanding to the traditional Methodist doctrines of human depravity and redemption. Whedon admitted that humans inherited a depraved, sinful nature from Adam because the "law of descent" requires that "the nature of the primogenitor is the nature of all his generations," but, in effect, he dismissed the relevance of human depravity in soteriology on two grounds. First, he argued that humans lacked moral responsibility for their nature because their nature prevented them from acting otherwise. Whedon explained that "there can be no guilt for not obeying a motive which was never in the agent's reach; nor can there be any guilt for the existence of the nature which excludes, the power of the volition and the motive. . . . The man no more made himself than he made Satan; and he is no more responsible for his own nature than for Satan's nature."[84]

Second, and more importantly, Whedon focused his attention on the restoration of moral accountability through Christ's redemptive work, which permitted "the return of the Holy Spirit to every soul of man as soon as born." This brought "the revelation of the system of divine truth to his developed intellect" that transforms the sinful nature of all humans and restores their free agency.[85] By emphasizing the elimination of the effects of depravity in the process of recreating human freedom, particularly in the process of salvation, Whedon left human depravity only a symbolic place in Methodist theology. Humans did not need to fight the sinfully depraved aspect of the self because Jesus already conquered it, and even if he had not, humans had little impetus to battle their nature since God did not hold humans accountable for acts performed under its direction in the first place.

By emphasizing the freedom of the will over against a sinfully depraved nature, Whedon, like Palmer, constructed a theology that helped shift Methodist thought and practice away from language of militant struggle. Methodism's evolving conceptions of God's nature and work in the world, as well as the moral and soteriological responsibilities of humans, established divine nurture and intimacy as not only the product of salvation as it always had been in Methodist thought, but now also the mechanism that, along with human initiative, led to salvation and communal relations with other Christians. For most Methodists, conversion and sanctification remained integral to Christian identification. However, by emphasizing a peaceful path to the divine, Methodists less commonly made their identification with God or other believers contingent upon suffering and warfare. They now saw the path to salvation as bereft of pain, a movement toward a welcoming and loving savior.

This concomitantly influenced the nature of Methodist understandings of human relationships. For instance, Methodists began to stress to parents the need to imitate God's love in their relations with each other and their children in order to lead children to Christianity. As one writer explained: "If in the family circle a mutual forbearance, submission, and love are visible . . . what may we expect of the children of that family. . . ? Is not the stamp of Christianity on their minds, and will it not remain there, and stand forth in perpetual characters at the end of time?"[86] Conversely, John Corrigan has recently argued that family life, especially child rearing, was assumed to be based on the expression of love and intimacy, and these emotions became, over the course of the second half of the nineteenth century, the context for people's conceptions of their relationship with God.[87]

If Methodist relations with a peaceful and loving God became the foundation for engaging other humans with affection, the Civil War represented a stark contrast. Methodist rhetoric about the war described God as a God of war and called Christians to take up arms against their fellow human beings. Ministers preached that the war was a sacred cause and the religious periodicals waxed romantically on the heroism of the Christian soldier. The zealous commitment to war on the part of Methodists in both the North and South, and the way Methodists spoke of the war as part of the great cosmic battle between good and evil, demonstrate the preservation of the cosmic battle as a critical tool for interpreting the functioning of society. Although Methodists were less likely to struggle against spiritual forces or their own sinful nature for their salvation in any profound way, they believed Christians had a responsibility to counter temporal struggles, not so much for the health of their personal faith, but for the defense of the nation they believed God had blessed.

Methodism and the Civil War

Methodists' adoption of a more peaceful and loving devotional life in the mid-nineteenth century did not preclude God's punishment and vengeance. Likewise, their more optimistic assessment of human nature did not extinguish sin and evil from the world. As Mark Noll has recently shown, Protestant evangelicals of all stripes in the Civil War era, including Methodists, proclaimed that they could identify such weighty matters as sin, evil, and the divine will in the world through a careful analysis of Scripture and the use of reason.[88] The confidence this evoked proved to be particularly problematic when northern and southern Christians each imagined that God had blessed them with divine favor and poured wrath out on the other. As the Union disintegrated in 1861, Methodists assumed an active role in interpreting the conflict as far more than a political dispute. Methodists cast the controversy as part of the cosmic battle between good and evil and called Christians to war.

White northerners, as Harry Stout helpfully uncovers, coalesced around the defense of the Union as a motive for war.[89] But these northerners saw more than the preservation of the Union at stake. While the Union became the primary rallying point, the belief in the Union as God's new Israel and its citizens as God's chosen people firmly united white northern Christians around the religious significance of the war. In May 1861, as the North prepared for war after the fall of Fort Sumter, Methodist Robert Allyn wrote that the war symbolized the opportunity, through "the glorious form of a genuine liberty upheld by a pure Christianity," to restore "Union and peace, for and by means of truth and justice."[90] The editors of the *Christian Advocate* spoke even more forcefully in defense of the sacred cause of the war when it rooted the Union's creation and preservation in the divine decree: "Hath not he [God] who placed Moses in Mount Sinai to utter law over the wilderness, placed us on this continent to shout the Gospel over two oceans? Will he suffer the mission to be confounded? Hath not he who bound us in one language, laws, and religion, also riveted our states together by the mountains, and cemented them by the streams?" Most northern Methodists answered this line of questioning with an unequivocal yes.[91]

Against northern arguments for the preservation of the Union, southerners countered that the defense of their rights denied them by the North obligated their government to go to war. The Rev. Robert Newton Sledd argued as much when he preached before a group of Confederate cadets that because God intended their happiness, "if a state of independence be most conducive to our happiness and to our accomplishment of the objects of life, then have we an inalienable moral right to that state, and to the unmolested fruition of its advantages." The North's denial of that right, urged Sledd, not only necessitated war, it also prompted God's blessing of the South: "God, by His providence, if not by his word, bid us buckle on our armour, and 'behave ourselves valiantly for our people, and for the cities of our God.'"[92]

As these arguments about states' rights and the preservation of the Union imply, the war symbolized far more than the defense of political values. Methodists integrated the war into the greater cosmic battle between good and evil. Such sentiment appeared commonly in the pages of the *Christian Advocate and Journal,* where, for instance, the following writer envisioned the war as perhaps the last and greatest battle in the process of restoring God's dominion through the final conquering of sin and Satan.

> What we see to-day is but an extraordinary, perhaps a final, outbreaking of a warfare that has raged nearly six thousand years; sometimes secretly, often openly; an irrepressible conflict between good and evil, right and wrong, truth and error; God and all heaven on one side, Satan and all hell on the other. . . . Today it would seem the powers of hell are marshaled on the plains of the earth for what may prove to be a more terrible conflict than ever before convulsed the moral universe of God. But just as sure as there is a God in heaven truth will gain the victory on earth.[93]

Similarly, another Union supporter viewed all of America's wars as unambiguous battles between good and evil. The American Revolution, he declared, wrested liberty from the clutches of Satan. With the Civil War, Americans once again enlisted in "a contest between Christ and Belial" for human liberty and the expansion of God's kingdom.[94]

These sacred values provided the foundation for war when Methodists integrated them into their belief that the nation's rulers had a responsibility to defend the people's rights. As they did in previous conflicts, Methodists looked to the Bible, particularly God's commands to the people of Israel to make war on their enemies, to justify military action. In addition, Methodists drew upon the just war tradition to articulate the proper use of violence. Christian just war thought reaches back at least to Augustine (354–430). Thomas Aquinas (c. 1225–1274) provided Christians the first systematic treatment of what we identify as just war theory in his *Summa Theologica*. Aquinas challenged what appeared to be incontrovertible evidence in the New Testament, human reason, and ecclesiastical policy that "it is always sinful to wage war," by offering three conditions upon which a Christian could enter into war. First, that the proper authorities, the nation's sovereign power, declare and oversee the war. Second, supporters of war needed to gather some consensus that the cause leading to the war was just. For this, Aquinas referred to Augustine's contention that a sovereign must respond when a nation refused to "make amends for the wrongs inflicted by its subjects, or to restore what it has seized unjustly." Third, those fighting the war needed to possess the proper intentions, namely the "advancement of good, or the avoidance of evil."[95] Others developed Aquinas's notions further by emphasizing that those entering into a just war could do so only as a last resort, when they had a reasonable probability of success, used methods for carrying out the war that were proportional to the conflict's goals, and discriminated between legitimate targets and noncombatants. These criteria provided the foundation for identifying both the legitimacy of going to war (*jus ad bellum*) and the importance of appropriate conduct in warfare (*jus in bello*).[96]

A Union supporter summarily reflected the integration of just war thinking into Methodist interpretations of the war when he wrote in the *Christian Advocate and Journal* in 1861.

> It [the Union] should be sustained. It was constitutionally elected; it has pursued a conciliatory policy; it has given ample assurance of its determination not only to abstain from any warfare upon Southern institutions, but to fulfill all its constitutional obligations however odious and painful; it has abstained from any act of aggression; and has been moving only on the defensive.[97]

Just war thought helped define the moral parameters of the war and motivate Christians to enlist. In fact, as one proponent of the war declared, the Christian's duty to go to war to defend the nation was every bit "as sacred as prayer, as solemn as sacraments." Even more, "we cannot live that life to better purpose than to serve God in serving our country. Death cannot come to us at a higher post of duty than when we strike for this blood-hallowed, prayer hallowed Union."[98] Others, such as the popular Soldier's Tract Association of the Methodist Episcopal Church, South, even suggested that war could make one a better Christian because "the long night watches . . . lonely hours . . . and the imminent danger of death" brought many to prayer and contemplation.[99] In another tract, the association explained that war "teaches us to fear God, and not man; to risk and sacrifice all for right and duty," all traits of the good Christian.[100] Even in defeat on the battlefield, Methodists saw war as offering an opportunity, albeit a dreadful one, for religious growth and improvement. War, as the Southern bishop George Foster Pierce declared in 1862, arrested the "corruption of prosperity . . . by upheaving the incrustations imposed by long years of peace and security, to let into our darkened minds the light of truth and ventilate the dormant conscience."[101]

Methodists tempered their exuberance for war by continually reminding themselves that in addition to the moral necessity and benefits of war, a just war depended on appropriate behavior on the battlefield. Methodists responded by urging soldiers toward proper conduct: "We must watch against its [war's] savageness, its hate, its revengefulness, its murderous rancor. When public justice smites with her sword on the neck of crime there is no passion in her stroke, only a stern and awful sorrow. I have read of a minister of the Gospel who went into battle, and dispatched one after another a score of unerring bullets, and as each took effect he apostrophized from afar the victim, 'My poor fellow, God have mercy on your soul.' That is the spirit in which to fight and in which to wait."[102]

Because all participants recognized the importance of divine intervention in the conflict, Methodists feared that "unchristian" practices could endanger the campaign by bringing God's wrath on the armies. Failure to recognize God's authority and moral law, intemperance, Sabbath violations, and barbarous behavior on the field of battle all concerned Methodist ministers and laypeople as a violation of just war practices that would call forth God's condemnation. Conversely, Methodists contended that a properly fought campaign "mindful of the demands of our Christian civilization and Christian character" would ensure divine aid and ultimate victory.[103]

The ease with which Methodists embraced the war as a cosmic struggle and the comfort they took in their valorization of themselves as God's warriors is startling when placed within the context of their rhetoric about their inner religious lives, which rejected militant language in favor of an emphasis on God's nurture and love. In the very years that vivid battles between spiritual forces for individual salvation declined, Methodists participated in the bloodiest war the nation had ever seen—and they did so under the guise of the war as a sacred battle. The confidence Methodists placed in the war's relation to the spiritual battle could no longer draw support from the ways they imagined the basic contours of their piety. If anything, the religious life that Methodists based on the creation and maintenance of bonds of affection with a loving God and fellow Christians challenged the rhetoric of a great battle between good and evil. Battling evil was simply not as significant to their path to salvation or their image of the Christian community as it had once been. Yet because evil remained a presence at the social level, Methodists rushed to destroy their enemies on the battlefield by casting the political conflict as a spiritual war.

This distinction between the ways Methodists spoke of their devotional practices and the ways they spoke of their social activity is important for how it perpetuated a longer tradition among American Methodists. Civil War–era Methodists, like the earliest generation of Methodists, created a chasm between their piety and community on the one hand and their participation in their nation's war on the other hand. But Methodists in 1861 evinced a nearly complete reversal of this duality. Revolutionary War–era Methodists championed a highly conflicted practice of the Christian life but rejected the application of that conflict to the war with England. However, in the Civil War era, Methodists increasingly celebrated images of peacefulness and experiences of love in their religious lives, but defended the use of violence against other humans by associating that violence with God's intentions for the greater battle against evil. As Methodists defined away the struggle for their own salvation and their collective identity of the church as an army of soldiers, they elevated political struggles, and the violence that attended them, to cosmic proportions. In the process, they assumed the right to take human life and legitimated that right by linking it with their responsibility to destroy evil.

Is there more than just irony in these reversals? Did Methodists lose some of their ability to resist social violence when they embraced a more genteel image of Christian devotion? We have seen that in the Revolutionary War era, American Methodists argued that their spiritual battles for salvation made them less interested in political conflict and so less inclined to participate in war. It is certainly overly simplistic to think that we could solely attribute the vigor with which early Methodists adhered to the Christian's warfare with their resistance to social violence. However, recent scholarship on the intersection of religion and violence might prove helpful in establishing just how far the two might have been connected and what this connection might mean for understanding the history of religion and violence in American Protestantism.

violent language and rituals and the ways religious belief and practice influence religious adherents to participate in or refrain from violent activity. I do this for two reasons. First, entering into broader conversations about religion and violence from a perspective of greater historical and theoretical distance will help us acquire additional insight into why Methodists might have placed such value in a cosmology of conflict and how that cosmology shaped Methodist participation in social violence. Second, the commonalities between Methodists' good fight for salvation and the religious thought and practice addressed in this broader literature leads us to explore the ways that images of a great cosmic battle are woven into the fabric of American Protestant religious life.

Violence and Religious Worlds

John Wesley defined the religious life as a very real war against sin and evil. Against the backdrop of a cosmos infused by battle, the Christian fought for salvation and the eternal peace that accompanied Satan's final defeat. The earliest American Methodists followed Wesley's lead. They fought the "good fight" to deliver penitents from sin to salvation, initiate them into the community of saints, and destroy the forces of evil that plagued their communities. Methodists understood that part of this process required God to wound them as a necessary step toward their own salvation and that they emerged from their slaying as great soldiers, called to battle sin, Satan, and the world. The quest for Christian peace required nothing less than martial attacks against the collective forces of evil.

Many Methodists described this feature of the Christian life as a kind of violence. Interpreting the nature of this violence is fraught with difficulty. I explained in previous chapters that one aspect of what Methodists meant when they described their religious lives as violent is that they imagined themselves as victims of assaults by Satan, and in some cases even God, and they called one another to inflict harm on spiritual entities. In this light, we should recall the caution raised in the introduction about the use of the term "violence" in relation to Methodist spirituality. Very often modern interpreters attach a sense of immorality or illegality, either implicitly or explicitly, to their understanding of the word "violence." Applying this evaluative perspective proves problematic for interpreting what Methodists meant when they described their religious lives as violent. Many aspects of Methodist religious life and thought presented in this book could easily fit within the parameters of violence as an immoral or illegal act, particularly acts of physical harm perpetrated by Methodists against other human beings. However, these evaluative categories would lead us to misrepresent other aspects, particularly Methodist conceptions of the nature of the spiritual life as a battle that involved believers in spiritual and physical conflicts against God, Satan, and the self. Because of the discordance created by an anachronistic imposition of modern assumptions of violence onto the past, I have referred to violence in ways that resonate more clearly with Methodists' use of the term. I defined violence in the introduction as "the use of force in order to cause injury or harm to someone or something." This definition does not impose a moral evaluation upon violence, but it does capture its aggressive nature. As a result, Methodist spirituality that emphasized the destruction of what adherents saw as the very real and dangerous forces of evil, or God "killing" the penitent in conversion, has been called violent, as has the more traditional conceptions of violence such as participation in the state's warfare or physical conflicts with other human beings. I do not mean to suggest that the two forms of action are identical. There is a difference between a spiritual battle against Satan's temptations and a physical battle that results in one soldier killing another on the field of battle. But sensitivity to the ways Methodists spoke of their religious lives as violent helps us see the places where Methodists' conflicts with spiritual forces shared similar intentions, efforts, and even results with physical conflicts between human beings. When Methodists said they felt physical pain when God struck them to the ground or when Satan assaulted them, the differences between spiritual warfare and physical violence begin to blur.

This more expansive understanding of the word "violence" allows the depths and nuances of Methodist religious life to emerge. I focused the first five chapters of this book on how Methodists understood their violent religious lives. The remainder of this book draws more freely on an "outsider's" analysis of the violence of Methodist religion.

Belief in cosmic battles, divine warriors, and destructive demons have garnered interest, albeit much too limited, from scholars who have observed these traits in religious traditions across the world. These scholars often ask two questions of the religious communities they study. First, how do theologies and cosmologies of warfare and battle function religiously? Second, what connections do these theologies and cosmologies have to social experiences? T. M. Luhrmann asks perceptively, "Why would you choose to see God (or the Goddess) as destructive, chaotic, fearsome or cruel? And why, in so many religions, should violence be associated with the sacred?"[1] Luhrmann's reflection on violent images of the divine present in her studies of witchcraft and feminist spirituality led her to see these images as functioning to validate and give meaning to feelings of pain and anger and also to help adherents overcome social ambivalence and dislocation. Luhrmann postulates that the confrontation with a violent image of the Goddess acted as a cathartic means for her followers to overcome experiences of violence in everyday life. "For these women who see so clearly the frustrating irritation of their lives, the dark Goddess becomes perhaps the means to transform frustration into tolerable vividness."[2]

A similar function applies to the early Methodist cosmology of warfare. Images of God as a destructive and yet simultaneously redemptive force might have helped Methodists make sense of their own experiences of suffering, whether in the form of social dislocation, economic marginalization, or religious persecution. For instance, the promise of divine judgment clearly joined with other aspects of early Methodist religion to provide hope to slaves, all of whom knew too well the injustice meted out to them by white slaveholding society. Albert Raboteau's classic work on slave religion explains: "Old Testament prophecies of the destruction of Israel's enemies easily and naturally fit the slaves' desire that whites suffer just retribution for the brutality of slavery."[3] It has been less common to identify similar themes when explaining the attraction of Methodism to women, who constituted the majority of early Methodist church members. More often, scholars have observed the social freedoms and opportunities that early Methodism allowed women and the "women's language . . . of tender and uncontrollable emotionalism" in which "preachers and believers felt and wept, trembled and groaned; persons melted and softened and sank into God; hearts were 'tendered' and filled and comforted." While this discourse featured images of nurture and love, some have observed militant language in women's narratives.[4] Speaking of the appeal that violent images of God's retribution had for evangelical women, historian Catherine Brekus noted, "Longing for the reassurance that God would punish their adversaries, they searched for evidence of his anger as well as his compassion."[5] Like their enslaved coreligionists, women drew upon the language of war and violence to express feelings of frustration, anger, and hope concerning the social and political opportunities denied them and in some cases to enlarge the qualities that defined women's nature in the late eighteenth and early nineteenth centuries. Violent imagery was not the only thing that drew people to Methodism, but it certainly could have addressed certain deeply felt experiences.

In addition to helping Methodists make sense of suffering and offering hope for justice, images of the divine as violent or aggressive may simply be a typical human response to God's transcendence or otherness. Luhrmann draws from the theologies of Rudolph Otto and Søren Kierkegaard and the psychoanalytic theory of Jacques Lacan to contend that violent images of the divine can be a response to "the radical otherness of God. If the sacred is what is set apart, and different, then to confront the sacred . . . should invite the annihilating terror of one's own nonbeing." Relations with the divine are a paradox in which God is wholly other and yet intimately present. God's otherness requires that God's ways are not the ways of humans and this fact is evident in biblical narratives where God seems to ask the unthinkable, as when Abraham is told to sacrifice Isaac or Job is caused to suffer. Yet it is through these very encounters of otherness that one is said to gain a deeper, more profound knowledge of God. Imagining God in violent ways, then, might go hand in hand with the attempt to gain knowledge of a God defined as the inscrutable other.[6]

The ways scholars have seen violent images as orienting adherents in the world and helping them make sense of God's otherness has a parallel in religious rituals that integrate symbolic or actual violence. Maurice Bloch contends that because religion deals in the transformation of the material processes of life, rituals often invert everyday understandings of life. In "ritual representations, instead of birth and growth leading to successful existence, it is weakening and death which lead to a successful existence." For example, initiation frequently begins with a symbolic "killing" of the initiates, "which negates their birth and nurturing." The reversal that valorizes death, Bloch contends, enables the person to enter into the "world beyond" that transcends the present, temporal life.[7]

To account for the process of transformation, Bloch draws from Van Gennup and Turner's threefold dialectical process of separation, liminality, and reintegration. Bloch stresses that this dialectic relies upon violence or conquest. In the case of initiation rites, for instance, the initiate often undergoes either symbolic or literal "violence" in the form of beatings and/or kidnappings to instigate separation from the temporal and entrance into the liminal. In reintegration, the practitioner returns from the liminal as a conqueror, bringing the transcendent into domination over the "here and now." "In the case of initiation, the initiate does not merely return to the world he had left behind. He is a changed person, a permanently transcendental person who can therefore dominate the here and now of which he previously was a part."[8]

Bloch's work nicely illuminates important features of Methodist religious life that we have considered in this book, particularly the conversion experience. Methodists' narrations of their conversion as a kind of ritual death through which God slays the sinner who is then resurrected to new life conforms to what Bloch finds an integral part of religious rituals. Like Bloch's subjects, Methodists considered an experience of suffering—whether mental, bodily, or some combination of both—as central to their religious transformations.

In chapter 2 I showed how the social effects of the drama of conversion have been a source of interest for interpreters of early Methodism. Like Bloch, many of these interpreters draw upon Victor Turner's notions of liminality to introduce what Turner defined as a "betwixt and between" state in which an individual or group moves to the peripheries of everyday life and social status. The dominant signs of social position do not apply in the liminal sphere, and this contributes to the formation of social relationships or bonds that Turner called "communitas." Such bonds are equalitarian and unstructured and thereby represent a direct opposition to dominant social relations.[9] Interpreters have used this process to understand how conversion liberated slaves and women, at least psychologically, from their positions of social subordination and in some cases even helped them claim religious authority.[10]

As insightful as these analyses of the social implications of Methodist conversion are, they often overlook the particularly violent images and experiences evoked in early Methodist conversion. As a result they are unable to establish the critical links between violence and transformation that Bloch argues are so important. For early Methodists, as with those whom Bloch studied, an essential path to personal spiritual transformation and reconstituted social relations was a ritual death and transformation. Even more, because these interpreters overlook this violent discourse and the practices associated with it, they fail to consider the ways religious experiences and rhetoric might contribute to less laudable outcomes than countercultural egalitarianism and social empowerment. Consider, for instance, the serious mental distress that accompanied the struggle for conversion and holiness. Jarena Lee contemplated suicide on at least three occasions before her conversion. James B. Finley recalled the temptations to shoot himself that arose from "the horror of darkness and despair that enveloped my wretched, ruined soul" after he feared he had committed the unpardonable sin and lost his salvation.[11] Freeborn Garrettson told of a man who wanted to kill himself because he believed he lost his salvation and another who he said went mad for the same reason.[12] Itinerant preacher William Swayze suffered from a "nervous disease" brought on by doubts about his salvation that made him feel as if he literally resided in hell. Swayze's description of his suffering exemplifies the seriousness of his condition: "I frequently called aloud for 'water to cool my tongue; for here,' said I, 'I am tormented in this flame.' It not infrequently took two men to keep me on the bed." Swayze once even attempted to commit suicide by throwing himself on the kitchen fire.[13] These and many similar accounts suggest that though the Christian's warfare could induce profound social transformations that led to communitas, it could also lead to more problematic consequences.[14]

A careful examination of the social impact of ritual violence in early Methodism also raises a point of difference with Bloch's theory. For Bloch, one or several members of the community always carries out the "violence" against another. This claim reflects Victor Turner's assertion that "we are always dealing not with solitary individuals but with systems of social relations—we have drama, not merely soliloquy."[15] The ritual reflects and even helps constitute social relations. However, in the case of Methodist conversion, the agent of violence was not another member of the community; Methodists said it was God. There may still have been drama rather than soliloquy in Methodist conversions, but the main actors were the initiate and their perception of the divine. God wounded the person, not some representative or official within the community. It should come as no surprise, then, that the system of social relations created through Methodist conversion privileged the relation with the divine first and the human community second. Methodists regularly highlighted the importance of their identity as children of God above all others. Only after the creation of this bond with God did Methodists say they gave attention to their social position within and without the earthly community of saints.

If we can attribute important personal and social transformation to the turmoil so characteristic of the battles of Methodist conversion, how might we also understand the connections we have observed between Methodist conceptions of their world beset by cosmic warfare and the social conflicts that Methodists experienced in the eighteenth and nineteenth centuries? Are the same tensions and intersections between cosmic struggles and social violence evident in other religious traditions? If so, how might these similarities contribute to our perspectives on contemporary manifestations of cosmic struggles in American Protestantism?

The Violent Implications of the
Cosmic Battle for Salvation

Thus far, the images of great cosmic battles, a wrathful God, and even ritual practices that involve violence have not been reduced to socially destructive acts or individual pathology. Rather, by looking at Methodist history and contemporary scholarship, I have tried to show how the mythic and ritual aspects of Methodism's good fight for salvation helped adherents make sense of the world and orient themselves within it. However, as James Jones has recently argued in his book exploring the psychology of religious violence, if recent acts of terrorism throughout the world teach us anything, it is that religion not only provides "meaning and value, but . . . is also a container for aggression, self-hatred, sacrifice, and various anxieties."[16] In fact, belief in cosmic struggles between good and evil, apocalyptic predictions of God's divine judgment of the sinful world, theologies that characterize the world as deeply sinful and in need of purification, and images of humans as divine warriors are all characteristics that scholars have associated with religious violence.[17]

In unpacking the intersection between religion and acts of violence, many have turned to the influence of religious ritual on social violence. Maurice Bloch, used earlier to help characterize the role of violence in removing converts from the temporal and transferring them into a liminal space, argues that initiates respond to the violence experienced as part of the entrance into the liminal by enacting violence upon their return to the temporal. Bloch calls this rebounding violence. "The element of violence involved in the renunciation of vitality [in separation from the temporal] leads to the return of vitality in a form which brings about aggressive reproduction of the community through the consumption of the vitality of outsiders, whether other species or other humans." Thus, "rebounding violence can take either a reproductive form in which vitality is regained from creatures . . . or an aggressive form in which this recovery becomes extended to involve more ambitious expansionist aims."[18]

What Bloch found of other religious traditions, namely the violent actions that often follow the violent experiences of ritual, has some resonance with Methodist history. Of course, many early American Methodists who underwent the liminal transformation of conversion eschewed the use of social violence. Even more, they argued that their conversions initiated them into a battle greater than the political conflicts of the nation. However, this commitment quickly evaporated as countless Methodists condoned and even celebrated violence as a means to further God's kingdom and the nation's conquest of North America in a way all too similar to Bloch's claims about rebounding violence. The expansionist designs to which many American Methodists committed themselves in the West and the concomitant justification of the destruction of Native peoples described in chapter 4 conform to Bloch's assertion that those transformed through the wrenching violence that introduces liminality can return to the "here and now" with a violent resolve to extend the community. Although Methodist resistance to the Revolutionary War demonstrates that the struggles Methodists experienced to achieve the liminal state of conversion did not lead to social violence in a direct way, these struggles might have contributed to Methodist participation in violence in later years by introducing or reinforcing a belief that violence was a means to purify evil.

The prospect that conversions that ritualize death and resurrection reinforce certain beliefs about the propriety of physical violence is intriguing. However, it is important to note that the point at which American Methodists disentangled their "good fight" for salvation from the everyday practice of the Christian life was also the point at which they most readily used the cosmic battle to justify war. As Civil War–era Methodists distanced themselves from bodily struggles with God or Satan and envisioned the Christian life as less conflicted, they nevertheless drew upon the notion of the cosmic battle between good and evil to justify the war as sacred. Conversely, the most ardent period of American Methodist commitment to the Christian's warfare lived out in the daily religious practices of the believer's life was also the period of strongest opposition to the use of social violence. The belief in a cosmic struggle remained consistent over this period, but American Methodists' ritual practices of spiritual warfare were inversely related to their practice of social violence.

While this inverse relationship between social violence and ritual practice might have been coincidental, some theorists, most notably René Girard, have raised the possibility of a more direct connection between ritual violence and the suppression of social violence without dismissing the prospect that ritual violence might also lead to social violence. Recall that Girard posits the foundation of human society in the scapegoating of an innocent victim. Religious rituals that re-enact the community's founding and myths that relate the sacred significance of the scapegoating event pass on rules for the maintenance of society to future generations, particularly a belief that God decrees violence as the necessary mechanism for the creation and protection of social order.[19] These myths and rituals are meant to control violence by diffusing mimetic rivalry. However, they can only do so for a time. Eventually they will break down or otherwise prove insufficient. The system founded on violence inevitably returns to violence and the cycle of myths and rituals that institutionalize and memorialize that violence are recycled and reinstituted.

The function and malfunction of myths and rituals to control violence may well apply to nineteenth-century American Methodism's perspectives on violence. The importance of rituals and myths of cosmic struggle in early Methodism helped direct adherents' focus away from social conflict during the American Revolution. Methodists found a greater battle to fight and they defined this battle as pre-eminent over all others. As the vitality of these myths and rituals waned, Methodists lost one of the chief contributors to their resolve to resist social violence.

This failure of myths and rituals to direct religious adherents away from social conflict only tells part of the story, though. Methodists also began to attach greater significance to certain social struggles within their cosmic warfare. As Methodists became more involved in the political life of the nation over the course of the nineteenth century, they applied deeper religious categories to the political realm in order to sanctify the structures in which they participated. This sacralizing effort brought those structures into the cosmic realm in more significant ways than simply being a part of God's providential oversight. Methodists came to imagine the United States as a nation called by God for a unique task in sacred history. They then read the events that shaped the nation as either confirmation of God's plan or an attempt to undermine that plan. When events undermined it, Methodists easily folded the controversy into the battle between good and evil. As Methodists interpreted political and social events through the lens of the spiritual battle, they drew upon their commitment to violently struggle against the forces of evil to justify violent social behavior as part of the larger cosmic struggle.

This move to accept and justify violent behavior also depended on several other features. First, Methodists defined certain political struggles in morally absolute terms of good and evil, righteousness and wickedness. American Methodists did this most clearly in the Civil War when they described the war as part of the cosmic battle preceding the millennial kingdom, if not the climax to the millennium. Second, Methodists' ability to resort to violence not only depended on a dualistic interpretation of social events as good and evil, but also an identification of the proper authorities to carry out the violence. Not everyone had an equal right to commit violence against another. Methodists usually granted the government this right, but they also legitimated individual acts of violence in the West by defining the early pioneers' use of violence against Native peoples as defensive, though they blurred the lines between defensive and offensive when they depicted individual pioneers taking pre-emptive action. Third, Methodists tried to establish the terms of appropriate conduct in battle by defining Christian behavior as defensive, temperate, and dispassionate and by urging the observance of Christian ritual life such as Sabbath keeping, prayer, Bible reading, and attendance at preaching. Their emphasis on moral conduct in warfare allowed them to escape the association between sin and violence and perpetuate their identity as holy warriors.

All these forces shaped Methodist perspectives on social violence. Methodists' temporal struggles took on cosmic significance and fueled the community's participation in acts Methodists saw as furthering God's kingdom. Early American Methodists might be an unlikely group to be the focus of a discussion of the intersection of religion and violence, but they show how deeply rooted and complex violence has been in the history of American Protestantism. The largest and arguably most important religious group in America for much of the nineteenth century made a certain kind of violence a central component of its religious life, and that violent religious life had important, thought divergent, relations with social violence. A proper understanding of Methodist history, and by association American religious history, depends on the recognition of these various aspects of violence.

Cosmic Warfare and Contemporary Mainstream Protestantism

Manifestations of cosmic struggle in American Protestantism are not confined to eighteenth- and nineteenth-century Methodists. Cosmic struggles have been and continue to be an important part of the way mainstream American Protestants imagine the world. Tim LaHaye and Jerry B. Jenkins's *Left Behind* fiction series offers the most popular contemporary example of the vitality of cosmic warfare in American Protestantism. LaHaye and Jenkins published the first volume of their series, *Left Behind: A Novel of the Earth's Last Days,* in 1995. Since then, the thirteen books and three prequels that constitute the series have sold more than sixty-three million copies worldwide and spawned a feature film, Internet sites, newsletters, and a host of companion books.[20] Influenced by the apocalypticism of dispensational premillennial theology, LaHaye and Jenkins describe the world after God's rapture of Christians to heaven. The earth falls under the brutal control of the Antichrist, Nicolae Jetty Carpathia, a former secretary-general of the United Nations. The protagonists of the stories are a small remnant who, after the rapture, realize their error and convert to Christianity. Called the Tribulation Force, this group tries to convert others through the Internet while conducting armed resistance against Carpathia and his empire, the Global Community.

LaHaye and Jenkins emphasize that they based their fictionalized novels on what they and their faithful readers believe to be the Bible's clear description of God's intentions for the end of the world. The work has even inspired a veritable cottage industry devoted to informing followers about the truth behind the books, including LaHaye's own *Popular Encyclopedia of Bible Prophecy* and the Tim LaHaye School of Prophecy on the campus of Liberty University. The authors' attempts to represent the beliefs of their followers in their series make it impossible to dismiss the books as merely imaginative works of fiction. An apocalyptic struggle rests at the center of the way LaHaye, Jenkins, and many of their readers imagine the world and its future.

The series' commitment to dispensational premillennialism—a particular type of premillennial belief that emerged in the second half of the nineteenth century—distinguishes it quite clearly from the theology manifest in early Methodism. Millennialism of any type was not a significant feature of Methodist theology until well into the nineteenth century. Once Methodists evinced a stronger attraction to millennial theology, they more commonly adhered to a postmillennial position that identified Christ's return occurring at the conclusion of the millennium rather than at the beginning.

The difference in millennial influences notwithstanding, the series shares two essential traits with the cosmic battles of early Methodists. First, both the series and early Methodists embrace a cosmology of conflict that embroils humans in a battle between good and evil. Christians have a responsibility to participate in this battle by resisting the work of the devil, most commonly through prayer, Scripture reading, evangelism, and seeking the mutual support of other believers. However, the two movements also identify a more physical role for the Christian warrior. Early Methodists primarily focused human responsibility on participation in the nation's wars that they defined as sacred battles. LaHaye and Jenkins focus their battle against the Antichrist, who will establish a bloody regime on earth. The authors' description of the characters' motives for forming the Tribulation Force underscore the Christians' ability to assume active military revolution. Bruce Barnes, a pastor to those who convert after the rapture, asks provocatively of the "sort of Green Berets" he hopes to form: "It's one thing to hide in here, studying, trying to figure out what's going on so we can keep from being deceived. . . . But doesn't part of you want to jump into battle?"[21] Barnes's colleagues agree and "jump in" by arming themselves to resist the evil that has taken over the earth.

Second, the authors of the *Left Behind* series share with early Methodists a belief that ultimately God wins the battle. While Methodists focused on God's empowerment of human beings to fight wars and protect the innocent, LaHaye and Jenkins's eschatological focus directs them to God's justice meted out by Jesus. LaHaye and Jenkins illustrate God's role in graphic detail in their depiction of Jesus' defeat of the Antichrist in book twelve of the series, *Glorious Appearing*:

> Tens of thousands of foot soldiers dropped their weapons, grabbed their heads and their chests, fell to their knees, and writhed as they were invisibly sliced asunder. Their innards and entrails gushed to the desert floor, and as those around them turned to run, they too were slain, their blood pooling and rising in the unforgiving brightness of the glory of Christ.[22]

Out of this carnage, God's millennial kingdom emerges with Jesus, "the hem of his robe turning red in the blood of his enemies," establishing a thousand-year reign on earth.[23]

As gory as the details might be, LaHaye and Jenkins explain that death is not all that awaits those who refused to repent. The final installment of the series, *The Kingdom Come*, opens and closes with divine judgment and eternal damnation. In the book's prologue, Jesus summons all those who somehow survived the violent battle that accompanied Christ's return. Jesus' followers amass on his right while the greater number, those of the enemy, group to his left. All bow and proclaim "Jesus Christ is Lord," but Jesus condemns the "goats." They "beat their breasts and fell wailing to the desert floor, gnashing their teeth and pulling their hair. Jesus merely raised one hand a few inches and a yawning chasm opened in the earth, stretching far and wide enough to swallow all of them. They tumbled in, howling and screeching, but their wailing was soon quashed and all was silent when the earth closed itself again."[24]

The violent drama prefacing LaHaye and Jenkins's millennium pales to that which ends it. War and famine are absent from the thousand-year reign of Christ, but many born after the initial judgment choose to reject Christ's rule. By the end of the millennium, millions join what LaHaye and Jenkins call the forces of the "Other Light." They constitute a great army from across the world and arm themselves with weapons greater than any the world has ever seen. As this army encircles Jerusalem, Satan stands at their fore, released from hell by God in accordance with LaHaye and Jenkins's reading of Revelation 20. The authors make the significance of the event clear, "the cosmic battle of the ages between the forces of good and evil, light and darkness, life and death, was about to commence." As promised, Satan calls his forces to war with a shrieking, "Charge!" The Son of God counters "quietly, I AM WHO I AM." Readers cannot confuse the response with meekness; terrible destruction follows. The heavens pour forth flames to vaporize the army "in an instant." Satan is left alone, speechless and "shuddering."

Just as at the start of the millennium, Jesus' victory in battle transitions quickly to judgment. The initial focus is Satan. Jesus declares the glory from which Satan fell and chronicles the sins the Evil One committed. God permits only one end for such rebellion, even as Satan finally admits that Jesus truly is Lord. Hell, full of flames and black smoke, swallows Satan. LaHaye and Jenkins make clear that Satan would be "tormented day and night forever and ever in the lake of fire and brimstone." Jesus proceeds to usher the untold millions of the "unbelieving dead" from all ages into "the lake of fire" to join Satan and those already cast into hell at the start of the book. This act completes God's banishment of evil from the cosmos and allows a new and proper world to emerge from the carnage. The masses in hell pass from view, and we assume from the thoughts of those who enjoy God forever in a new heaven and new earth. God's violent retribution, we hope, has ceased, at least for those who inhabit the new creation. Those in hell, on the other hand, prove that God's ability to inflict terrible harm is simply a part of the very nature of God's being.

The immense popularity of the *Left Behind* series testifies to the fact that belief in cosmic battles is not limited to a radical fringe within American Protestantism. It remains critical for how millions of Americans view the universe. Belief in a great war between good and evil also continues to shape the way American Protestants interpret world events, as when they read natural disasters as God's judgment on sinners or when political leaders define their nation's "enemies" as evil, as President George W. Bush did in his State of the Union speech in 2002 when he identified Iran, Iraq, North Korea, and their allies as an "axis of evil."[25] We have seen here that belief in cosmic warfare helps orient people in the world and can help them make sense of social marginalization and feelings of anger. As Amy Johnson Frykholm observes of the readers of the *Left Behind* books, the "apocalyptic language and belief in the rapture gave them hope, both cultivated and assuaged fear, and compelled them toward compassion for the world."[26]

The meaning so many find in cosmic struggle suggests that violent images of God and martial ways of defining the religious life will remain prominent parts of many adherents' religious imagination. If connections do exist between cosmic warfare and social violence, then the endurance of such beliefs and practice in mainstream Protestantism raise important concerns. I am not suggesting that somehow readers of the *Left Behind* series or other religious practitioners who find religious value in cosmic warfare are inherently violent or dangerous. I have tried to show in this chapter that more than just belief in cosmic warfare is necessary to compel religious adherents to commit violence. However, the ways cosmic warfare perpetuate beliefs that God sanctions violence, and that this sanctioning extends to humans' use of violent means to carry out God's plans in the world, can contribute to violent behavior. Insofar as the *Left Behind* books perpetuate the vitality of cosmic battle in American Protestantism, they preserve one aspect of the religious sanctioning of social violence.

Any solution to the cosmic battle's influence on social violence will not come from trying to eliminate militant discourse and practices from religion, but from finding ways to diffuse the tendency of religious communities to apply cosmic dimensions to human conflicts in order to motivate and justify their violent behavior. Mark Juergensmeyer's groundbreaking study on religious terrorism provides important insight in this regard by identifying the conditions that encourage religious communities to transfer their cosmic battle onto the temporal realm. Juergensmeyer found that three factors were most critical. First, adherents perceive the worldly struggle as a defense of identity and dignity. Second, they imagine that losing the temporal conflict would cause irreparable damage to the community by unleashing dangerous and perhaps even destructive forces upon it. Third, the religious community believes it cannot rectify the problem in real time or through worldly means.[27] When these conditions appear, the community begins to view the problem as a manifestation of the transcendent battle between ultimate forces of good and evil.

By directing attention to the conditions that encourage religious adherents to apply cosmic dimensions to temporal events, Juergensmeyer makes an essential contribution to diffusing conflicts that lead to religious violence. A meaningful challenge to religious violence must also avoid the opposite tendency of attempting to prevent religious communities from applying a theological interpretation to temporal events. Such limitations deny religious adherents the ability to bring religious thought to bear on social ills in order to benefit their communities. With such concerns in mind, Juergensmeyer has suggested a mediating position that encourages religious social action when positive and peaceful while discouraging the potentially destructive influence of religion, which he locates in religion's application of absolutism to its political perspectives. Juergensmeyer encourages the place of religion in the public realm because he sees religion infusing a sense of purpose and morality, especially among political leaders, that can serve as a counterweight to political motivations based solely on the accretion and protection of power. He also contends that religion provides the motivation necessary to ameliorate the conditions of injustice—especially poverty, political alienation, and social upheaval—that help create the urge to commit violence.[28] Juergensmeyer balances these positive contributions by warning of religion's absolutist aspects that help justify violent action by defining ideas and movements as either entirely holy or entirely evil. Juergensmeyer favors a religion moderated by Enlightenment ideals that undercut religion's ability to confer such absolutes while challenging those aspects of Enlightenment political philosophy that separate religion from the political.[29]

Juergensmeyer's ability to preserve a place for religion in the modern public sphere even as he seeks to dismantle religion's ability to fuel violent action makes his work perhaps the most insightful and promising analysis of religion and violence. It is less clear whether belief in cosmic battle would survive his challenge to religious absolutes. Could religious adherents successfully preserve a belief in cosmic warfare between good and evil while refusing to apply the battle's absolutes to the temporal world? Only time and the significant efforts of those seeking to counteract religious violence will tell. For the sake of a world torn by violence, let us hope these efforts will inspire meaningful strategies to avoid following a very old tradition of sacralizing violence.

Notes

Introduction

The epigraph is from Charles Wesley, "Soldiers of Christ Arise," in *The United Methodist Hymnal*, 513.

1. Harriet Crabtree observes the decline of martial imagery within mainline Christianity's hymns as part of larger changes in mainline Christian symbolism as a whole. Crabtree, *The Christian Life*, 87–92. In the final chapter we will have the opportunity to explore the ways that martial imagery is still an important part of American popular religion.

2. For more on the organization of Wesley's collection, see Wesley, *The Works of John Wesley*, vol. 7, *A Collection of Hymns for the Use of the People Called Methodists*, ed. Franz Hilderbrandt and Oliver Beckerlegge, 1–75. In Bicentennial Edition (Nashville: Abingdon Press, 1984–), hereafter abbreviated *Works*.

3. *Works* 9:31–46.

4. John Fletcher, "The Kingdom of Heaven Suffereth Violence, and the Violent Take it by Force" reprinted in Jeffrey, *A Burning and Shining Light*, 352–354.

5. Asbury, *The Journal and Letters of Francis Asbury*, vol. I, hereafter abbreviated *J&L*. For examples of Asbury's struggles against Satan, see *J&L* 1:17, 24, 32, 45, 53, 71, 72, 80, 92, 106, 110, 112, 132, 136, 165, 169, 182, 185, 187, 188, 189, 235.

6. Abbott, *The Experience and Gospel Labours of the Rev. Benjamin Abbott*, 32–33.

7. One might challenge my claim about Schneider's book as the most significant on the basis of the more recent and exhaustive work of Lester Ruth in *Early Methodist*

Life and Spirituality: A Reader (Nashville: Kingswood Books 2005). Ruth's book is important. However, the book is primarily an introduction to primary texts rather than a thorough analysis of early Methodist spirituality. As a result, I believe Schneider's work remains the best critical analysis of early Methodist spirituality.

8. Schneider, *The Way of the Cross Leads Home*.

9. Ibid., 54–57.

10. On the positive affections generated by Methodist religious experience, see Steele, *Heart Religion in the Methodist Tradition and Related Movements*; Henry H. Knight III, "The Transformation of the Human Heart: The Place of Conversion in Wesley's Theology" in Collins and Tyson, *Conversion in the Wesleyan Tradition*, 43–55. On the social implications of Methodist religious experience, see Catherine Brekus, "Female Evangelism in the Early Methodist Movement," in Hatch and Wigger, *Methodist and the Shaping of American Culture*, 135–173; Donald G. Mathews, "Evangelical America—The Methodist Ideology," in Richey, Rowe, and Schmidt, *Perspectives on American Methodism*, 29–30; Schmidt, *Grace Sufficient*, 51, 73–74; Douglas Strong, "A Real Christian Is An Abolitionist" and Estrelda Alexander, "Conversion and Sanctification in Nineteenth-century African American Wesleyan Women," in Collins and Tyson, *Conversion in the Wesleyan Tradition*, 69–82, 83–100. Bruce Hindmarsh's recent analysis of the evangelical conversion narrative is a notable exception to the trend emphasizing the positive emotions created through conversion. While Hindmarsh rightly emphasizes that the rhetorical emphasis in conversion narratives is on joyful release from despair, he not only emphasizes that the process leading to conversion was "agonistic," but he also helpfully reminds readers that Methodism's Arminian theology meant that converts could never rest secure in the joy of conversion. Backsliding could also result in later periods of despair that could, in the best cases, result in a new conversion. *The Evangelical Conversion Narrative*, 130–161, 226–260.

11. Richey, *Early American Methodism*, 1–20. Cynthia Lyn Lyerly called early Methodists "cultural critics" who boldly challenged race, class, gender, and religious norms. *Methodism and the Southern Mind*, 8. John Wigger argued similarly in *Taking Heaven By Storm*.

12. Nathan O. Hatch, "The Democratization of Christianity and the Character of American Politics," in Noll and Harlow, *Religion and American Politics*, 101. Hatch finds William Warren Sweet's work on frontier Methodists and Baptists as exemplary of his argument.

13. Hall, *Lived Religion in America*; Maffley-Kipp, Schmidt, and Valeri, *Practicing Protestants*; Schmidt, *Holy Fairs*; Schmidt, *Consumer Rites*; Schmidt, *Hearing Things*; McDannell, *Religions of the United States in Practice*; Orsi, *The Madonna of 115th Street*; Orsi, *Thank You, St. Jude*.

14. See especially Girard, *Violence and the Sacred*; Girard, *I See Satan Fall Like Lightning*. For a general overview of Girard's work, see Williams, *The Girard Reader*.

15. Girard sees Christianity, at least in its ideal, as the exception to the rule. Christianity, for Girard, exposes the scapegoat as innocent. *I See Satan Fall Like Lightning*.

16. *Works* 21:377.

17. *Oxford English Dictionary*, 2d ed., s.v. "violence."

18. This definition is not only useful for the purposes of this work, but is also helpful for identifying other forms of aggression, such as the destruction of the environment, as violent.

1. Fighting the Good Fight

1. Wesley's reference to righteousness, peace, and joy is drawn from Romans 14:17: "For the kingdom of God is not food and drink but righteousness and peace and joy in the Holy Spirit." It is essential to Wesley's sermon "The Way to the Kingdom," particularly in his equation of "true religion" with the kingdom that he defined as righteousness, peace, and joy. *Works* 1:218–232. The reference also appears in numerous other sermons. *Works* 1:151, 157, 218–232, 291, 298, 307, 336, 390, 449, 481, 482, 557, 582, 691; 2:46, 139, 132, 208, 215, 343, 488, 491, 527; 3:185, 607; 4:32 as well as in Wesley's journals: 20:200; 22:321.

2. For the most developed treatment of the importance of "heart religion" in the Wesleyan tradition, see Steele, *Heart Religion in the Methodist Tradition and Related Movements.*

3. Wesley's command to fight the good fight appears in numerous sermons. *Works* 1:137, 169, 313, 333, 413; 2:87, 143; 3:114, 198, 209, 328, 381; 4:38, 47, 116.

4. *Works* 22:287.

5. *Works* 19:288. The letter also appears in Wallace, *Susanna Wesley: The Complete Writings,* 370. Wallace's collection of Susanna's letters provides a fine introduction to her religiosity in general and her influence on John in particular. For secondary sources on the childhood religious education of John and his siblings, see Newton, *Susanna Wesley and the Puritan Tradition in Methodism.* Philip Greven featured Susanna's parenting methods in *The Protestant Temperament,* 21–148.

6. *Works* 18:325.

7. *Works* 18:360. Background for my relation of Wesley's early spiritual formation depends heavily upon two main sources: Heitzenrater, *Wesley and the People Called Methodists,* 33–58; and Rack, *Reasonable Enthusiast,* 61–106.

8. For an excellent treatment of the interpretation of Wesley's Aldersgate experience, particularly on whether historians have placed too much emphasis upon Wesley's early statements that he was not a Christian before Aldersgate, see Maddox, *Aldersgate Reconsidered.*

9. Heitzenrater, *Wesley and the People Called Methodists,* 77–95; Rack, *Reasonable Enthusiast,* 137–157.

10. *Works* 18:245–250.

11. *Works* 18:247.

12. *Works* 18:250.

13. *Works* 1:264.

14. Hymns were such an integral part of the early Methodist movement that some have wondered whether the movement would have succeeded without them (*Works* 7:1). For more on the importance of hymns in early Methodism, see Hempton, *Methodism,* 68–74; Kimbrough, *Charles Wesley: Poet and Theologian*; Ruth, *A Little Heaven Below.* For broader treatments on hymns in eighteenth- and nineteenth-century evangelicalism, see Marini, "Hymnody as History," 273–306; Mouw and Noll, *Wonderful Words of Life.*

15. *Works* 7:74, 257–284, 398–436.

16. *Works* 7:403.

17. Ibid., 409.

18. Ibid., 413.

19. Ibid., 404.

20. Ibid., 399.

21. Ibid., 412–413.

22. *Works* 2:170–185, 400–412.

23. For references to sinners as dead, see *Works* 2:190; 19:95. For humans as created in the image of Satan, see Ibid., 19:97.

24. Quoted in Collins, *The Scripture Way of Salvation*, 37.

25. *Works* 3:207.

26. *Works* 3:199–209. For more on Wesley's doctrine of human depravity and "responsible" grace, see Maddox, *Responsible Grace*, 65–93.

27. The importance of human struggle is one of the critical causes of Wesley's fallout with the Moravians. For Wesley, seekers should participate in the sacraments with all diligence as part of their quest for salvation rather than merely waiting for saving grace. See *Works* 19:131–134.

28. *Works* 3:73.

29. Ibid., 73–74.

30. *Works* 2:155–169.

31. *Works* 3:127–140. For more on the love Wesley desired Christians to show toward nonbelievers, see *Works* 3:142–152. For more on abstention from worldly pleasures, see *Works* 2:266–280; 3:228–246, 248–261.

32. *Works* 9:38.

33. Luke 9:23.

34. *Works* 2:243–244.

35. Ibid.

36. *Works* 19:348. For a similar account of Wesley claiming he did not feel pain when assaulted, see Ibid., 19:297. Wesley records several instances in which he and his followers were attacked, sometimes brutally. Ibid., 19:343, 349; 20:10–14, 23–24, 29, 168–169, 286–310, 332, 338–339; 21:100. For most, the threat of death was more perceived than real, though Wesleyan convert William Seward died of wounds acquired during a mob attack. *Works* 19:172.

37. See chapter 2 for a larger discussion of mob violence against Methodists.

38. Accusations that Methodism could drive its followers insane were deeply intertwined with more general concerns about Methodist "enthusiasm." The connection was twofold. First, a common argument of Methodism's opponents was that Methodists' claims to receiving direct communication from the Holy Spirit sprung either from hypocrisy or insanity. Second, some people were driven mad by the ascetic behavior they adopted in the pursuit of justification and sanctification and the bodily religious exercises they experienced as part of what they considered conversion. The best treatment of these accusations remains Lyles's, *Methodism Mocked*, 36–43, 108–110.

39. *Works* 18:123–133.

40. Rubin, *Religious Melancholy and Protestant Experience in America*, 7. See also King, *The Iron of Melancholy*.

41. *Works* 20:322. Wesley found evidence that religious melancholy struck some of his followers. Ibid., 21:61–62. For opponents' accusations that Methodism encouraged religious melancholy, see Lavington, *The Enthusiasm of Methodists and Papists Compared*; Lyles, *Methodism Mocked*, 108–110.

42. *Works* 2:222–235. For examples of heaviness in Wesley's journals, see *Works* 19:89, 122, 164–165.

43. *Works* 2:205–208.

44. *Works* 23:333. For other examples in Wesley's journals, see *Works* 19:136; 20:484; 21:61–62; 22:39; 23:23.

45. *Works* 2:214–221.

46. *Works* 2:158.

47. Ibid.

48. On the prominence and meaning of Methodist death narratives, see Hempton, *Methodism*, 65–68; Ruth, *Early Methodist Life and Spirituality*, 287–308; Schneider, *The Way of the Cross Leads Home*, 49–51.

49. *Works* 22:91–95.

50. Ibid.

51. A. Gregory Schneider has argued that death became one of the foundational concepts in Methodism. Christianity became, in Schneider's words, "a preparation for death." Methodists continually anticipated physical death by "dying with Christ" in the present life in order that they might live with Christ in the next life. Therefore, Schneider contends that the actual physical death of the believer became the pivotal point at which the success or failure of one's ability to imitate Christ came to fruition. *The Way of the Cross Leads Home*, 50–51.

52. *Works* 23:401; see also *Works* 7:138.

53. *Works* 21:497; 22:237–238; 23:407–408.

54. Midelfort, *Exorcism and Enlightenment*, 7.

55. For the changing relationship between religion and the supernatural, see Thomas, *Religion and the Decline of Magic*; Hall, *Worlds of Wonder, Days of Judgment*; Midelfort, *Exorcism and Enlightenment*; Daston and Park, *Wonders and the Order of Nature*; Mullin, *Miracles and the Modern Religious Imagination*.

56. Almond, *Demonic Possession and Exorcism in Early Modern England*, 2–9.

57. Johnstone, *The Devil and Demonism in Early Modern England*, 1–8.

58. Russell, *Mephistopheles: The Devil in the Modern World*, 66–127. See also Muchembled, *A History of the Devil*, 167–196.

59. See *Works* 22:136 n. 13 on Wesley's reading of Joseph Glanville's *Saducismus Triumphatus*. I am indebted to Midelfort's *Exorcism and Enlightenment* for uncovering sources related to the English interpretive controversy.

60. For more on Sykes, see John Stephens, "Sykes, Arthur Ashley," in Matthew and Harrison, *Oxford Dictionary of National Biography*, vol. 53.

61. [Arthur Ashley Sykes], *An Enquiry into the Meaning of Demoniacks in the New Testament*, 2–78. In support of Sykes, see [Gregory Sharpe], *A Review of the Controversy about the Meaning of Demoniacks in the New Testament*.

62. For more on Church, Twells, and Whiston, see *Oxford Dictionary of National Biography*.

63. See Church, *A Reply to the Farther Enquiry into the Meaning of the Demoniacks in the New Testament*; Twells, *An Answer to the Enquiry into the Meaning of the Demoniacks in the New Testament*; Whiston, *An Account of the Demoniacks*.

64. Hempton, *Methodism*, 32–54. For the Enlightenment's influence on the emergence of the evangelical movement as a whole, see Noll, *The Rise of Evangelicalism*, 146–151.

65. See for instance *Works* 20:132–134; 21:115.

66. Wesley only preached from Ephesians 6:12 once (1759). *Works* 3:3. As I explain later, the vitality of Wesley's belief in Satan and demons is more apparent in his Journals.

67. *Works* 3:21–22.

68. Ibid., 22–23.

69. Ibid., 24.

70. Ibid., 25–27.

71. *Works* 20:374–375; see also *Works* 19:120 and 20:101.

72. *Works* 19:252.

73. *Works* 1:246, 327, 592; 2:18; 4:144, 226.

74. See for instance, *Works* 19:248; 20:106.

75. *Works* 19:296; 20:106.

76. *Works* 19:149–150; 21:468; 20:356.

77. *Works* 22:237–238. See also *Works* 20:128. For a brief defense of witchcraft, see *Works* 22:135–146.

78. *Works* 19:109–111. Wesley records Sally Jones's problems beginning in October 1739. Jones's struggles with Satan continued until at least January 1741. *Works* 19:178.

79. *Works* 4:429–433. For other accounts of demon possession, see *Works* 19:23, 34, 54–55, 110–111, 112, 150, 177–178, 256, 311–312; 20:363, 421, 460–463; 21:29, 204, 429–433; 22:7.

80. *Works* 19:312.

81. The whole armor of God refers to Ephesians 6:11.

82. The shield of faith is a reference to Ephesians 6:16; the helmet of salvation refers to Ephesians 6:17 and 1 Thessalonians 5:8.

83. *Works* 3:27–29.

84. *Works* 19:171.

85. *Works* 20:164–165. The danger of divine wrath even extended to converts in good standing who resisted the leadings of God. Wesley spoke, for instance, of God plaguing a woman with "fits" until she agreed to obey the divine call to preach. *Works* 23:426–427.

86. See for instance *Works* 2:217; 3:152; 19:110, 176, 228, 252; 20:93, 218, 281, 352, 432; 21:376–377; 22:253.

87. *Works* 7:250n.

88. Wesley, *Explanatory Notes Upon the Old Testament*, 131.

89. Ibid.

90. *Works* 2:211. For Wesley's commentary on Matt. 11:12–13, see Wesley, *Explanatory Notes Upon the New Testament*, 35. Wesley references the verse in several other sermons: *Works* 2:108; 3:114, 235, 246, 328.

91. *Works* 20:98; 21:110, 127, 166; 22:315, 363, 426; 23: 62, 80.

92. Cohen, *God's Caress*, 81. See also Caldwell, *The Puritan Conversion Narrative*, 9.

93. Taves, *Fits, Trances, and Visions*; Knox, *Enthusiasm*.

94. Wesley commonly uses the term "as dead" when speaking of falling out. See *Works* 19:57, 73, 178, 276, 302, 336; 21:148, 377, 450; 22:254. Ann Taves finds the biblical precedent for falling out in Ezekiel 21:7: "and every heart shall melt, and all hands shall be feeble, and every spirit faint, and all knees shall be weak as water," and Ezekiel 21:14: "I have set the point of the sword against all their gates, that their heart may faint." *Fits, Trances, and Visions*, 108.

95. *Works* 19:317. It is interesting to note that in letters written by some of Wesley's followers, they suggest that men "fell out" more than women, *Works* 21:196, 219–220. However, there is ample evidence that women commonly fell out, so it would be difficult to support a claim about the gendered nature of the experience.

96. *Works* 19:135.

97. *Works* 19:82, 99, 112–113.

98. *Works* 19:100; 19:52.

99. *Works* 19:53.

100. Ann Taves, *Fits, Trances, and Visions,* 57–58. For evidence in Wesley's own work, see especially *Works* 21:235.

101. *Works* 19:317; 21:199, 450; 23:389. Wesley's point is reinforced by the Scottish revivalist John Erskine (1721–1803) in ibid., 19:75–76.

102. *Works* 19:302.

103. *Works* 21:199.

104. *Works* 20:309.

105. *Works* 20:335.

106. *Works* 19:74.

107. *Works* 1:524–525.

108. Holifield, *Health and Medicine in the Methodist Tradition,* 70. Holifield also notes ambivalence within the Wesleyan tradition over suffering. While Wesley attributed the potential for spiritual growth to suffering, he also emphasized the necessity of Christians to work to counter suffering through love. To Wesley, suffering was an enemy to be overcome, not simply a means for spiritual growth. Holifield concludes that, in general, the Wesleyan tradition emphasizes that suffering is not a central purpose to human life, though it can become meaningful when it works to enhance human capacity for love. 63–84.

109. Of course, aside from legitimate bodily exercises, Wesley also believed that such effects could arise from purely natural and therefore illegitimate sources in the individual as a result of an overheated imagination emerging from an imbalance in bodily humors.

110. *Works* 19:317.

111. Gunter, *The Limits of 'Love Divine',* 151. Gunter bases his claims on remarks Wesley made in his journal dated April 3, 1786. Here Wesley denounced a group of people that, though he believed had been justified and sanctified, were being led by Satan to "extravagance" in screaming, falling down, jumping, and so on.

112. Ibid., 154–155.

113. Taves, *Fits, Trances, and Visions,* 57–58.

114. *Works* 21:234.

115. Wesley, *Explanatory Notes Upon the Old Testament,* 131.

116. *Works* 1:426–427.

117. *Works* 2:510.

2. Contesting the Good Fight

1. See for instance, Turley, "John Wesley and War," 96–111; Raymond, "'I Fear God and Honour the King'," 316–328; Hynson, "War, the State, and the Christian Citizen," 204–219; Coppleston, "John Wesley and the American Revolution," 89–105; Holland,

"John Wesley and the American Revolution," 199–213; Gerdes, "John Wesley's Attitude Toward War."

2. Ephesians 6:12. For Wesley's references to this battle as primary, see especially his sermon "Of Evil Angels," which is based on this verse. *Works* 3:16–21. See also 1:280, 317; 2:64, 144, 213, 314; 4:195, 235.

3. *The Letters of the Rev. John Wesley,* hereafter abbreviated *Letters.*

4. John Wesley, "How Far Is it the Duty of a Christian Minister to Preach Politics?" in Maddox, *Political Writings of John Wesley,* 42–43.

5. *Works* 1:189–190.

6. *Works* 1:425.

7. *Works* 3:74; 292–307. See also Marquardt, *John Wesley's Social Ethics,* 103–109.

8. *Works* 3:585.

9. John Wesley, "Thoughts Upon Slavery," in Maddox, *The Political Writings of John Wesley,* 103–105.

10. Hynson, "John Wesley's Theology of the Kingdom."

11. *Works* 1:517–518. On Christians loving their enemies, see ibid., 79.

12. *Works* 2:268–273.

13. See for instance *Works* 19:168, 246, 297, 325, 339, 343–349; 20:10–14, 74–77, 168–169, 242–243, 244, 245, 285–290, 337–338, 414–415. For more on the persecution of the Methodists, see Walsh, "Methodism and the Mob in the Eighteenth Century," in Cuming and Baker, *Popular Belief and Practice,* 213–227.

14. Ibid., 19:297, 339, 347; 20:242–243. For the most concise examples of mob attacks against Wesley's followers, see ibid., 20:285–290.

15. *Works* 19:246, 339, 348; 20:11–12, 74–75.

16. *Works* 19:333.

17. Ibid., 348.

18. *Works* 19:344.

19. *Works* 9:336.

20. Matthew 5:10; *Works* 1:521–528; 19:168.

21. *Works* 1:521–528; Rack, *Reasonable Enthusiast,* 272.

22. *Works* 19:297.

23. Minutes of the 1744 Conference reprinted in *The Church and War.* In 1744, England faced war with France and the attempt by Charles Edward Stuart, "the Pretender," to recapture the British throne for the Stuart family that was lost when his grandfather, King James II, was banished from England in 1688 during the "Glorious Revolution."

24. *Works* 20:32, 352.

25. John Wesley, "The Doctrine of Original Sin," in *The Works of John Wesley,* vol. IX, 237–238.

26. John Wesley, "Thoughts Concerning the Origin of Power" in Maddox, *Political Writings of John Wesley,* 51–52. For a more complete discussion of Wesley's theology as it relates to war, see Gerdes, "John Wesley's Attitude Toward War," 57–59, 146–149. For Gerdes, Wesley's conclusion that war is the result of sin means that God could never be the direct cause of war without being the cause of sin. God's providence can use war to punish and correct humans in the sense that divine foreknowledge perceives human action and then uses it for good, but war does not originate with God.

27. Weber, *Politics in the Order of Salvation,* 452 n. 47.

28. Turley, "John Wesley and War," 107; Gerdes, "John Wesley's Attitude Toward War," 148.

29. On Wesley's efforts during the Seven Years' War, see *Letters* 3:165. On Thomas Webb, see Harvey, "The Wesleyan Movement," 265.

30. John Wesley, "Free Thoughts on the Present State of Public Affairs. In a Letter to a Friend," in Maddox, *Political Writings of John Wesley*, 149. Weber, *Politics in the Order of Salvation*, 112.

31. *Letters* 6:156, 161.

32. *Letters* 6:142.

33. For background on the sermon's publication and title, see *Works* 3:564–565.

34. *Works* 3:566–576. Psalm 79:3. A similar theme is frequently a part of the Bible's apocalyptic narratives in which the waters are turned to blood because of God's judgment upon the people. Isaiah 15:9; Ezekiel 32:6; Revelation 8:8, 11:6, 16:4.

35. *Works* 3:575–576.

36. John Wesley, "A Calm Address to Our American Colonies," in Maddox, *Political Writings of John Wesley*, 178.

37. Weber, *Politics in the Order of Salvation*, 123.

38. For more on Wilkes, see Weber, *Politics in the Order of Salvation*, 90–92.

39. These essays are reprinted in Maddox, *Political Writings of John Wesley*, 44–52, 137–159, 160–173.

40. John Wesley, "Some Observations On Liberty. Occasioned by a Late Tract," in Maddox, *Political Writings of John Wesley*, 53–84.

41. Ibid., 69.

42. Gerdes, "John Wesley's Attitude Toward War," 162.

43. Weber, *Politics in the Order of Salvation*, 261–267.

44. Ibid., 68–69.

45. Wesley, "Some Observations on Liberty," 80. On just war, see chapter 5.

46. *Works* 3:595–608.

47. John Wesley, "A Seasonable Address to the More Serious Part of the Inhabitants of Great Britain, Respecting the Unhappy Contest Between Us and Our American Brethren: With an Occasional Word Interspersed to Those of a Different Complexion. By a Lover of Peace," in Maddox, *Political Writings of John Wesley*, 186–197.

48. Ibid., 190–191.

49. John Wesley, "A Compassionate Address to the Inhabitants of Ireland," in *The Works of John Wesley*, 154.

50. Quoted in Andrews, *The Methodists and Revolutionary America*, 54.

51. See Harvey, "The Wesleyan Movement," 156–158.

52. *J&L* 1:377, 181.

53. See for instance, *J&L* 1:204.

54. *J&L* 3:21.

55. *J&L* 1:164. For a similar concern about war distracting people from thoughts about their eternal state, see *J&L* 1:180, 184.

56. *J&L* 1:184.

57. *J&L* 1:195.

58. *J&L* 1:271–272.

59. Harvey, "The Wesleyan Movement," 181–226, 265.

60. See Freeborn Garrettson's reference to this in *American Methodist Pioneer,* 68, 150 n. 52.

61. Ibid.

62. Harvey, "The Wesleyan Movement," 322–323.

63. Ibid., 323. See also Cox, *Pioneers and Perfectors of our Faith.*

64. MacClenney, *The Life of Rev. James O'Kelly and the Early History of the Christian Church in the South,* 42–43. For other examples of Methodists who joined the military, see Andrews, *The Methodists and Revolutionary America,* 53

65. Even an incomplete list of Methodist preachers either refusing to take an oath of loyalty or actually serve in the military would include Francis Asbury, Benjamin Abbott, David Abbott, Edward Dromgoole, William Duke, Freeborn Garrettson, Philip Gatch, William Glendinning, Joseph Hartley, John Littlejohn, Jesse Lee, Nathan Perigrau, Daniel Ruff, Sater Stephenson, William Watters, William Wren, Robert Wooster, and John Young.

66. Williams, *The Garden of American Methodism,* 50.

67. The committee consisted of William Watters, Philip Gatch, Edward Dromgoole, Daniel Ruff, and William Glendinning. Watters, *A Short Account of the Christian Experience and Ministerial Labours of William Watters,* 57.

68. For population statistics, see *Minutes of the Methodist Conference,* 12. William Lux to Gov. Thomas Johnson, March 3, 1778, quoted in Harvey, "The Wesleyan Movement," 316. The central problem with the oath appears to have been that it included a clause pledging the person's willingness to fight for the colony. Williams, *Garden of American Methodism,* 41.

69. Lee, *Memoir of the Rev. Jesse Lee With Extracts From His Journals,* 25–28.

70. Ibid., 33.

71. Ibid., 32.

72. Andrews, *The Methodists and Revolutionary America,* 47–62; Lyerly, *Methodism and the Southern Mind,* 18–26; Norwood, *The Story of American Methodism,* 82–93.

73. Isaac, *The Transformation of Virginia,* 168–177.

74. Heimert, *Religion and the American Mind.*

75. Ruth Bloch, "Religion and Ideological Change in the American Revolution," in Noll and Harlow, *Religion and American Politics,* 47–63; Bloch, *Visionary Republic.*

76. Bloch, *Visionary Republic,* xiii.

77. Ibid., xiv.

78. For statistics on American loyalism, see Clark, *The Language of Liberty,* 298.

79. Clark, *The Language of Liberty,* 296–381.

80. See, for instance, Bonomi, *Under the Cope of Heaven,* 161–216; Stout, "Religion, Communication, and the Ideological Origins of the American Revolution," 519–541.

81. Gordon Wood, "Religion and the American Revolution," in Stout and Hart, *New Directions in American Religious History,* 173–205.

82. Juergensmeyer, *Terror in the Mind of God,* 161–162. Juergensmeyer postulated that the choice of religions to impose cosmic significance on secular crises occurs when three fundamental conditions appear. First, the temporal struggle "is perceived as a defense of basic identity and dignity." Second, that losing the struggle would be unthinkable to participants. Third, the solution to the struggle appears impossible in human terms and thus reconceived on a spiritual plane.

83. Young, "Follow Peace with all men and Holyness [*sic*] without which men shall not see the Lord," 1–9.

84. For more on this topic, see chapter 3.

85. Young, "Autobiography," 18.

86. Watters, *A Short Account of the Christian Experience and Ministerial Labours of William Watters*, 49–52, 60–61, 70.

87. Gatch, *Sketch of Rev. Philip Gatch*, 97–98.

88. Garrettson, *American Methodist Pioneer*, 50, 88.

89. Ibid., 62.

90. Abbott, *The Experience and Gospel Labours of the Rev. Benjamin Abbott*, 30–31.

91. Ware, *Sketches of the Life and Travels of Rev. Thomas Ware*, 62.

92. Ibid., 25–29, 44–46. Frederick Norwood incorrectly identifies Ware as an example of a Methodist who served in the military. However, Ware became a Methodist after he enlisted. Norwood, *The Story of American Methodism*, 89.

93. Everett, "An Account of the Most Remarkable Occurrences in the Life of Joseph Everett," 561.

94. Turner, *Dramas, Fields and Metaphors*, 45–53.

95. Mathews argues that this happens through the imposition of a language that serves as a mechanism for shared communication and morality with whites, legitimacy in white society through the erection of the public institution of the church, the power to define themselves independent of white power, and finally the preservation of social institutions, especially the class meeting, where communitas reigned. Donald G. Mathews, "Evangelical America—The Methodist Ideology," in Richey, Rowe, and Schmidt, *Perspectives on American Methodism*, 29–30.

96. Schmidt, *Grace Sufficient*, 51, 73–74. Others outside the Methodist tradition have also used the theoretical lens of liminality to interpret evangelical religious experiences similar to those of Methodists. Among those who have sought to refine the discussion of liminality, Susan Juster emphasized differences in the experience of liminality based on gender. Juster found that while conversion and other evangelical rites of passage facilitated the formation of communitas, "the nature of the boundaries to be overcome through liminal reversal was perceived very differently by evangelical men and women." While men pursued the restoration of bonds with their fellow human beings, women sought a more individualized experience of self-transcendence, turning "their energies inward in search of perfect physical subsumption into the body of Christ." Nevertheless, for Juster, the end result of liminality is the same, the eradication of traditional boundaries in order to experience deeper relations with one another and the divine as well as the empowerment of traditionally marginalized figures. Juster, *Disorderly Women*, 19, 72–73.

97. Gatch, *Sketch of Rev. Philip Gatch*, 45–46.

98. *J&L* 1:5. The idea of suffering as confirmation of one's chosen status or a means for deeper communion with God was actually central to Asbury's thinking and dominates his journal writings. See *J&L* 1:5, 103, 104, 120–121, 122, 129, 146, 229, 240, 250, 266, 339, 357, 499, 527.

99. Richey, *Early American Methodism*, 39–41.

100. Mathews, *Slavery and Methodism*, 296–298.

101. Norwood, *The Story of American Methodism*, 186.

102. Ibid., 191–192. Richard Carwardine, "Methodist Ministers and the Second Party System," in Richey, Rowe, and Schmidt, *Perspectives on American Methodism*, 134–147.

103. Carwardine, *Evangelicals and Politics in Antebellum America*, 18.

3. The Power to "Kill and Make Alive"

1. *Minutes of the Methodist Conferences, Annually Held in America*.

2. Wigger, *Taking Heaven By Storm*, 3, 197–199.

3. Cooper, *Beams of Light on Early Methodism in America*, 88–89.

4. Finley, *Autobiography*, 170.

5. Early, "Diary," 34 (1926): 300. Pilmore, *The Journal of Joseph Pilmore*, 61. See also Smith, *Recollections and Reflections of an Old Itinerant*, 126, 128.

6. Catherine Garrettson, Diary.

7. Diane Lobody, "'That Language Might Be Given Me': Women's Experience in Early Methodism," in Richey, Rowe, and Schmidt, *Perspectives on American Methodism: Interpretive Essays*, 144.

8. Methodist Episcopal Church, Hymn CCVII, *The Methodist Pocket Hymn-Book*.

9. Allen, *A Collection of Hymns and Spiritual Songs from Various Authors*, 94–95.

10. Gatch, *Sketch of the Rev. Philip Gatch*, 109–111; Early, "Diary" 37 (1929): 136, 138, 257–258.

11. Smith, *Recollections and Reflections of an Old Itinerant*, 83. On people falling out, see 53, 54, 56, 61, 73, 74, 82.

12. Young, *Autobiography of a Pioneer*, 41–43.

13. Lee, *A Short History of the Methodists in the United States of America*, 128.

14. Newell, *Memoirs of Fanny Newell*, 29–35.

15. Bradley, *A Narrative of the Life and Christian Experience of Mrs. Mary Coy Bradley*, 77.

16. Tucker, *Itinerant Preaching in the Early Days of Methodism*, 31.

17. On conversion and gender in the late eighteenth and early nineteenth centuries, see Brereton, *From Sin to Salvation*, 3–40; Epstein, *The Politics of Domesticity*, 45–65; Juster, *Disorderly Women*, 181–208; Estrelda Alexander, "Conversion and Sanctification in Nineteenth Century African American Wesleyan Women," in Collins and Tyson, *Conversion in the Wesleyan Tradition*, 83–100. Christine Leigh Heyrman has argued that the loss of control inherent in bodily religious experiences was problematic to southern men and so was increasingly discouraged in the nineteenth century. *Southern Cross*, 212–214.

18. Lee, *A History of the Methodists in the United States*, 129.

19. Gatch, *Sketch of the Rev. Philip Gatch*, 86–87, 110.

20. Taves, *Fits, Trances, and Visions*, 76.

21. [Watson], *Methodist Error*, 9, 17.

22. Ibid., 24.

23. Taves, *Fits, Trances, and Visions*, 78, 87–88, 95–98, 103.

24. Capers, *Life of William Capers*, 53.

25. Johnson, *Recollections of the Rev. John Johnson and His Home*, 27.

26. Young, *Autobiography of a Pioneer*, 135–137; Capers, *Life of William Capers*, 53–54.

27. Cartwright, *Autobiography*, 46 (page citations are to the reprint edition).

28. Young, *Autobiography of a Pioneer*, 136.

29. Cartwright, *Autobiography*, 46.

30. Lewis Garrett, *Recollections of the West*, 67.

31. Ibid.

32. Capers, *Life of William Capers*, 53–54.

33. Young, *Autobiography of a Pioneer*, 135–137.

34. See, for instance, Arminius, "Account of the Rise and Progress of the Work of God in the Western Country," 41–43.

35. Griffith, *Born Again Bodies*, 19–47.

36. Hibbard, *Memoirs*, 162–165.

37. Finley, *Autobiography*, 367.

38. Giles, *Pioneer*, 75; Swayze, *Narrative of William Swayze*, 41.

39. Brunson, *A Western Pioneer*, vol. 1, 29, 63–64.

40. See chapter 1.

41. Weber, *The Protestant Ethic and the Spirit of Capitalism*.

42. Miller, *The Works of Jonathan Edwards*, 91–461.

43. Mark Noll, "The Irony of the Enlightenment for Presbyterians in the Early Republic," in Hart, *Reckoning with the Past*, 132.

44. Griffith, *Born Again Bodies*; Lindman and Tarter, *A Centre of Wonders*; Bryan Turner, "The Body in Western Society," in Coakley, *Religion and the Body*.

45. John Wesley, "We Wrestle Not Against Flesh and Blood," *The Methodist Magazine*, February 1797, 1.

46. "A Strange Account," *The Methodist Magazine*, June 1797, 273.

47. Garrettson, *American Methodist Pioneer*, 41–44.

48. Ibid., 44–45.

49. Ibid., 53.

50. Ibid., 291–292.

51. Ibid., 96.

52. Ibid., 113

53. Ibid., 162.

54. Abbott, *The Experience and Gospel Labours of the Rev. Benjamin Abbott*, 11.

55. Delbanco, *The Death of Satan*, 45.

56. Watters, *A Short Account of the Christian Experience and Ministerial Labours of William Watters*, 57.

57. Glendinning, *The Life of William Glendinning*, 16–17.

58. Ibid., 19–20.

59. Ibid., 22.

60. Ibid., 29. On his attempts to commit suicide, see pp. 17, 28.

61. Ibid., 31–32.

62. Ibid., 35.

63. Ibid., 49–50.

64. *J&L* 3:105–106.

65. Glendinning, *The Life of William Glendinning*, 69–70.

66. *J&L* 3:111.

67. Glendinning, *The Life of William Glendinning*, 50, 53.

68. Ibid., 54–55.

69. *J&L* 1:659.

70. Ibid., 3:107. Interpreting this remark is difficult. Asbury could be suggesting that he believed that Satan actually possessed Glendinning. However, this is not likely for two reasons. First, Asbury later stayed in Glendinning's home and on one occasion even embraced Glendinning "in peace." See *J&L* 2:752; Boehm, *Reminiscences, Historical and Biographical,* 337–338. It seems hard to believe that Asbury would have stayed in the home of a man he believed was possessed by Satan. Second, as I will explain below, there is reason to think that saying Satan was "in" someone may have developed into a reference to Satan influencing someone to do something evil rather than literal possession.

71. *J&L* 1:237.

72. Ibid., 422, 447, 407, 339, 250–251.

73. Ibid., 71.

74. Ibid., 314.

75. Ibid., 1:262.

76. Ibid., 319–320.

77. See, for instance, Lee, *A Short History of the Methodists in the United States of America,* 118–119; and Boehm, *Reminiscences, Historical and Biographical,* 337–338.

78. Rush, *The Autobiography of Benjamin Rush,* 220–221.

79. Heyd, *Be Sober and Reasonable,* 165–173.

80. Cartwright, *Autobiography,* 199.

81. Jarena Lee, "The Life and Religious Experiences of Jarena Lee," in Andrews, *Sisters in the Spirit,* 30–31.

82. Benjamin Lakin, "The Journal of Benjamin Lakin," in Sweet, *The Methodists,* 217–218.

83. Ibid., 208–213.

84. Early, "Diary," 36 (1926): 286–287.

85. Smith, *Recollections and Reflections,* 100; Boehm, *Reminiscences, Historical and Biographical,* 107.

86. See, for instance, Cartwright, *Autobiography,* 104, 123; Smith, *Recollections and Reflections,* 100; Finley, *Autobiography,* 224.

87. Finley, *Autobiography,* 174–175.

88. Giles, *Pioneer,* 301.

89. Swayze, *Narrative of William Swayze,* 81–82.

90. Finley, *Autobiography,* 251–252.

91. Hibbard, *Memoirs,* 176–177.

92. Young, *Autobiography of a Pioneer,* 252–253. For similar references, see also Hibbard, *Memoirs,* 204; Cartwright, *Autobiography,* 203; Brunson, *A Western Pioneer,* vol. 1, 87.

93. On evangelical women's battles with Satan, see Juster, *Disorderly Women,* 57–62; Brekus, *Strangers and Pilgrims,* 40–42.

94. Muchembled, *A History of the Devil,* 148–226; Delbanco, *The Death of Satan,* 57–89.

95. Delbanco, *The Death of Satan,* 69.

96. Ibid., 76.

97. Ibid., 150–151.

98. *J&L* 1:754.

4. Beating Their Plowshares into Swords

1. Arminius, "Account of the Rise and Progress of the Work of God in the Western Country," 184–185.

2. Finley, *Autobiography*, 25.

3. Young, *Autobiography of a Pioneer*, 415–417. See also Garrett, *Recollections of the West*, 17; F. B. "Early Scenes in the West," *Western Christian Advocate*, May 23, 1834, 16; Stevens, *History of the Methodist Episcopal Church in the United States*, vol. 2, 358–359; "The Autobiography of the Rev. William Burke," in Finley, *Sketches of Western Methodism*, 44.

4. Tucker is not listed in the minutes as a traveling preacher nor is his death noted in the minutes in accordance with custom in the early nineteenth century. Therefore, it is likely that Tucker was a local preacher.

5. See, for instance, Cherry, *God's New Israel*, 61–110.

6. Richey, *Early American Methodism*, 36–43.

7. Appleby, *Inheriting the Revolution*, 262.

8. Stiles, *The United States Elevated to Glory and Honor*. Excellent treatments on the religious descriptions of the new nation can be found in Cherry, *God's New Israel*.

9. The conference inserted Article XXIII, "Of the Rulers of the United States," into the Articles of Religion composed by Wesley. The article included the following note: "As far as it respects civil affairs, we believe it the duty of Christians, and especially of all Christian Ministers, to be subject to the supreme authority of the country where they may reside, and to use all laudable means to enjoin obedience to the powers that be; and therefore it is expected that all our Preachers and People, who may be under the British or any other Government, will behave themselves as peaceable and orderly subjects." Quoted in Wheeler, *History and Exposition*, 365.

10. Stevens, *History of the Methodist Episcopal Church in the United States*, 348–349.

11. On the image of America as an asylum for the oppressed in notions of American empire, see Hudson, *Nationalism and Religion in America*, 55.

12. Richard Carwardine, "Methodist Ministers in the Second Party System," in Richey and Rowe, *Rethinking Methodist History*, 137.

13. Norwood, *The Story of American Methodism*, 86.

14. Andrews, *The Methodists and Revolutionary America*, 71–72.

15. Andrews, *The Methodists and Revolutionary America*, 190. William Henry Williams makes a similar point about Methodist concern for the establishment of religion. *The Garden of American Methodism*, 170–172.

16. Richard Carwardine, "Methodist Ministers in the Second Party System," in Richey and Rowe, *Rethinking Methodist History*, 137.

17. For Methodist political identification, see Richard Carwardine, "Methodist Ministers in the Second Party System," in Richey and Rowe, *Rethinking Methodist History*; Andrews, *The Methodists and Revolutionary America*, 187–196; Carwardine, *Evangelicals and Politics in Antebellum America*.

18. Richard Carwardine, "Methodist Ministers in the Second Party System," in Richey and Rowe, *Rethinking Methodist History*, 140.

19. Noll, *America's God*, 340.

20. Ibid.

21. In this sense, the War of 1812 functioned for Methodists in ways that Ruth Bloch has argued the Revolution functioned for other evangelicals. Bloch argued that the Revolution raised fundamental questions that required religious interpretation. Ruth Bloch, "Religion and Ideological Change in the American Revolution," in Noll and Harlow, *Religion and American Politics*, 47–64.

22. Silverstone, *Divided Union*, 89–90. See also Horseman, *The Causes of the War of 1812*; Mahan, *The War of 1812*.

23. Silverstone, *Divided Union*, 87–90.

24. Clark, *Life and Times of Rev. Elijah Hedding*, 221–222.

25. Newell, *Life and Observations of Rev. E. F. Newell*, 168–170.

26. *J&L* 2:705. See also 2:708.

27. Giles, *Pioneer*, 90–93.

28. See, for instance, Finley, *Autobiography*, 17–18, 394; Cartwright, *Autobiography*, 25; Young, *Autobiography of a Pioneer*, 244; Lewis, *Recollections of a Superannuate*, 76; Beggs, *Pages From the Early History of the West and North-West*, 9; Stewart, *Highways and Hedges*, 15; Capers, *Life of William Capers*, 12–24.

29. Brunson, *A Western Pioneer*, 30–31. Billy Hibbard expressed similar sentiments in his autobiography, *Memoirs*, 52–53.

30. Dr. Henry Wilkins to William M'Kendree Aug. 11, 1813, reproduced in Paine, *The Life and Times of William M'Kendree*, 240–242. See chapter 2 for William Lux's comment to the governor of Maryland concerning Methodist refusal to sign the loyalty oath.

31. Lewis, *Recollections of a Superannuate*, 293–296.

32. Ibid., 101–102.

33. Ibid., 293–296.

34. Ibid.

35. Ibid., 78–79.

36. Ibid., 99.

37. Cartwright, *Autobiography*, 179.

38. Brunson, *A Western Pioneer*, vol. 1, 113–115, 154–155.

39. Hibbard, *Memoirs*, 327.

40. "Memoir of Charles Black," *Western Christian Advocate*, September 16, 1836, 84.

41. Merritt, *Discourse on the War with England*, 1–16.

42. Ibid., 14.

43. Bartlett, *The New Country*, 39.

44. Smith, *Virgin Land*, 12.

45. Dwight, *Greenfield Hill*, 52.

46. Slotkin, *Regeneration Through Violence*.

47. Ibid., 313–368.

48. Smith, *Virgin Land*, 123.

49. Ibid., 127–128.

50. *Minutes of the Methodist Conferences.*

51. Sweet, *The Methodists,* 60.

52. *Minutes of the Methodist Conferences,* 547. For a similar statement see the *Methodist Magazine,* September 1822, 359.

53. Finley, *Sketches of Western Methodism,* 17.

54. Philip Gatch to Edward Dromgoole, " Dromgoole Letters," in Sweet, *The Methodists,* 153–154.

55. Gatch, "Dromgoole Letters," in Sweet, *The Methodists,* 152, 155. For similar motives, see Roe, *Recollections of Frontier Life,* 68; Hinde, "Short Sketches of Revival of Religion among the Methodists in the Western Country," *Methodist Magazine,* July 1822, 268–269; John Sale to Edward Dromgoole, February 20, 1807, "Dromgoole Letters," in Sweet, *The Methodists,* 160. Congress barred slavery from the Old Northwest in 1787.

56. Frederick Bonner to Edward Dromgoole, July 19, 1807, "Dromgoole Letters," in Sweet, *The Methodists,* 170–171.

57. James Haw to Francis Asbury, quoted in Stevens, *History of the Methodist Episcopal Church,* 362; John Sale to Edward Dromgoole, February 20, 1807, "Dromgoole Letters," in Sweet, *The Methodists,* 160.

58. On the application of biblical metaphors to the nation and their implications for the intersection of nationalism and religion in the early American republic, see Cherry, *God's New Israel;* Hudson, *Nationalism and Religion in America;* Jewett and Lawrence, *Captain America and the Crusade Against Evil;* Tuveson, *Redeemer Nation.* There is a bitter irony in the fact that the same biblical typologies used to condemn the South for the injustice of slavery were also used to justify the removal and destruction of Native peoples during western expansion.

59. Hinde scattered biographical information throughout his writings. On his family history and religious influence, see *Methodist Magazine,* June 1827, 260–263; July 1827, 309–312; August 1827, 369–371; September 1827, 410–414; January 1828, 32–35. See also *J&L* 2:409, 709. Boehm, *Reminiscences, Historical and Biographical,* 405.

60. Hinde first compiled his hymnal in 1810 and published it as *The Pilgrim's Songster* in 1815. It was reprinted in 1828 and again in 1853. *Methodist Magazine,* May 1828, 190.

61. Arminius, "Account of the Rise and Progress of the Work of God in the Western Country" *Methodist Magazine,* May–June 1819, 186–187, 222–223.

62. Ibid., July 1819, 274.

63. Ibid., August 1819, 303. See also September 1819, 350

64. Ibid., August 1819, 306–308; September 1819, 350–353.

65. Ibid., October 1819, 394.

66. Ibid., 394–395.

67. Ibid., 395.

68. Ibid.

69. Ibid., 396.

70. Ibid., October–November 1819, 395–396, 434–439.

71. Hinde, "Short Sketches of Revivals on Religion," 223.

72. *Methodist Magazine,* March 1828, 110–113.

73. "Western Life," *Western Christian Advocate,* May 9, 1834, 5.

74. Barclay, *History of Methodist Missions*, vol. 1, 205–212.

75. Ibid.

76. "Address of the Missionary and Bible Society, of the Methodist Episcopal Church," *Methodist Magazine*, August 1819, 303. The connection between Isaiah 35 and Indian conversion was frequent. See also "Address to the Editors," *Methodist Magazine*, January 1823, 5.

77. See, for instance, "Third Anniversary of the Missionary Society of the Methodist Episcopal Church," *Methodist Magazine*, August 1822, 316–317, 320; "Fifth Annual Report of the Missionary Society of the Methodist Episcopal Church," *Methodist Magazine*, June 1824, 232.

78. "Sixth Anniversary of the Missionary Society of the Methodist Episcopal Church," *Methodist Magazine*, July 1825, 278.

79. "Third Anniversary of the Missionary Society of the Methodist Episcopal Church," *Methodist Magazine*, August 1822, 317.

80. For brief histories of the formation of these missions, see Barclay, *History of Methodist Missions*, vol. 2, 112–151.

81. "Stanzas on Hearing the Success of the Wyandot Mission," *Methodist Magazine*, September 1825, 367.

82. Vaughan, *New England Frontier*, 238, 260–280.

83. Hutchinson, *Errand to the World*, 15–42.

84. Ibid., 65.

85. Coke, *An Address to the Pious and Benevolent*.

86. Among such offhand comments, see Coke's reference to the civilization of the Caribbean natives, *An Address to the Benevolent Subscribers*, 15–16. See also Coke's comments on the bodily presentation of Antiguans. Vickers, *The Journals of Dr. Thomas Coke*, 75–76. Civilizing discourse might have appeared problematic in Coke's reports on West Indian missions given the successful efforts that were made to evangelize slaves in the Caribbean. Slave owners may have perceived any goal to civilize even the nonslave community as dangerous. Coke makes the West Indian slave owners' suspicions of Christianity clear in his narratives of their persecution of those who preached to slaves. Vickers, *The Journals of Dr. Thomas Coke*, 109–110, 180.

87. Vickers, *Thomas Coke: Apostle of Methodism*, 290–291. Vickers concludes that Coke must have had a hand in writing the proposal, though it is interesting if he did since the word "civilization" does not appear elsewhere in his writing.

88. Vickers, *The Journals of Dr. Thomas Coke*, 101.

89. See for instance Coke's rationalization of the fire that destroyed Cokesbury College as evidence that Methodists should restrict their activity to "the salvation of souls." *Journals of Dr. Thomas Coke*, 229–230.

90. Vickers, *The Journals of Dr. Thomas Coke*, 128–129.

91. "Address of the Missionary and Bible Society, of the Methodist Episcopal Church," *Methodist Magazine*, August 1819, 301.

92. [No title], *Methodist Magazine*, June 1820, 225.

93. Quoted in Prucha, *The Great Father*, 151.

94. William Capers, "Extract from the Journal of William Capers," *Methodist Magazine*, July 1822, 272.

95. *Methodist Magazine*, August 1822, 318–319.

96. Berkhofer, *Salvation and the Savage*, 6–7.

97. McLoughlin, *Cherokees and Missionaries*, 171–172.

98. Bowden, *American Indians and Christian Missions*, 169.

99. *Methodist Magazine*, December 1827, 482.

100. Finley, *Life Among the Indians*, 445–446.

101. On the history of the Wyandot Mission, see Barclay, *History of Methodist Missions*, vol. 1, 203–205, and vol. 2, 117–126.

102. Joshua Soule, "Letter from Bishop Soule, Giving Account of a Visit to the Indian Mission, at Upper Sandusky," *Methodist Magazine*, January 1825, 32–38.

103. John L. Leib, "Extract from Judge Leib's Report to the Department of War," *Methodist Magazine*, August 1827, 414–415.

104. Lewis, *Recollections of a Superannuate*, 242–244.

105. See, for instance, Pearce, *Savagism and Civilization*. Among the first academic studies of civilization in American history is Beard and Beard, *The American Spirit*. On the role of civilization and American civil religion, see Cherry, *God's New Israel*, 14.

106. The family history and style of writing indicates that the author is undoubtedly the Methodist preacher James B. Finley. Why Finley masked his identity is not clear. Finley used his own name in letters and missionary reports submitted to the *Methodist Magazine* and *Western Christian Advocate* for years prior to this series and also applied his name to histories of the West that he published later in the 1830s and throughout the 1840s and 1850s.

107. F. B., "Early Scenes in the West," *Western Christian Advocate*, May 23, 1834, 30.

108. Ibid., June 13, 20, 27; July 4, 1834.

109. *J&L* 2:743.

110. Finley, *Autobiography*, 43, 66–68, 118, 143.

111. Ibid., 125–126.

112. Ibid., 36–40.

113. Ibid., 124.

114. "Anniversary of the Female Missionary Society of New-York," *Methodist Magazine*, September 1826, 348–354.

115. Stephen Olin, "An Address," *Methodist Magazine*, August 1824, 30.

116. McLoughlin, *Cherokees and Missionaries*, 179.

117. Barclay, *The History of American Missions*, vol. 2, 128–129.

118. *Christian Advocate*, October 29, 1830, 34.

119. On opposition to removal in the *Christian Advocate*, see McLoughlin, *Cherokees and Missionaries*, 292.

120. Quoted in McLoughlin, *Cherokees and Missionaries*, 294.

121. Ibid., 299.

122. On the decline of the Methodist mission to the Cherokee, see Barclay, *History of Methodist Missions*, vol. 2, 133.

123. Finley, *Life Among the Indians*, 548.

124. On the cultural value of violence in nineteenth-century America, see Bellesiles, *Lethal Imagination*; Wyatt-Brown, *Honor and Violence in the Old South*; Brown, *No Duty to Retreat*; Bruce, *Violence and Culture in the Antebellum South*; Courtwright, *Violent Land*; Gorn, "'Gouge and Bite, Pull Hair and Scratch,'" 20.

5. Methodist Respectability and the Decline of the
Good Fight for Salvation

1. Tevis, *Sixty Years in a School-Room*, 250.

2. Ibid., 247–253.

3. "Amorous, and Extravagant Expressions, and Action," *Christian Advocate and Journal*, November 8, 1833, 42. "Reprinted, Revised, and Enlarged," *Christian Advocate and Journal*, December 13, 1833, 61. On opposition to bodily experiences in the South, see Heyrman, *Southern Cross*, 217. The loss of control often associated with bodily religious experiences was particularly problematic for nineteenth-century conceptions of manhood. Rotundo, *American Manhood*; Bederman, *Manliness and Civilization*.

4. Cott, *The Bonds of Womanhood*; Epstein, *The Politics of Domesticity*; Matthews, *"Just a Housewife"*; Romero, *Domesticity and Its Critics*; Ryan, *The Empire of the Mother*; Sklar, *Catherine Beecher*.

5. Schneider, *The Way of the Cross Leads Home*.

6. "Position and Influence of Women," *Ladies' Repository and Gatherings of the West*, January 1850, 20.

7. Bushman, *The Refinement of America*, xvii.

8. Ibid., 321.

9. Elliott, *The Life of the Rev. Robert R. Roberts*, 405–406.

10. "Importance of Intelligence in the Christian Ministry," *Christian Advocate and Journal*, January 24, 1836, 176.

11. See, for instance, *J&L* 2:75; 3:171; Vickers, *The Journals of Dr. Thomas Coke*, 229–230.

12. Duvall, *The Methodist Episcopal Church and Education*, 75–83.

13. *General Conference Journals*, vol. I, 186, quoted in Duvall, *The Methodist Episcopal Church and Education*, 63.

14. Ibid., 66.

15. Bradley J. Longfield, "'Denominational' Colleges in Antebellum America? A Case Study of Presbyterians and Methodists in the South," in Mullin and Richey, *Reimagining Denominationalism*, 300.

16. The periodical in question was the *Methodist Magazine* published from 1788–1790.

17. "Address," *Methodist Magazine*, January 1818, 1.

18. "Prospectus," *The Methodist Magazine and Quarterly Review*, January 1830, 2.

19. "Prospectus," *The Methodist Quarterly Review*, January 1841, 6.

20. "Prospectus," *The Quarterly Review of the Methodist Episcopal Church, South*, January 1847, 5–8, 10.

21. Noll, *America's God*, 332–336. For more on the intellectual development of Methodism in the nineteenth century, see Farrelly, "'God Is the Author of Both,'" 659–687.

22. Stevenson, *Biographical Sketch of the Rev. Valentine Cook*, 9–11.

23. Ibid., 15.

24. *Ladie's Repository*, April 1850, 122; ibid., December 1850, 407.

25. "Baths and Cleanliness," *Christian Advocate and Journal*, March 1, 1848, 36.

26. See for instance, "Address to Mothers," *Western Christian Advocate*, February

19, 1841, 176; "Value of Character to a Young Man," *Western Christian Advocate,* May 8, 1840, 12.

27. "Husband and Wife," *Western Christian Advocate,* May 8, 1840, 12. The April 7, 1843, edition of the *Western Christian Advocate* exemplifies the way Western Methodists also defined male relationships in terms of mutual affection. See "Beautiful Exemplification of Paternal, Filial, and Fraternal Affection," 204.

28. "Golden Rules, To Render Young Tradesmen Respectable, Prosperous and Wealthy," *Western Christian Advocate,* May 16, 1834, 12; "Cleanliness in Church," *Western Christian Advocate,* August 1, 1834, 56.

29. Wigger, *Taking Heaven By Storm,* 181.

30. Cartwright, *Autobiography,* 61–62.

31. Ibid., 265.

32. Ibid., 144.

33. Quinn, *Sketches of the Life and Labors of James Quinn,* 183.

34. Giles, *Pioneer,* 174.

35. Ibid., 33.

36. Stevens, *Sketches and Incidents,* vol. 2, 80–81.

37. Ibid., 161–162.

38. Waugh, *Autobiography of Lorenzo Waugh,* 53.

39. Taylor, *Story of My Life,* 36.

40. "The Seven Protracted Meetings," *Christian Advocate and Journal,* January 9, 1835, 78.

41. "Ministerial Inefficiency," *Christian Advocate and Journal,* September 21, 1865, 300.

42. Rubenstein, *The Spiritual Self in Everyday Life,* 182.

43. "God Is Love," *Christian Advocate and Journal,* February 9, 1848, 24.

44. Thomas O. Summers, "Divine Benevolence," *Ladies' Repository and Gatherings of the West,* July 1841, 203–204.

45. Ibid., 204.

46. John T. Brame, "The Love of God," *Ladies' Repository and Gatherings of the West,* November 1841, 346.

47. S. J. Howe, "Trust in God," *Christian Advocate and Journal,* February 23, 1848.

48. W. F. Lowrie, "Deity and Nature," *Ladies' Repository and Gatherings of the West,* September 1841, 268–269. The article appeared from September 1841 to April 1842.

49. "God a Defense," *Ladies' Repository and Gatherings of the West,* March 1841, 84.

50. I. N. K., "The Flowers of Spring," *Christian Advocate and Journal,* May 16, 1850, 76.

51. M. H. Wetherbee, "God's Love," *Ladies' Repository and Gatherings of the West,* December 1843, 363.

52. Miss M. B. Baker, "Deity," *Ladies' Repository and Gatherings of the West,* January 1843, 30.

53. Prothero, *American Jesus,* 53.

54. Ibid., 43–86; See also Fox, *Jesus in America,* 201–306.

55. William J. Thompson, "A Marriage in Heaven," *Ladies' Repository and Gatherings of the West,* November 1850, 370.

56. Caldwell, *Walking with God.*

57. Hibbard, *Memoirs,* 208.

58. John Randon, "Letter of a Dying Soldier," *Christian Advocate and Journal,* September 23, 1826, 12.

59. Haven, *Autobiography of Erastus O. Haven,* 38.

60. "An Account of the Conversion and Happy Death of Mr. J," *Christian Advocate and Journal,* September 23, 1846, 37.

61. Smith, *An Autobiography,* 79.

62. Stokes, *Footprints in My Own Life,* 25.

63. Merritt, *The Christian's Manual,* 31–61.

64. Palmer, *Faith and Its Effects,* 27th ed., 24, 260.

65. Ibid., 79, 84.

66. Ibid., 310.

67. Ibid., 344.

68. White, *The Beauty of Holiness,* 136.

69. Raser, *Phoebe Palmer: Her Life and Thought,* 259.

70. Palmer, *The Way of Holiness,* 30.

71. Palmer, *Faith and Its Effects,* 25.

72. Ibid., 29–30.

73. Ibid., 162.

74. Buck, *The History of American Methodism,* vol. 2, 611.

75. Palmer, *The Way of Holiness,* 79, 102.

76. "What Is it to Be Holy?" *Ladies' Repository and Gatherings of the West,* March 1844, 89–90.

77. Morehouse, *Autobiography of A. C. Morehouse,* 11–13.

78. For the transformations in Methodist theology in the nineteenth century, see Chiles, *Theological Transition in American Methodism;* Langford, *Practical Divinity.*

79. See chapter 1.

80. Whedon, *The Freedom of the Will,* 15.

81. Ibid., 23.

82. Ibid., 39, 367, 423.

83. Ibid., 438.

84. Daniel Whedon, "The Arminian View of Fall and Redemption," in Whedon and Whedon, *Essays, Reviews, and Discourses,* 43.

85. Ibid., 86.

86. F., "Love," *Christian Advocate and Journal,* May 30, 1850, 85. This contrasts in interesting ways with Philip Greven's claims about earlier evangelical parents who sought to break the child's will, often through physical punishment, in order to lead them to Christian faith. *The Protestant Temperament.*

87. Corrigan, *Business of the Heart,* 163–185.

88. Noll, *The Civil War as a Theological Crisis,* 18–19.

89. Stout, *Upon the Altar of a Nation,* 38–39.

90. Robert Allyn, "Love of Country," *Christian Advocate and Journal,* May 30, 1861, 170.

91. "Editorial Notes," *Christian Advocate and Journal,* April 18, 1861, 125.

92. Sledd, *A Sermon Delivered in the Market Street M.E. Church,* 6–7.

93. H. B. Collins, "The Conflict," *Christian Advocate and Journal,* May 9, 1861, 2.

94. J. M. Howe, "Christ Is King, And Not Cotton!" *Christian Advocate and Journal,* July 25, 1861, 234.

95. Aquinas, *Summa Theologica,* 2–2.40.

96. For the development of the just war tradition in Christianity, see Cahill, *Love Your Enemies;* Russell, *The Just War in the Middle Ages;* Ramsey, *The Just War.* For the best treatment of the application of just war theory in the Civil War, see Stout, *On the Altar of the Nation.*

97. "The War," *Christian Advocate and Journal,* April 25, 1861, 4.

98. "War and Its Duties," *Christian Advocate and Journal,* May 9, 1861, 5.

99. Soldiers Tract Association, "The Camp and the Cross," n.d., 8.

100. Soldiers Tract Association, "An Address to the Soldiers of the Southern Armies," n.d., 15.

101. Pierce, *The Word of God a Nation's Life,* 17–18.

102. "War and Its Duties," *Christian Advocate and Journal,* May 9, 1861, 5.

103. W. Hunter, "The Morals of our Soldiers," *Christian Advocate and Journal,* August 22, 1861, 265. See also Anonymous, "Duty of Christians in the Present Emergency," *Christian Advocate and Journal,* May 30, 1861, 172; "A Plea for the Sabbath in War," *Christian Advocate and Journal,* August 29, 1861, 274.

6. The Christian's Warfare and Social Violence

1. Luhrmann, "The Ugly Goddess," 115.

2. Ibid., 141.

3. Raboteau, *Slave Religion,* 312.

4. On the predominance of nurturing language in women's writings, see Diane Lobody, "'That Language Might Be Given Me': Women's Experience in Early Methodism," in Richey, Rowe, and Schmidt, *Perspectives on American Methodism: Interpretive Essays,* 140–144; Brekus, *Strangers and Pilgrims,* 211–212.

5. Brekus, *Strangers and Pilgrims,* 215.

6. Luhrmann, "The Ugly Goddess," 133–141.

7. Bloch, *From Prey Into Hunter,* 4.

8. Ibid., 5.

9. Turner, *Dramas, Fields and Metaphors,* especially pp. 45–53.

10. Donald G. Mathews argues that this happens through the imposition of a language that served as a mechanism for shared communication and morality with whites, legitimacy in white society through the erection of the public institution of the church, the power to define themselves independent of white power, and finally the preservation of social institutions, especially the class meeting, where communitas reigned. Donald G. Mathews, "Evangelical America—The Methodist Ideology," in Richey, Rowe, and Schmidt, *Perspectives on American Methodism,* 29–30. Schmidt, *Grace Sufficient,* 51, 73–74. Others outside the Methodist tradition have also used the theoretical lens of liminality to interpret evangelical religious experiences similar to those of Methodists. Among those who have sought to refine the discussion of liminality, Susan Juster has emphasized differences in the experience of liminality based on gender. Juster found that while conversion and other evangelical rites of passage facilitated the formation of communitas, "the nature of the boundaries to be over-

come through liminal reversal was perceived very differently by evangelical men and women." While men pursued the restoration of bonds with their fellow human beings, women sought a more individualized experience of self-transcendence, turning "their energies inward in search of perfect physical subsumption into the body of Christ." Nevertheless, for Juster the end result of liminality is the same, the eradication of traditional boundaries in order to experience deeper relations with one another and the divine as well as the empowerment of traditionally marginalized figures. Juster, *Disorderly Women*, 19, 72–73.

11. Finley, *Autobiography*, 174–175.

12. Garrettson, *American Methodist Pioneer*, 198.

13. Swayze, *Narrative of William Swayze*, 103.

14. For similar conclusions about evangelical conversions, see Rubin, *Religious Melancholia and Protestant Experience in America*.

15. Turner, *Dramas, Fields and Metaphors*, 69.

16. Jones, *Blood That Cries Out From the Earth*, 142.

17. See for instance, Gorringe, *God's Just Vengeance*; Jensen, "Religious Cosmologies and Homicide Rates among Nations," 1–14; Bromley and Melton, *Cults, Religion, and Violence*; Hall, Schuyler, and Trinh, *Apocalypse Observed*; Juergensmeyer, *Terror in the Mind of God*; Kimball, *When Religion Becomes Evil*.

18. Bloch, *From Prey Into Hunter*, 4–6, 60–61.

19. See especially *Violence and the Sacred* and *I See Satan Fall Like Lightning*. For a general overview of Girard's work, see Williams, *The Girard Reader*.

20. This number is reported in Jones, *Blood That Cries Out From the Earth*, 91, and Unger, "American Rapture," 204.

21. LaHaye and Jenkins, *Left Behind*, 419–421.

22. LaHaye and Jenkins, *Glorious Appearing*, 226.

23. Ibid., 228.

24. LaHaye and Jenkins, *The Kingdom Come*, xxii–xxv.

25. In this same speech, President Bush asserted that world events made clear that "evil is real, and it must be opposed." Bush went on to promise that "in this great conflict . . . we will see freedom's victory." Available at http://www.whitehouse.gov/news/releases/2002/01/20020129-11.html (accessed September 26, 2008).

26. Frykholm, *Rapture Culture*, 8.

27. Juergensmeyer, *Terror in the Mind of God*, 161–163.

28. Ibid., 238–243.

29. Ibid.

Bibliography

Primary Sources

PERIODICAL SOURCES

Christian Advocate and Journal, 1833–1865 (New York)
Ladies' Repository and Gatherings of the West, 1841–1867 (Cincinnati)
Methodist Magazine, 1797–1798 (Philadelphia)
Methodist Magazine, 1818–1828 (New York)
Methodist Magazine and Quarterly Review, 1830–1840 (New York)
Methodist Quarterly Review, 1841–1884 (New York)
Methodist Quarterly Review, 1847–1930 (Nashville)
Western Christian Advocate, 1834–1883 (Cincinnati)

BOOKS, MANUSCRIPTS, MINUTES

Abbott, Benjamin. *The Experience and Gospel Labours of Benjamin Abbott.* Philadelphia: Ezekiel Cooper, 1801.

Allen, Richard. *A Collection of Spiritual Songs and Hymns Selected From Various Authors.* Philadelphia: John Ormrod, 1801.

———. *The Life Experience and Gospel Labors of the Rt. Rev. Richard Allen.* New York: Abingdon Press, 1960.

Andrews, William L., ed. *Sisters of the Spirit: Three Black Women's Autobiographies of the Nineteenth Century.* Bloomington: Indiana University Press, 1986.

Arminius, Theophilus [Thomas S. Hinde]. "Account of the Rise and Progress of the Work of God in the Western Country." *Methodist Magazine,* May–November 1819.

Asbury, Francis. *The Journal and Letters of Francis Asbury In Three Volumes.* Edited by Elmer T. Clark. Nashville: Abingdon Press, 1958.

Beggs, S. R. *Pages From the Early History of the West and North-West: Embracing Reminiscences and Incidents of Settlement and Growth, and Sketches of the Material and Religious Progress of the States of Ohio, Indiana, Illinois, and Missouri, with Especial Reference to the History of Methodism.* Cincinnati: Methodist Book Concern, 1868.

Boehm, Henry. *Reminiscences, Historical and Biographical of Sixty-Four Years in the Ministry.* New York: Carlton & Porter, 1866.

Boyd, Robert. *Personal Memoirs: Together With a Discussion Upon the Hardships and Sufferings of Itinerant Life.* Cincinnati: Methodist Book Concern, 1860.

Bradley, Mary Coy. *A Narrative of the Life and Christian Experience of Mrs. Mary Coy Bradley.* Boston: Strong and Brodhead, 1849.

Brooks, John. *Life and Times of Rev. John Brooks.* Nashville: Nashville Christian Advocate, 1848.

Brown, George. *The Lady Preacher: Or, The Life and Labors of Mrs. Hannah Reeves, Late the Wife of the Rev. W. M. Reeves, D.D., of the Methodist Church.* Philadelphia: Daughaday & Becker, 1870. Reprint, New York: Garland, 1987.

Brunson, Alfred. *A Western Pioneer: Or, Incidents of the Life and Times of Rev. Alfred Brunson.* Cincinnati: Hitchcock and Walden, 1872.

Caldwell, Nancy. *Walking With God: Leaves From the Journal of Mrs. Nancy Caldwell.* Edited by Rev. James O. Thompson. Keyser, W.V., 1886.

Capers, William. *Life of William Capers, D.D.* Nashville: Southern Methodist Publishing House, 1859.

Cartwright, Peter. *Autobiography of Peter Cartwright. The Backwoods Preacher.* New York: Hunt & Eaton, 1856.

Church, Thomas. *A Reply to the Farther Enquiry into the Meaning of the Demoniacks in the New Testament.* London: J. Roberts, 1738.

Clark, D. W. *Life and Times of Rev. Elijah Hedding, D.D., Late Senior Bishop of the Methodist Episcopal Church.* New York: Carlton and Phillips, 1855.

———, ed. *The Methodist Episcopal Pulpit: A Collection of Original Sermons by Living Ministers of the M.E. Church.* New York: Lane & Tippett, 1848.

Clark, Laban. *Laban Clark: Circuit Rider for the Methodist Episcopal Church,* trans. E. Farley Sharp. Rutland, Vt.: Academy Books, 1987.

Coke, Thomas. *An Address to the Benevolent Subscribers for the Support of the Missions Carried on by Voluntary Contributions in the British Isles, in the West Indies, for the Benefit of the Negroes and Caribs.* London, 1789.

———. *An Address to the Pious and Benevolent Proposing an Annual Subscription for the Support of Missionaries in the Highlands and Adjacent Islands of Scotland, the Isles of Jersey, Guernsey, and Newfoundland, the West Indies, and the Provinces of Nova Scotia and Quebec.* London, 1786.

Cole, George. *Heroines of Methodism; or, Pen and Ink Sketches of the Mothers and Daughters of the Church.* New York: Carlton & Porter, 1857.

Cooper, Ezekiel. *Beams of Light on Early Methodism in America.* Edited by George Phoebus. New York: Phillips and Hunt, 1887.

Dawson, William. *Memoirs of the Rev. David Stoner: Containing Copious Extracts from His Diary and Epistolary Correspondence.* New York: J. Emory and B. Waugh, 1832.

Dwight, Timothy. *Greenfield Hill: A Poem in Seven Parts.* New York: Childs and Swain, 1794.

Early, John. "Diary of John Early, Bishop of the Methodist Episcopal Church, South." *Virginia Magazine of History and Biography,* 33–40 (1925–1932): 166–174, 283–287; 130–137, 237–251, 299–312; 7–12, 280–286; 175–179, 239–248, 328–332; 130–138, 256–260; 251–258; 41–45, 146–151; 70–74, 147–154.

Elliott, Charles. *The Life of the Rev. Robert R. Roberts.* New York: Lane & Tippett, 1846.

Erwin, James. *Memoirs of Early Circuit Life.* Toledo, Ohio: Spear, Johnson, & Co., 1884.

Everett, Joseph. "An Account of the Most Remarkable Occurrences in the Life of Joseph Everett." *Arminian Magazine* 2 (1790): 558–604.

Finley, James B. *Autobiography of Rev. James B. Finley; Or, Pioneer Life in the West.* Edited by W. P. Strickland. Cincinnati: Methodist Book Concern, 1854.

———. *Life Among the Indians, Or, Personal Reminiscences and Historical Incidents Illustrative of Indian Life and Character.* Edited by D. W. Clark. Cincinnati: Curts & Jennings, 1857.

———, ed. *Sketches of Western Methodism: Biographical, Historical, and Miscellaneous Illustrative of Pioneer Life.* Cincinnati: Methodist Book Concern, 1854.

Gannaway, Robertson. "Autobiography of Rev. Robertson Gannaway." *Virginia Magazine of History and Biography* 37 (1929): 316–322; 38 (1930): 137–144.

Garrett, Lewis. *Recollections of the West.* Nashville: Western Methodist Office, 1834.

Garrettson, Catherine. Diary, Garrettson Family Papers, Drew University Methodist Collection, Madison, New Jersey, December 1787.

Garrettson, Freeborn. *American Methodist Pioneer: The Life and Journals of Freeborn Garrettson, 1752–1827.* Edited by Robert Drew Simpson. Rutland, Vt.: Academy Books, 1984.

Gatch, Philip. *Sketch of the Rev. Philip Gatch.* Edited by John McLean. Cincinnati: Swarmstedt & Poe, 1854.

Giles, Charles. *Pioneer: A Narrative of the Nativity, Experience, Travels, and Ministerial Labours of Rev. Charles Giles.* New York: G. Lane & P. P. Stanford, 1844.

Glendinning, William. *The Life of William Glendinning, Preacher of the Gospel Written By Himself.* Philadelphia: W. W. Woodward, 1795.

Haven, Erastus O. *Autobiography of Erastus O. Haven, D.D., LL.D., One of the Bishops of the Methodist Episcopal Church.* New York: Phillips & Hunt, 1883.

Hibbard, Billy. *The Life and Travels of B. Hibbard, Minister of the Gospel.* New York: J. C. Totten, 1825.

Hinde, Thomas. "Short Sketches of Revivals on Religion Among the Methodists in the Western Country, and Reflections on the Western Country Generally." *Methodist Magazine,* August 1822–May 1827.

Hodges, Graham Russell, ed. *Black Itinerants of the Gospel: The Narratives of John Jea and George White.* New York: Palgrave, 2002.

Ingraham, Sarah R., comp. *Walks of Usefulness, or Reminiscences of Mrs. Margaret Prior*. New York: American Female Moral Reform Society, 1843. Reprint, New York: Garland Publishing, 1987.

Jeffrey, David Lyle, ed. *A Burning and Shining Light: English Spirituality in the Age of Wesley*. Grand Rapids, Mich.: Eerdmans, 1987.

Jenkins, James. *Experience, Labours, and Sufferings of the Rev. James Jenkins of the South Carolina Conference*. N.p.: printed for the author, 1842. Reprint, Columbia, S.C.: State Commercial Printing Co., 1958.

Johnson, Susannah. *Recollections of the Rev. John Johnson and His Home: An Autobiography*. Nashville: Southern Methodist Publishing House, 1869.

LaHaye, Tim, and Jerry B. Jenkins. *Glorious Appearing*. Carol Stream, Ill.: Tyndale House, 2004.

———. *The Kingdom Come*. Carol Stream, Ill.: Tyndale House, 2007.

———. *Left Behind: A Novel of the Earth's Last Days*. Carol Stream, Ill.: Tyndale House, 1995.

Lavington, George. *The Enthusiasm of Methodists and Papists Compared. In Three Parts*, vol. 1–2. London: J. and P. Knapton, 1749.

Lee, Jesse. *Memoir of the Rev. Jesse Lee With Extracts from His Journals*. Edited by Minton Thrift. New York: Arno Press, 1969.

———. *A Short History of the Methodists in the United States of America*. Baltimore: Magill and Clime, 1810.

Lewis, David. *Recollections of a Superannuate: Or, Sketches of Life, Labor, and Experience in the Methodist Itinerancy*. Cincinnati: Methodist Book Concern, 1857.

Maddox, Graham, ed. *Political Writings of John Wesley*. Bristol: Thoemmes Press, 1998.

Maynard, Sampson. *The Experience of Samson Maynard, Local Preacher of the Methodist Episcopal Church (Written By Himself.) To Which is Prefixed an Allegorical Address to the Christian World, or, a Thimble Full of Truth to Blow Up the World of Error*. New York: printed for the author, 1828.

Merritt, Timothy. *The Christian's Manual: A Treatise on Christian Perfection*. Cincinnati: Swormstedt & Poe, 1854.

———. *Discourse on the War with England; Delivered in Hallowell on Public Fast, April 7, 1814*. Hallowell: N. Cheever, 1814.

Methodist Church (US), General Conference. *The Church and War*. Silver Bay, N.Y.: Epworth Fund, 1944.

Methodist Episcopal Church, *Collection of Hymns for the Use of the Methodist Episcopal Church*. New York: Nathan Bangs and T. Mason, 1821.

———. *The Methodist Pocket Hymn-Book, Revised and Improved: Designed as a Constant Companion for the Pious of all Denominations. Collected From Various Authors, the Twenty-Eighth Edition*. Philadelphia: Solomon W. Conrad, 1803.

———. *Minutes of the Methodist Conference, Annually Held in America; From 1773–1813*. New York: Daniel Hitt and Thomas Ware, 1813.

Miller, Perry, ed. *The Works of Jonathan Edwards*, vol. 2, *Treatise on Religious Affections*. New Haven, Conn.: Yale University Press, 1959.

Morehouse, A. C. *Autobiography of A.C. Morehouse: An Itinerant Minister of the New York and New York East Conference of the Methodist Episcopal Church*. New York: Tibbals Book Co., 1895.

Morrell, Thomas. *The Journals of the Rev. Thomas Morrell.* Madison, N.J.: Historical Society, Northern New Jersey Conference, MEC, 1984.

Mudge, Enoch. *The American Camp-Meeting Hymn Book. Containing a Variety of Original Hymns, Suitable to be Used at Camp-Meetings; and at Other Times in Private and Social Devotions.* Boston: Joseph Burdakin, 1818.

Newell, Ebenezer F. *Life and Observation of Rev. E.F. Newell, Who Has Been More Than Forty Years an Itinerant Minister in the Methodist Episcopal Church, New England Conference.* Worcester, Mass.: C. W. Ainsworth, 1847.

Newell, Fanny. *Memoirs of Fanny Newell; Written By Herself, and Published by the Desire and Request of Numerous Friends.* Springfield and New York: O. Scott and E. F. Newell, 1832.

Osborn, Elbert. *Passages in the Life and Ministry of Elbert Osborn, An Itinerant Minister of the Methodist Episcopal Church.* New York: Joseph Longking, 1853.

Paddock, Zachariah. *Memoir of Rev. Benjamin Paddock, with Brief Notes of Early Ministerial Associates.* New York: Nelson and Phillips, 1875.

Paine, Robert. *The Life and Times of William M'Kendree: Bishop of the Methodist Episcopal Church.* Nashville: Pub. House of the Methodist Episcopal Church, South, 1893.

Palmer, Phoebe. *Faith and Its Effects.* New York: Palmer and Hughes, 1867. Reprint, New York: Garland 1985.

———. *The Way of Holiness, with Notes By The Way.* New York: Palmer & Hughes, 1867. Reprint, New York: Garland, 1985.

Pierce, George Foster. *The Word of God a Nation's Life.* Augusta, Ga.: Office of the Constitutionalist, 1862.

Pilmore, Joseph. *The Journal of Joseph Pilmore, Methodist Itinerant for the Years August 1, 1769 to January 2, 1774.* Edited by Frederick E. Maser and Howard T. Maag. Philadelphia: Message Publishing Co., 1969.

Porter, James. *The True Evangelist: Or, An Itinerant Ministry, Particularly That of The Methodist Episcopal Church, Explained, Guarded, and Defended.* Boston: Waite, Pierce, and Company, 1847.

Quinn, James. *Sketches of the Life of James Quinn.* Edited by John F. Wright. Cincinnati: Methodist Book Concern, 1851.

Rankin, Thomas. "The Diary of Reverend Thomas Rankin, One of the Helpers of John Wesley." Garrett Evangelical Theological Seminary Library, Evanston, Ill., n.d.

Richards, Lucy. *Memoirs of the Late Miss Lucy Richards, of Parris, Oneida County, N.Y.* New York: Lane & Sanford, 1842.

Roe, Elizabeth A. *Recollections of Frontier Life by Mrs. Elizabeth A. Roe, Wife of the Late Dr. John Roe. Of Rock River Memory.* Rockford, Ill.: Gazette Publishing House, 1885. Reprint, New York: Arno Press, 1980.

Rogers, Hester Ann. *An Account of the Experience of Hester Ann Rogers; And Her Funeral Sermon, by Rev. Dr. Coke. To Which Are Added Her Spiritual Letters.* New York: Carlton & Phillips, 1853.

Rush, Benjamin. *The Autobiography of Benjamin Rush.* Edited by George W. Corner. Princeton, N.J.: Princeton University Press, 1948.

Ruth, Lester, ed. *Early Methodist Life and Spirituality: A Reader.* Nashville: Kingswood Books, 2005.

[Sharpe, Gregory]. *A Review of the Controversy about the Meaning of Demoniacks in the New Testament*. London: J. Roberts, 1739.

Sledd, Robert Newton. *A Sermon Delivered in the Market Street M.E. Church*. Petersburg, Va.: A. F. Crutchfield, 1861.

Smith, Amanda. *An Autobiography: The Story of the Lord's Dealings with Mrs. Amanda Smith, The Colored Evangelist*. Chicago: Meyer & Brother, 1893.

Smith, Henry. *Recollections and Reflections of an Old Itinerant*. Edited by George Peck. New York: Lane & Tippett, 1848.

Stevens, Abel. *History of the Methodist Episcopal Church in the United States of America*. New York: Carlton and Porter, 1864.

——. *Sketches and Incidents; or A Budget From the Saddle-Bags of a Superannuated Itinerant*. Cincinnati: E. P. Thompson, 1848.

Stevenson, Edward. *Biographical Sketch of the Rev. Valentine Cook, A.M. with an Appendix Containing His Discourse on Baptism*. Nashville: J. B. M'Ferrin, 1858.

Stewart, Ellen. *Life of Mrs. Ellen Stewart, Together With Biographical Sketches of Other Individuals. Also, a Discussion with Two Clergymen, and Arguments in Favor of Women's Rights*. Akron, Ohio: Beebe & Elkins, 1858.

Stewart, John. *Highways and Hedges; or, Fifty Years of Western Methodism*. Cincinnati: Hitchcock and Walden, 1872.

Stiles, Ezra. *The United States Elevated to Glory and Honor. A Sermon*. New Haven, Conn.: Thomas and Samuel Green, 1783.

Stokes, E. H. *Footprints in My Own Life*. Asbury Park, N.J.: M., W & C Pennypacker, 1898.

Strickland, W. P. *The Life of Jacob Gruber*. New York: Carlton and Porter, 1860.

Swayze, William. *Narrative of William Swayze, Minister of the Gospel. Written By Himself. Including His Juvenile Mission. Volume 1*. Cincinnati: Methodist Book Room, 1839.

Sweet, William Warren. *The Methodists: A Collection of Source Material*. Religion on the American Frontier Series, Vol. 4. Chicago: University of Chicago Press, 1946.

Sykes, Arthur Ashley [T.P.A.P.O.A.B.I.T.C.O.S., pseud.]. *An Enquiry into the Meaning of Demoniacks in the New Testament, Second Edition, Corrected and Amended*. London: J. Roberts, 1737.

Taylor, William. *Story of My Life: An Account of What I Have Thought and Said and Done in My Ministry of More Than Fifty-Three Years in Christian Lands and Among the Heathen*. New York: Eaton and Mains, 1895.

Tevis, Julia A. *Sixty Years in a School-Room: An Autobiography of Mrs. Julia A Tevis, Principal of Science Hall Female Academy. To Which is Prefaced an Autobiographical Sketch of Rev. John Tevis*. Cincinnati: Western Methodist Book Concern, 1878.

Travis, Joseph. *Autobiography of the Rev. Joseph Travis, A.M., a Member of the Memphis Annual Conference. Embracing a Succinct History of the Methodist Episcopal Church, South; Particularly in Part of Western Virginia, the Carolinas, Georgia, Alabama, and Mississippi*. Edited by Thomas O. Summer. Nashville: Stevenson & F. O. Owens, 1856.

Tucker, Mary Orne. *Itinerant Preaching in the Early Days of Methodism. By a Pioneer Preacher's Wife*. Boston: B. B. Russell, 1872. Reprint, *The Nineteenth-Century Amer-*

ican Methodist Itinerant Preacher's Wife. Edited by Carolyn DeSwarte Gifford. New York: Garland Publishing, 1987.

Twells, Leonard. *An Answer to the Enquiry into the Meaning of the Demoniacks in the New Testament*. London, 1737.

United Methodist Publishing House. *The United Methodist Hymnal*. Nashville: The United Methodist Publishing House, 1989.

Vickers, John A., ed. *The Journals of Dr. Thomas Coke*. Nashville: Kingswood Books, 2005.

Wallace, Charles, Jr., ed. *Susanna Wesley: The Complete Writings*. New York: Oxford University Press, 1997.

Ware, Thomas. *Sketches of the Life and Travels of Rev. Thomas Ware*. New York: T. Mason & G. Lane, 1840.

[Watson, John Fanning]. *Methodist Error: Or Friendly, Christian Advice, To Those Methodists Who Indulge in Extravagant Emotions and Bodily Exercises*. Trenton, N.J.: D & E Fenton, 1819.

Watters, William. *A Short Account of the Christian Experience and Ministerial Labours of William Watters*. Alexandria, Va.: S. Snowden, 1806.

Waugh, Lorenzo. *Autobiography of Lorenzo Waugh*. San Francisco: Francis, Valentine & Company, 1888.

Wesley, John. *Explanatory Notes Upon the New Testament*. London: William Bowyer, 1755.

———. *Explanatory Notes Upon the Old Testament*, vol. 1. Bristol: William Pine, 1765.

———. *Hymns and Sacred Poems, 4th edition*. Bristol: Felix Farley, sold by A. Bradford in Philadelphia, 1743.

———. *The Letters of the Rev. John Wesley*, vol. III. Edited by John Telford. London: Epworth Press, 1931.

———. *The Works of John Wesley*. Oxford: Clarendon Press, 1975– (Oxford Edition); Nashville: Abingdon Press, 1984–(Bicentennial Edition).

———. *The Works of John Wesley* vol. IX. Edited by Thomas Jackson. Grand Rapids, Mich.: Zondervan, 1958.

Whedon, Daniel. *The Freedom of the Will as a Basis of Human Responsibility and a Divine Government*. New York: Carlton & Lanahan, 1864.

Whedon, J. S., and D. A. Whedon. *Essays, Reviews, and Discourses*. Freeport, N.Y.: Books for Libraries Press, 1972.

Whiston, William. *An Account of the Demoniacks, and of the Power of Casting out Daemons, both in the New Testament, and in the First Four Centuries*. London: printed for John Whiston, 1737.

White, George. *A Brief Account of the Life, Experience, Travels and Gospel Labors of George White, an African: Written By Himself, and Revised by a Friend*. New York: John C. Totten, 1810.

Woolsey, Elijah. *The Supernumerary: Or, Lights and Shadows of Itinerancy. Compiled from the Pages of Rev. Elijah Woolsey*. Edited by George Coles. New York: Lane & Tippett, 1845.

Young, Dan. *Autobiography of Dan Young*. New York: Carlton & Porter, 1860.

Young, Jacob. *Autobiography of a Pioneer: Or, The Nativity, Experience, Travels, and Ministerial Labors of Rev. Jacob Young*. Cincinnati: Cranston & Curtis, 1857.

Young, John. "Autobiography." Rare Book, Manuscript and Special Collection Library, Duke University, Durham, N.C.

——. "Follow Peace with all men and Holyness [*sic*] without which men shall not see the Lord." Rare Book, Manuscript and Special Collection Library, Duke University, Durham, N.C.

Secondary Sources

Almond, Philip C. *Demonic Possession and Exorcism in Early Modern England.* New York: Cambridge University Press, 2004.

Andrews, Dee. *The Methodists and Revolutionary America, 1760–1800: The Shaping of an Evangelical Culture.* Princeton, N.J.: Princeton University Press, 2000.

Andrews, William L. ed. *Sisters in the Spirit: Three Black Women's Autobiographies of the Nineteenth Century.* Bloomington: Indiana University Press, 1986.

Appleby, Joyce. *Inheriting the Revolution: The First Generation of Americans.* Cambridge, Mass.: Harvard University Press, 2000.

Aquinas, Thomas. *Summa Theologica.* Translated by Fathers of the English Dominican Province. Notre Dame, Ind.: Christian Classics, 1981.

Baker, Frank. *From Wesley to Asbury: Studies in Early American Methodism.* Durham, N.C.: Duke University Press, 1976.

Barclay, Wade Crawford. *History of Methodist Missions,* vol. 1–3. New York: The Board of Mission and Church Extension of the Methodist Church, 1949.

Bartlett, Richard A. *The New Country: A Social History of the American Frontier 1776–1890.* New York: Oxford University Press, 1976.

Beard, Charles, and Mary Beard. *The American Spirit: A Study of the Idea of Civilization in the United States.* New York: Macmillan, 1942.

Bederman, Gail. *Manliness and Civilization: A Cultural History of Gender and Race in the United States, 1880–1917.* Chicago: University of Chicago Press, 1995.

Bellesiles, Michael, ed. *Lethal Imagination: Violence and Brutality in American History.* New York: New York University Press, 1999.

Berkhofer, Robert F. *Salvation and the Savage: An Analysis of Protestant Missions and American Indian Response, 1787–1862.* Lexington: University of Kentucky Press, 1965.

Bloch, Maurice. *From Prey Into Hunter: The Politics of Religious Experience.* New York: Cambridge University Press, 1992.

Bloch, Ruth H. *Visionary Republic: Millennial Themes in American Thought, 1756–1800.* New York: Cambridge University Press, 1985.

Bonomi, Patricia. *Under the Cope of Heaven: Religion, Society, and Politics in Colonial America.* New York: Oxford University Press, 1986.

Bowden, Henry Warner. *American Indians and Christian Missions: Studies in Cultural Conflict.* Chicago: University of Chicago Press, 1981.

Brekus, Catherine. *Strangers and Pilgrims: Female Preaching in America 1740–1845.* Chapel Hill: University of North Carolina Press, 1998.

Brereton, Virginia Lieson. *From Sin to Salvation: Stories of Women's Conversion, 1800 to the Present.* Bloomington: Indiana University Press, 1991.

Bromley, David. G., and J. Gordon Melton, eds. *Cults, Religion, and Violence.* New York: Cambridge University Press, 2002.

Brown, Richard Maxwell. *No Duty to Retreat: Violence and Values in American History and Society.* New York: Oxford University Press, 1991.

Bruce, Dickson. *And They All Sang Hallelujah: Plain Folk Camp-Meeting Religion, 1800–1845.* Knoxville: University of Tennessee Press, 1974.

———. *Violence and Culture in the Antebellum South.* Austin: University of Texas Press, 1979.

Buck, Emory, ed. *The History of American Methodism,* vol. II. Nashville: Abingdon Press, 1964.

Bushman, Richard L. *The Refinement of America: Persons, Houses, Cities.* New York: Vintage Books, 1993.

Bynum, Caroline Walker. *Fragmentation and Redemption: Essays on Gender and the Human Body in Religion.* New York: Zone Books, 1991.

———. *Holy Fast, Holy Feast: The Religious Significance of Food To Medieval Women.* Berkeley: University of California Press, 1987.

Cahill, Lisa Sowle. *Love Your Enemies: Discipleship, Pacifism, and Just War Theory.* Minneapolis: Fortress Press, 1994.

Caldwell, Patricia. *The Puritan Conversion Narrative: The Beginnings of American Expression.* New York: Cambridge University Press, 1983.

Camporesi, Piero. *The Incorruptible Flesh: Bodily Mutation and Mortification in Religion and Folklore.* Translated by Tania Croft-Murray. New York: Cambridge University Press, 1988.

Carwardine, Richard. *Evangelicals and Politics in Antebellum America.* New Haven, Conn.: Yale University Press, 1993.

Cherry, Conrad. *God's New Israel: Religious Interpretations of American Destiny.* Chapel Hill: University of North Carolina Press, 1998.

Chiles, Robert E. *Theological Transition in American Methodism: 1790–1935.* Nashville: Abingdon Press, 1965.

Clark, J. C. D. *The Language of Liberty.* New York: Cambridge University Press, 1994.

Coakley, Sarah, ed. *Religion and the Body.* Cambridge: Cambridge University Press, 1997.

Cohen, Charles Lloyd. *God's Caress: The Psychology of Puritan Religious Experience.* New York: Oxford University Press, 1986.

Collins, Kenneth J. *The Scripture Way of Salvation: The Heart of John Wesley's Theology.* Nashville: Abingdon Press, 1997.

Collins, Kenneth J., and John H. Tyson, eds. *Conversion in the Wesleyan Tradition.* Nashville: Abingdon Press, 2001.

Coppleston, Tremayne. "John Wesley and the American Revolution." *Religion in Life* 45 (Spring 1976): 89–105.

Corrigan, John. *Business of the Heart: Religion and Emotion in the Nineteenth Century.* Berkeley: University of California Press, 2002.

Cott, Nancy. *The Bonds of Womanhood: "Women's Sphere" in New England, 1780–1835.* New Haven, Conn.: Yale University Press, 1977.

Courtwright, David T. *Violent Land: Single Men and Social Disorder from the Frontier to the Inner City.* Cambridge, Mass.: Harvard University Press, 1996.

Cox, James Reed. *Pioneers and Perfectors of our Faith: A Biography of the Rev. Green Hill.* Nashville: Parthenon Press, 1975.

Crabtree, Harriet. *The Christian Life: Traditional Metaphors and Contemporary Theologies*. Minneapolis: Fortress Press, 1991.

Cuming, G. J., and Derek Baker, eds. *Popular Belief and Practice*. London: Cambridge University Press, 1972.

Daston, Lorraine, and Katherine Park. *Wonders and the Order of Nature, 1150–1750*. New York: Zone Books, 1998.

Davis, Hugh, and Ted Robert Gurr, eds. *Violence in America: Historical and Comparative Perspectives*. Beverly Hills, Calif.: Sage Publications, 1979.

Delbanco, Andrew. *The Death of Satan: How Americans Have Lost the Sense of Evil*. New York: Farrar, Straus and Giroux, 1995.

Duvall, Sylvanus. *The Methodist Episcopal Church and Education Up To 1869*. New York: Teachers College, Columbia University, 1928.

Dvorak, Katherine L. "Peter Cartwright and Charisma." *Methodist History* 26, no. 2 (January 1998): 113–126.

Epstein, Barbara Leslie. *The Politics of Domesticity: Women, Evangelism and Temperance in Nineteenth-Century America*. Middletown, Conn.: Wesleyan University Press, 1981.

Farrelly, Mary Jane. "'God Is the Author of Both': Science, Religion, and the Intellectualization of American Methodism." *Church History* 77, no. 3 (September 2008): 659–687.

Fox, Richard Wightman. *Jesus in America: Personal Savior, Cultural Hero, National Obsession*. New York: HarperCollins, 2004.

Frykholm, Amy Johnson. *Rapture Culture: Left Behind in Evangelical America*. New York: Oxford University Press, 2004.

Gerdes, Egon. "John Wesley's Attitude Toward War." Ph.D. dissertation, Emory University, 1960.

Girard, René. *I See Satan Fall Like Lightning*. Translated by James Williams. New York: Orbis Books, 2001.

———. *Violence and the Sacred*. Translated by Patrick Gregory. Baltimore: Johns Hopkins University Press, 1977.

Gorn, Elliott J. "'Gouge and Bite, Pull Hair and Scratch': The Social Significance of Fighting in the Southern Backcountry." *The American Historical Review* 90, no. 1 (1985): 18–43.

Gorringe, Timothy. *God's Just Vengeance: Crime, Violence and the Rhetoric of Salvation*. New York: Cambridge University Press, 1996.

Greven, Philip. *The Protestant Temperament: Patterns of Child-Rearing, Religious Experience, and the Self in Early America*. New York: Alfred A. Knopf, 1977.

———. *Spare the Child: The Religious Roots of Punishment and the Psychological Impact of Physical Abuse*. New York: Alfred A. Knopf, 1991.

Griffith, R. Marie. *Born Again Bodies: Flesh and Spirit in American Christianity*. Berkeley: University of California Press, 2004.

Gunter, W. Stephen. *The Limits of 'Love Divine': John Wesley's Response to Antinomianism and Enthusiasm*. Nashville: Kingswood Books, 1989.

Hall, David D. *Worlds of Wonder, Days of Judgment: Popular Religious Belief in Early New England*. Cambridge, Mass.: Harvard University Press, 1989.

———, ed. *Lived Religion in America: Toward a History of Practice*. Princeton, N.J.: Princeton University Press, 1997.

Hall, John R., Philip Schuyler, and Sylvaine Trinh, eds. *Apocalypse Observed: Religious Movements in North America, Europe and Japan*. New York: Routledge, 2000.

Hart, D. G. ed. *Reckoning with the Past: Historical Essays on American Evangelicalism from the Institute for the Study of American Evangelicals*. Grand Rapids, Mich.: Baker Books, 1995.

Harvey, Marvin. "The Wesleyan Movement and The American Revolution." Ph.D. dissertation, University of Washington, 1962.

Hatch, Nathan. *The Democratization of American Christianity*. New Haven, Conn.: Yale University Press, 1989.

———. *The Sacred Cause of Liberty: Republican Thought and the Millennium in Revolutionary New England*. New Haven, Conn.: Yale University Press, 1977.

Hatch, Nathan, and John Wigger, eds. *Methodism and the Shaping of American Culture*. Nashville: Kingswood Books, 2001.

Heimert, Alan. *Religion and the American Mind From the Great Awakening to the Revolution*. Cambridge, Mass.: Harvard University Press, 1966.

Heitzenrater, Richard P. *Mirror and Memory: Reflections on Early Methodism*. Nashville: Kingswood Books, 1989.

———. *Wesley and the People Called Methodists*. Nashville: Abingdon Press, 1995.

Hempton, David. *Methodism: Empire of the Spirit*. New Haven, Conn.: Yale University Press, 2005.

———. *The Religion of the People: Methodism and Popular Religion c. 1750–1900*. New York: Routledge, 1996.

Heyd, Michael. *Be Sober and Reasonable: The Critique of Enthusiasm in the Seventeenth and Early Eighteenth Centuries*. Leiden: E. J. Brill, 1995.

Heyrman, Christine Leigh. *Southern Cross: The Beginnings of the Bible Belt*. Chapel Hill: University of North Carolina Press, 1997.

Hindmarsh, Bruce. *The Evangelical Conversion Narrative: Spiritual Autobiography in Early Modern England*. Oxford: Oxford University Press, 2005.

Holifield, E. Brooks. *Health and Medicine in the Methodist Tradition: Journey Toward Wholeness*. New York: Crossroads, 1986.

Holland, L. M. "John Wesley and the American Revolution." *Journal of Church and State* 5 (November 1963): 199–213.

Horseman, Reginald. *The Causes of the War of 1812*. Philadelphia: University of Pennsylvania Press, 1962.

Hudson, Winthrop S., ed. *Nationalism and Religion in America: Concepts of American Identity and Mission*. New York: Harper & Row, 1970.

Hutchinson, William R. *Errand to the World: American Protestant Thought and Foreign Missions*. Chicago: University of Chicago Press, 1987.

Hynson, Leon O. "John Wesley's Theology of the Kingdom." *Wesleyan Theological Journal* 23, no. 1–2 (Spring–Fall 1988): 46–57.

———. "War, the State, and the Christian Citizen." *Religion in Life* 45 (Summer 1976): 204–219.

Isaac, Rhys. *The Transformation of Virginia, 1740–1790*. Chapel Hill: University of North Carolina Press, 1982.

Jensen, Gary F. "Religious Cosmologies and Homicide Rates among Nations: A Closer Look." *Journal of Religion and Society* 8 (2006): 1–14.

Jewett, Robert, and John Shelton Lawrence. *Captain America and the Crusade Against*

Evil: The Dilemma of Zealous Nationalism. Grand Rapids, Mich.: Eerdmans, 2003.

Johnstone, Nathan. *The Devil and Demonism in Early Modern England.* New York: Cambridge University Press, 2006.

Jones, James W. *Blood That Cries Out From the Earth: The Psychology of Religious Terrorism.* New York: Oxford University Press, 2008.

Juergensmeyer, Mark. *Terror in the Mind of God: The Global Rise of Religious Violence.* Berkeley: University of California Press, 2000.

Juster, Susan. *Disorderly Women: Sexual Politics and Evangelicalism in Revolutionary New England.* Ithaca, N.Y.: Cornell University Press, 1994.

Kimball, Charles. *When Religion Becomes Evil: Five Warning Signs.* New York: HarperCollins, 2002.

Kimbrough, David. *Reverend Joseph Tarkington, Methodist Circuit Rider: From Frontier Evangelism to Refined Religion.* Knoxville: University of Tennessee Press, 1997.

Kimbrough, S. T., Jr., ed. *Charles Wesley: Poet and Theologian.* Nashville: Kingswood Books, 1992.

—— *Orthodox and Wesleyan Spirituality.* Crestwood, N.Y.: St. Vladimir's Seminary Press, 2002.

King, John Owen. *The Iron of Melancholy: Structures of Spiritual Conversion in America from the Puritan Conscience to Victorian Neurosis.* Middletown, Conn.: Wesleyan University Press, 1983.

Knox, Ronald. *Enthusiasm: A Chapter in the History of Religion, with Special Reference to the 18th and 19th Centuries.* New York: Oxford University Press, 1950.

Langford, Thomas. *Practical Divinity: Theology in the Wesleyan Tradition.* Nashville: Abingdon Press, 1983.

Lindman, Janet Moore, and Michele Liese Tarter, eds. *A Centre of Wonders: The Boy in Early America.* Ithaca, N.Y.: Cornell University Press, 2001.

Long, Kathryn. *The Revival of 1857–1858: Interpreting an American Religious Awakening.* New York: Oxford, 1997.

Luhrmann, T. H. "The Ugly Goddess: Reflections on the Role of Violent Images in Religious Experience." *History of Religions* 41, no. 2 (2001): 114–141.

Lyerly, Cynthia Lynn. "Francis Asbury and the Opposition to Early Methodism." *Methodist History* 31, no. 4 (1993): 224–235.

——. *Methodism and the Southern Mind.* New York: Oxford University Press, 1998.

Lyles, Albert. *Methodism Mocked.* London: Epworth Press, 1960.

MacClenney, W. E. *The Life of Rev. James O'Kelly and the Early History of the Christian Church in the South.* Raleigh, N.C.: Edwards and Broughton, 1910.

Maddox, Randy L., ed. *Aldersgate Reconsidered.* Nashville: Kingswood Press, 1990.

——. *Responsible Grace: John Wesley's Practical Theology.* Nashville: Kingswood Books, 1994.

Maffley-Kipp, Laurie, Leigh Schmidt, and Mark Valeri, eds. *Practicing Protestants: Histories of Christian Life in America 1630–1965.* Baltimore: Johns Hopkins University Press, 2006.

Mahan, John. *The War of 1812.* New York: De Capo Press, 1972.

Mariner, Kirk. "William Penn Chandler and Revivalism in the East, 1797–1811." *Methodist History* 25 (April 1987): 135–145.

Marini, Stephen. "Hymnody as History: Early Evangelical Hymns and the Recovery of American Popular Religion." *Church History* 7, no. 2 (2002): 273–306.

Marquardt, Manfred. *John Wesley's Social Ethics: Praxis and Principles.* Translated by John E. Steely and W. Stephen Gunter. Nashville: Abingdon Press, 1992.

Mathews, Donald. *Religion in the Old South.* Chicago: University of Chicago Press, 1977.

———. *Slavery and Methodism.* Princeton, N.J.: Princeton University Press, 1965.

———. "The Southern Rite of Human Sacrifice." *Journal of Southern Religion* 3 (2000), http://jsr.fsu.edu/mathews.htm.

Matthew, H. C. G., and Brian Harrison, eds. *Oxford Dictionary of National Biography: In Association with the British Academy: From the Earliest Times to the Present,* vol. 53. Oxford: Oxford University Press, 2004.

Matthews, Glenna. *"Just a Housewife": The Rise and Fall of Domesticity in America.* New York: Oxford University Press, 1987.

McDannell, Colleen, ed. *Religions of the United States in Practice,* 2 vols. Princeton, N.J.: Princeton University Press, 2001.

McGiffert, Michael. *God's Plot: Puritan Spirituality in Thomas Shepard's Cambridge.* Amherst: University of Massachusetts Press, 1994.

McLoughlin, William G. *Cherokees and Missionaries, 1789–1839.* Norman: University of Oklahoma Press, 1995.

———. "Mob Violence Against Dissent in Revolutionary Massachusetts." *Foundations* 14, no. 4 (October–December 1971): 294–317.

Midelfort, H. C. Erik. *Exorcism and Enlightenment: Joseph Gassner and the Demons of Eighteenth-Century Germany.* New Haven, Conn.: Yale University Press, 2005.

Mouw, Richard J., and Mark Noll, eds. *Wonderful Words of Life: Hymns in American Protestant History and Theology.* Grand Rapids, Mich.: Eerdmans, 2004.

Muchembled, Robert. *A History of the Devil From the Middle Ages to the Present.* Translated by Jean Birrell. Cambridge: Polity Press, 2003.

Mullin, Robert Bruce. *Miracles and the Modern Religious Imagination.* New Haven, Conn.: Yale University Press, 1996.

Mullin, Robert Bruce, and Russell E. Richey, eds. *Reimagining Denominationalism: Interpretive Essays.* New York: Oxford University Press, 1994.

Newton, John A. *Susanna Wesley and the Puritan Tradition in Methodism,* 2d ed. London: Epworth Press, 2002.

Noll, Mark. *America's God: From Jonathan Edwards to Abraham Lincoln.* New York: Oxford University Press, 2002.

———. *The Civil War as a Theological Crisis.* Chapel Hill: University of North Carolina Press, 2006.

———. *The Rise of Evangelicalism: The Age of Edwards, Whitefield and the Wesleys.* Downers Grove. Ill.: InterVarsity Press, 2003.

Noll, Mark, and Luke Harlow, eds. *Religion and American Politics: From the Colonial Period to the Present,* 2nd edition. New York: Oxford University Press, 2007.

Norwood, Frederick A. *The Story of American Methodism.* Nashville: Abingdon Press, 1974.

Orsi, Robert. *The Madonna of 115th Street: Faith and Community in Italian Harlem, 1880–1950.* New Haven, Conn.: Yale University Press, 1985.

———. *Thank You, St. Jude: Women's Devotion to the Patron Saint of Hopeless Causes.* New Haven, Conn.: Yale University Press, 1996.

Ownby, Ted. *Subduing Satan: Religion, Recreation, and Manhood in the Rural South, 1865–1920.* Chapel Hill: University of North Carolina Press, 1990.

Pearce, Roy Harvey. *Savagism and Civilization: A Study of the Indian and the American Mind.* Berkeley: University of California Press, 1988.

Posey, Walter Brownlow. *Religious Strife on the Southern Frontier.* Baton Rouge: Louisiana State University Press, 1965.

Prothero, Stephen. *American Jesus: How the Son of God Became a National Icon.* New York: Farrar, Straus and Giroux, 2003.

Prucha, Francis Paul. *The Great Father: The United States Government and the American Indians.* Lincoln: University of Nebraska Press, 1984.

Raboteau, Albert J. *Slave Religion: The "Invisible Institution" in the Antebellum South.* New York: Oxford University Press, 1978.

Rack, Henry D. *Reasonable Enthusiast: John Wesley and the Rise of Methodism,* 3d ed. London: Epworth Press, 2002.

Ramsey, Paul. *The Just War, Force and Political Responsibility.* New York: Scribner, 1968.

Raser, Harold E. *Phoebe Palmer: Her Life and Thought.* Lewiston, N.Y.: Edwin Mellen Press, 1987.

Raymond, Allan. "'I Fear God and Honour the King': John Wesley and the American Revolution." *Church History* 45, no. 3 (1976): 316–328.

Richey, Russell. *Early American Methodism.* Bloomington: Indiana University Press, 1991.

Richey, Russell, and Kenneth Rowe, eds. *Rethinking Methodist History.* Nashville: Kingswood Books, 1985.

Richey, Russell, Kenneth Rowe, and Jean Miller Schmidt, eds. *Perspectives on American Methodism: Interpretive Essays.* Nashville: Kingswood Books, 1993.

Romero, Lora. *Domesticity and Its Critics in the Antebellum United States.* Durham, N.C.: Duke University Press, 1997.

Rotundo, E. Anthony. *American Manhood: Transformations in Masculinity From the Revolution to the Modern Era.* New York: Basic Books, 1993.

Rubenstein, Richard. *The Spiritual Self in Everyday Life: The Transformation of Personal Religious Experience in Nineteenth-Century New England.* Boston: Northeastern University Press, 1989.

Rubin, Julius. *Religious Melancholy and Protestant Experience in America.* New York: Oxford University Press, 1994.

Russell, Frederick H. *The Just War in the Middle Ages.* New York: Cambridge University Press, 1975.

Russell, Jeffrey Burton. *Mephistopheles: The Devil in the Modern World.* Ithaca, N.Y.: Cornell University Press, 1986.

Ruth, Lester. *A Little Heaven Below: Worship at Early Methodist Quarterly Meetings.* Nashville: Kingswood Books, 2000.

Ryan, Mary P. *The Empire of the Mother: American Writing About Domesticity, 1830–1860.* New York: Institute for Research in History and Haworth Press, 1982.

Schmidt, Jean Miller. *Grace Sufficient: A History of Women in American Methodism, 1760–1939.* Nashville: Abingdon Press, 1999.

Schmidt, Leigh. *Consumer Rites: The Buying and Selling of American Holidays.* Princeton, N.J.: Princeton University Press, 1995.

———. *Hearing Things: Religion, Illusion, and the American Enlightenment.* Cambridge, Mass.: Harvard University Press, 2000.

———. *Holy Fairs: Scotland and the Making of American Revivalism.* Princeton, N.J.: Princeton University Press, 1989.

Schneider, A. Gregory. *The Way of the Cross Leads Home: The Domestication of American Methodism.* Bloomington: Indiana University Press, 1993.

Silverstone, Scott. *Divided Union: The Politics of War in the Early Republic.* Ithaca, N.Y.: Cornell University Press, 2004.

Sklar, Katheryn Kish. *Catherine Beecher: A Study in American Domesticity.* New Haven, Conn.: Yale University Press, 1973.

Slotkin, Richard. *Regeneration Through Violence: The Mythology of the American Frontier.* Middletown, Conn.: Wesleyan University Press, 1973.

Smith, Henry Nash. *Virgin Land: The American West as Symbol and Myth.* Cambridge, Mass.: Harvard University Press, 1978.

Steele, Richard, ed. *Heart Religion in the Methodist Tradition and Related Movements.* Lanham, Md.: The Scarecrow Press, 2001.

Stout, Harry S. "Religion, Communication, and the Ideological Origins of the American Revolution." *William and Mary Quarterly* 34 (1977): 519–541.

———. *Upon the Altar of a Nation: A Moral History of the Civil War.* New York: Penguin Books, 2006.

Stout, Harry S., and D. G. Hart, eds. *New Directions in American Religious History.* New York: Oxford University Press, 1997.

Taves, Ann. *Fits, Trances, and Visions: Experiencing Religion and Explaining Experience from Wesley to James.* Princeton, N.J.: Princeton University Press, 1999.

Thomas, Keith. *Religion and the Decline of Magic: Studies in Popular Beliefs in Sixteenth- and Seventeenth-Century England.* New York: Scribner, 1971.

Turley, Briane K. "John Wesley and War." *Methodist History* 22, no. 2 (1991): 96–111.

Turner, Victor. *Dramas, Fields and Metaphors: Symbolic Action in Human Society.* Ithaca, N.Y.: Cornell University Press, 1974.

Tuveson, Ernest Lee. *Redeemer Nation: The Idea of America's Millennial Role.* Chicago: University of Chicago Press, 1968.

Unger, Craig. "American Rapture." *Vanity Fair,* Dec. 2005.

Vaughan, Alden. *New England Frontier: Puritans and Indians 1620–1675.* Norman: University of Oklahoma Press, 1995.

Vickers, John A. *Thomas Coke: Apostle of Methodism.* Nashville: Abingdon Press, 1967.

Weber, Max. *The Protestant Ethic and the Spirit of Capitalism.* New York: Scribner, 1958.

Weber, Theodore. *Politics in the Order of Salvation.* Nashville: Kingswood Books, 2001.

Wheeler, Henry. *History and Exposition of the Twenty-five Articles of Religion of the Methodist Episcopal Church.* New York: Eaton and Mains, 1908.

White, Charles Edward. *The Beauty of Holiness: Phoebe Palmer as Theologian, Revivalist, and Humanitarian.* Grand Rapids, Mich.: Francis Asbury Press, 1986.

Wigger, John. *Taking Heaven By Storm: Methodism and the Rise of Popular Christianity in America*. New York: Oxford University Press, 1998.

Wightman, William. *Life of William Capers, D.D., One of the Bishops of the Methodist Episcopal Church South; Including an Autobiography*. Nashville: Southern Methodist Publishing House, 1858.

Williams, James G. *The Bible, Violence and the Sacred: Liberation From the Myths of Sanctioned Violence*. New York: HarperCollins, 1991.

——, ed. *The Girard Reader*. New York: Crossroads, 1997.

Williams, William Henry. *The Garden of American Methodism: The Delmarva Peninsula, 1769–1820*. Wilmington, Del.: Scholarly Resources, 1984.

Wyatt-Brown, Bertram. *Honor and Violence in the Old South*. New York: Oxford, 1986.

——. *The Shaping of Southern Culture: Honor, Grace and War*. Chapel Hill: University of North Carolina Press, 2001.

——. *Southern Honor: Ethics and Behavior in the Old South*. New York: Galaxy Books, 1982.

Index

JEFFREY WILLIAMS
*is Associate Dean for Academic
Affairs at Brite Divinity School,
Texas Christian University.*